Language Teacher Research in the Americas

Edited by Hedy M. McGarrell

Language Teacher Research Series

Thomas S. C. Farrell, Series Editor

Teachers of English to Speakers of Other Languages, Inc.

Typeset in Sabon and Adelon
by Capitol Communication Systems, Inc., Crofton, Maryland USA
Printed by United Graphics, Inc., Matoon, Illinois, USA
Indexed by Pueblo Indexing and Publishing Services, Pueblo West, Colorado, USA

Teachers of English to Speakers of Other Languages, Inc.
700 South Washington Street, Suite 200
Alexandria, Virginia 22314 USA
Tel. 703-836-0774 • Fax 703-836-6447 • E-mail info@tesol.org • http://www.tesol.org/

Publishing Manager: Carol Edwards
Copy Editor: Terrey Hatcher Quindlen
Additional Reader: Ellen Garshick
Cover Design: Tomiko Chapman

ISBN 9781931185424
Library of Congress Control Number: 2007924036

Table of Contents

Series Editor's Preface

The Language Teacher Research Series highlights the role language teachers at all levels play as generators of knowledge concerning all aspects of language teaching around the world. This idea may seem alien to many language teachers. Often, they think that they have nothing to say about their teaching or that what they have to say is of little significance. Teachers generally are accustomed to receiving knowledge from so-called *real* researchers.

In my opinion, language teachers have plenty to say that is valuable for colleagues around the world. One of the main reasons for the Language Teacher Research Series is to celebrate what is being achieved in English language classrooms each day, so educators can encourage and develop communities of like-minded language teaching professionals who are willing to share these important experiences.

In this manner, the TESOL community can extend its understanding of English language teaching in local, regional, and international settings. The series attempts to cover as many of these contexts as possible, with volumes covering Africa, the Americas, Asia, Australia and New Zealand, Europe, and the Middle East. Each account of research presented in the Language Teacher Research Series is unique in the profession. These studies document how individual language teachers at all levels of practice systematically reflect on their *own* practice (rather than on other teachers' practices).

When practicing language teachers share these experiences with teachers in other contexts, they can compare and contrast what is happening in different classrooms around the world. The ultimate aim of this series is to encourage an inquiry stance toward language teaching. Teachers can play a crucial role in taking responsibility for their own professional development as generators and receivers of knowledge about what it means to teach English language learning.

How This Series Can Be Used

The Language Teacher Research Series is suitable for preservice and in-service teacher education programs. The examples of teacher research written by practitioners at all levels of teaching and all levels of experience offer a window into the different worlds of English language teachers. In this series I have attempted to impose some order by providing authors with a template of headings for presenting their research. This format is designed so that language teachers with varied expertise and educational qualifications can pick up a book from any region and make comparisons about issues, background literature, procedures taken, results, and reflections without having to work too hard to find them. The details in each chapter will help readers compare and evaluate the examples of teacher research and even replicate some research, if so desired.

This Volume

This volume in the Language Teacher Research series, *Language Teacher Research in the Americas*, documents different forms of practitioner inquiry that involve systematic, intentional, and self-critical studies of language teaching in different settings. It will be interesting to compare and contrast these Americas research stories with studies not only from the Asian and European volumes that were published previous to this volume, but also from the volumes on the Middle East, Australia/New Zealand, and Africa that will follow.

Thomas S. C. Farrell, Brock University, Canada

CHAPTER 1

Language Teacher Research
in the Americas

Hedy M. McGarrell

Language teacher research is increasingly seen as a means for teachers to reflect on their own teaching, to enhance their professional development, and to contribute actively to the knowledge base on language learning and teaching (Richards & Farrell, 2005). Through a process of critical reflection, teachers embark on a path that enables them to take control over and transform their professional practices. By documenting and describing aspects of their daily classroom experiences, they promote change in the traditionally unidirectional relationship between teaching and research.

However, interest in the relationship between classroom teaching and research develops gradually for many teachers. Initially, their focus is on the day-to-day issues involved in the actual teaching; in other words, they are focused on surviving (Freeman, 1998). Many teachers feel overwhelmed by the sheer number of hours required to prepare and carry out classroom interaction, mark student work, respond to administrative requirements, and do similar tasks. As a result, occasional professional development opportunities such as attending one-day, in-house staff development sessions or external conferences tend to become quests for material that addresses the practical aspects of teaching. In other words, teachers look for how-to sessions or handouts that can be photocopied and used in class. Such practical material promises to make teaching more successful and preparation less time-consuming. But as the new learning becomes absorbed into the teacher's previous experiences, it can quickly fade from memory. Research, for teachers at this stage, offers information that is optional to and incompatible with their immediate practical needs.

As teachers gain confidence in their classroom practices, they tend to become keen observers of what does or does not work in their classrooms. Observations of their daily teaching environment become reflections that lead them to ask *why* or *how* questions related to their teaching. These kinds of questions readily lead to observing, comparing, analyzing, and valuing, which can move the teacher's practice closer to meeting unmet learner needs.

A major shift in the profession has resulted in widespread acceptance of the need for language teachers to have undergone extensive professional preparation. This shift coincides with an increasing expectation for language teachers to conduct research about their professional practice (Crookes, 1993, 1998; Nunan, 1989). A basic understanding of how to conduct research is viewed not only as an essential component of teacher education but also as an important part of language teachers' professional activities. However, support for language teacher research is varied so far, depending on the teaching context. Some institutions require language teachers to engage in at least some research activities; other institutions simply encourage teacher research; and still others discourage it, either directly or indirectly. This varying support for teacher research may be reflected in the contributions submitted for this volume; most came from language teachers based in or attached to tertiary institutions. No doubt, the culture of research is more visible in university settings than in other teaching contexts such as primary schools, secondary schools, and colleges. As language professionals start to pay more attention to teacher-driven research, its potential to explain and clarify pedagogical issues occurring in language classrooms will become more widely recognized. An additional shift, however, is likely needed to bring about widespread acceptance of language teacher research at all levels of language teaching.

Issues that capture teachers' attention and spur reflection and inquiry tend to depend on their teaching context. Although the teaching environment tends to cultivate many issues suited to reflection, circumstances often act as a barrier to teacher reflection and research. During a short discussion at a conference, I asked teachers to share some of the barriers to inquiry, and we drafted a long list of discouraging situations:

- Large classes.

- Multilevel classes.

- Lack of resources (including textbooks, Internet).

- Lack of teacher training.

- Syllabus development left to classroom teacher.

- Poor English skills and low self-esteem in students.

- Inexperienced instructors burdened with administrative responsibilities.

- Competing purposes of English as a foreign language (EFL) instruction.

    — to communicate with foreign students in exchange programs

    — to attend lectures given by international visiting specialists

    — to pass exams (national, international)

    — to read journal articles

- Classroom use of language that does not meet academic requirements for undergraduate and degree programs.

- Insufficient opportunities for lifelike examples and practice opportunities.

The contributors to this volume have also encountered many of these situations. Some contributors overcame potential barriers to teacher research, and some addressed these barriers directly in their contributions. In *Language Teacher Research in the Americas*, the authors show how they have moved beyond their day-to-day classroom activities to consider research-oriented questions that help them gain insights into *why* or *how* issues. They have developed skills such as observing, comparing, analyzing, and telling, and they draw on those skills to assume the teacher researcher role. While telling their stories of teacher-driven research, the authors reflect on how the research affected their growth and development as language professionals. Their contributions are arranged in alphabetical order, based on the surname of the first author.

The teaching context of the first contribution, "Understanding Practices: Bridging the Gap Between What Teachers Do and What Students Know," is a university setting in Colombia. Angela Bailey, Lourdes Rey, and Nayibe Rosado report on a study designed to help them understand why many students did not achieve the anticipated TOEFL Institutional Testing Program scores in reading and writing. The three teachers of English reading and writing classes discovered that part of the problem could be attributed to their own teaching. A careful analysis of their teaching practices suggested that including longer texts, explicitly teaching cohesive devices, and focusing more on vocabulary would enhance their classroom practices.

Sandra Burger and Catherine Danforth set up a variation of the peer review process between Danforth's English as a subsequent language (ESL) students and Burger's teachers in training at a Canadian university. In their chapter, "Revisiting Peer Review," the authors describe how the student teachers in Burger's classroom benefited from a learning environment in which they studied peer review and then applied their knowledge to real ESL writing. Danforth's

ESL students, meanwhile, benefited from additional feedback on their texts—feedback from a sympathetic, informed native speaker who was trying to understand the texts without evaluating them.

In "Film in the ESL Classroom: Hearing the Student's Voice," Andy Curtis explores what his university-level ESL students thought about three movies that provided them with language learning opportunities in their Canadian classroom. Curtis wanted to know how helpful his students considered each of the three movies, which led him to develop a basic questionnaire that provided some answers. However, he realizes that he needs to further explore the complex picture that emerges as he adapts his use of film for language learning.

Maria Dantas-Whitney reports on a study she carried out in an intensive English language program at a U.S. university. In "ESL Students as Ethnographers: Examining Academic Interactions," she describes how her students observed, analyzed, and reflected on interactions within the academic context. Their insights helped sensitize them to the communicative practices of the academic community. In her reflections, Dantas-Whitney notes that her curriculum innovation helped her understand how exposure to actual academic interaction prepares students for success when they leave her classroom.

Wendy Fraser and Janna Fox's contribution, "Studying Classroom Practices and Learner Perceptions to Improve Test Quality," stems from their teaching context in a Canadian university. They developed their study to find out why students often showed complex language capabilities in class (in terms of structure or vocabulary) that they did not show in tests outside the classroom. To tackle the problem, the authors experimented with adding tasks in the testing context that encouraged students to engage in reflection.

In Jami Gurkin's teaching context, an elementary ESL classroom in the United States, she questioned whether listening to stories would help her young students learn enough vocabulary to succeed academically. Her contribution, "Listening to Text and ESL Students: Facilitating Low-Frequency Vocabulary Acquisition Incidentally," reports on her efforts to help young learners increase their vocabulary learning opportunities. The positive results increased Gurkin's confidence in her teaching techniques and encouraged her to continue finding ways to facilitate her students' ESL development.

Andrea Jesus, Heliana Mello, and Deise Dutra report on their collaboration to support the use of more communicative techniques in Brazilian classrooms with young English language learners. In "Promoting Innovative Practices Through Reflective Collaboration," they describe how their collaborative sessions helped introduce a more communicative syllabus in two sixth-grade public school classes. Through regular exchanges, the three educators brainstormed and developed innovative classroom teaching practices. Jesus implemented the innovations in her classes and reported on the results so that all group members could learn from the experience. Their reflections indicate that their model of collaboration can help overcome common barriers to innovative classroom practices and foster a positive and successful learning environment.

In a study based in Jamaica, Mary Hills Kuck describes how speakers of a nonstandard variety of English at the Vocational Training Development Institute in Kingston view the use and purpose of the standard variety. Her study, "Mi and Myself: Dual Identity in Jamaican Contact Language Speakers," draws attention to the intricate interaction between identity and language, especially in the contact of two different varieties of English. In her reflections, Kuck highlights the positive effects her study has had on her own views and her teaching practice as she draws on the local nonstandard variety to teach standard English.

Kathleen McInerney's chapter explores using service learning in the Andean highlands of Ecuador to help preservice teachers understand their language students' culture and thereby enhance teaching practices. In "Local Cultures, Language Politics, and Service Learning in the TEFL Certificate Course," McInerney attempts to heighten the sensitivity of her students to the cultural and political situation of ESL learners. She reflects on how her students in the teaching EFL program might continue to incorporate local culture into classroom materials by drawing on constructivist teaching approaches.

Elizabeth Park's study, "Finding and Leveraging Vocabulary Strengths While Addressing Needs," is set in a U.S. middle school that draws on a student population from a broad range of cultures. Although the students learn to converse relatively quickly in English on everyday topics, Park is concerned with the difficult task her students face in developing broad-based vocabulary. Her study revealed that many of her students are unfamiliar with vocabulary typically considered easy in English: the one-syllable words young children growing up in an English language environment typically learn early on. As a result of her study, Park has developed lessons that address her students' vocabulary needs more directly. She also emphasizes the importance of collecting and analyzing data about students' learning needs.

Eliana Santana-Williamson investigates how native and nonnative adult speakers of English use a limited number of discourse markers and conversational hedges in "Are Nonnative Speakers Really Able to Converse?" For this study, Santana-Williamson analyzed selected segments from *The Michigan Corpus of American Spoken English* (Simpson, Briggs, Ovens, & Swales, 2002). She found that nonnative speakers' use of discourse markers and conversational hedges was limited in comparison to native speakers' use of the same expressions. Based on insights from her study, Santana-Williamson has modified her teaching practice to teach frequent discourse markers and conversational hedges explicitly, based on models from oral rather than written language.

In "Learning How to Learn: Metacognitive Strategy Training With Beginning EFL Students," Sharon Springer describes her exploratory work incorporating strategy training into beginner-level English lessons for her Spanish-speaking students in Costa Rica. Springer designed her study to find out whether a focus on metacognition would increase strategy use and improve performance in English. She also wanted to be sure the use of Spanish for the strategy training did not hinder students' progress in learning English. Although her results are not conclusive, Springer suggests that the study has encouraged her to use strategy training in future ESL courses.

Overall, this volume shows that language teachers are interested in a broad range of issues that arise in their classrooms. Moreover, they are capable of applying varied research methodologies—qualitative and quantitative—to explore these issues before drawing conclusions to improve learning and teaching. Regardless of the teaching context and geographic location, these authors have shown the capability to investigate aspects of their practice and share the results and reflections for the benefit of their colleagues everywhere.

Hedy M. McGarrell is Associate Professor in Applied Linguistics at Brock University in Canada. Her research interests include the development of ESL writing skills, technology in the development of writing skills, and language teacher education and development.

CHAPTER 2

Understanding Practices: Bridging the Gap Between What Teachers Do and What Students Know (*Colombia*)

Angela Bailey, Lourdes Rey, and Nayibe Rosado

Issue

Our research focused on identifying the problems that led a high percentage of students in the English program at the Universidad del Norte's Instituto de Idiomas to achieve disappointing scores on end-of-program assessments. All three of us—the authors and primary researchers—work for the Instituto de Idiomas in Barranquilla. Because educational research in Colombia is rarely mentioned in mainstream investigatory publications, we wanted to share the challenges in our English as a foreign language (EFL) program with others.

Universidad del Norte is one of 10 institutionally accredited universities in Colombia and one of the top three private universities in the nation. It serves about 10,000 students annually. Completing a modern language program, typically eight levels, is a graduation requirement for all majors. Most of the students choose English as their language program. The institute's courses are 64 hours per 16-week semester for its regular program, with a more intensive program for the medicine and nursing majors that includes fewer levels of completion due to their practicum hours. Each student is expected to finish the English program with a high-intermediate level of language and obtain a Test of EFL (TOEFL) Institutional Testing Program (ITP) score between 470 and 520.

After the initial administration of the TOEFL ITP in 2003, institute officials discovered that a high percentage of its students did not achieve the target scores for the program. This caused extreme concern within the institute's and the university's administration. In response, the program coordinators divided the program levels into investigative teams to take on and evaluate the various difficulties in their own classrooms. Levels 5 and 6 were assigned reading and writing. Three Level 5 classrooms and three Level 6 classrooms were chosen for this investigation, which lasted throughout the second semester of 2004 and the first semester of 2005. All three of us were involved in the investigation. The first teacher, Teacher A, investigated her Level 5 students; the second teacher, Teacher B, investigated both her Levels 5 and 6; and the third, Teacher C, studied her Level 6 students. The aim was to identify potential reasons for the low reading and writing scores that students in these levels achieved on the TOEFL ITP.

The 67 participating students from the Level 5 classes were between 17 and 23 years old. They focused on reading strategies and practices. A total of 63 students in the same age range participated from the Level 6 classes and focused on writing. The students came from a wide sampling of disciplines of the university—law, social communication, business administration, engineering (electrical, mechanical, and systems), psychology, early childhood education, and nursing. They were homogenous as far as first language and nationality, and most of the participants were from the northern region of Colombia.

Background Literature

Literacy research is a common theme in current Latin American studies. One of the more interesting reports comes from Seda-Santana (2000). She observed and investigated schools throughout Latin America and noted that many of them had what she calls "common literacy practices" (para. 17). Primary schools she observed taught sight and sound recognition, and once the students had mastered the sounds and symbols, they were considered literate. There was little critical focus on reading or writing even though the policies of the schools seemed to emphasize literacy skills and behaviors (para. 17). A similar observation study by Smith, Jimenez, and Martinez-Leon (2003) in Mexico noted that the practice of reading and writing in the classrooms was set "outside of course activities and focused more on form than content and was not considered important to the overall aspects of the course and the learning processes of the students" (p. 775). Similar observations have been noted in Colombia.

Barletta et al. (2002) investigated the reading competences in Spanish courses of first-semester students from 10 different UniNorte programs. Their study found that the majority of these students had difficulties with literacy practices. The Barletta study reported that the students tended to transcribe pertinent information and then elaborate texts literally. The study further indicated that the students had problems with semantic competence and did not seem to read at inferential levels or demonstrate global comprehension of intermediate-level texts. The comments indicated that teachers did not appear to take counter-measures to help the students reach higher reading levels. These findings suggest that subsequent language learning might also be affected by these first language practices. As Devine (1993) commented, developing reading and writing competence presents a substantial challenge to EFL and English as a second language students. Meeting those challenges by teaching the skills and strategies that are critical to students' academic success is imperative, she observed. Our goal at the institute then was to determine some of the major challenges our students faced and make necessary adjustments. Although the TOEFL ITP scores did reveal some of the issues, we needed to enter the classroom to be certain what the problems were.

Procedures

An adapted action research approach presented by Burns (1999), which involves exploring, identifying, planning, collecting, analyzing, hypothesizing, intervening, observing, and writing (p. 35), was chosen for this investigation. We used this approach to guide us to discover some of the learning and teaching practices used and perhaps suggest an explanation for some of the lower scores on the TEOFL ITP. As teacher researchers, we identified three specific objectives for exploring, collection, and analysis.

Our first objective was to reflect on our current teaching practices to determine what we were doing, what we felt we were accomplishing, and what we believed needed improvement. We identified three basic areas to evaluate:

1. What do we do to meet the objectives?

2. What objectives of the levels are met from what we do?

3. Which objectives of the levels are not met or need improvement?

We each answered the questions individually and then met to discuss the results. This gave us a basic perspective regarding our practices in the various courses and how they related to the institute's reading and writing objectives for Levels 5 and 6. Although this step was not an integral part of the classroom research, it permitted us to recognize how we were achieving the course objectives and later compare our practices with how our students were achieving these same objectives.

The second objective was to survey students' current reading and writing practices as well as their attitudes toward these activities in both their first language (L1) and their subsequent language (L2). This information was obtained by administering a questionnaire to classroom participants (see Appendix A). The beginning of the survey allowed us to determine if our students were entering the program with an English study background outside the institute's program or were continuing students within the program. Then, the survey uncovered feelings students had toward reading and writing, provided information about strategy awareness, and revealed some existing reading and writing practices in English (L2) and Spanish (L1). We considered it important to include questions regarding students' L1 practices to obtain general ideas about their current practices for comparison purposes.

The third objective was achieved through classroom study. Our objective was to observe, take notes, and clarify what strategies the students used and how they were using them in the classroom. This part of the investigation consisted of three distinct paths to achieve our specific objective: (1) observations, (2) evaluations of classroom activities, and (3) semistructured, whole-class interviews. Each of us observed her students working on a classroom activity, revised the activity, and later returned with questions that had arisen. The observations, the analysis of final products, and the interviews were expected to provide us with a clearer representation of what our students' practices really were.

We decided that observation by the classroom teacher would be the best choice for the first part of the classroom study because it allowed natural interaction without the interference of external observers and the resulting pressure to give appropriate responses (Lerner, 1997). Before the observations, we decided the specific areas we wanted to observe while the students worked to complete the assignments. These specific areas, which came from our own contextual knowledge and experience, were the following:

- Interaction—Did the students choose to work together or alone? If they worked together, what were some of the things discussed?

- Language choices—Did the students use Spanish or English to interact and share? In the final product, what tense aspects and vocabulary did they choose?

- Strategy use—Were there any specific noticeable strategies the students used?

- Correction—What types of correction strategies, if any, did the students demonstrate before they turned in the product?

- Final product—What were the final products like? Were there any notable concerns? What do we want to ask our students during the interviews?

Each of the observations took place during a class session. The Level 5 students, with their teachers A and B, participated in the reading study. They went to the library, where they read an article from an English language magazine they had previously chosen. During the reading activity, they were given the following instructions to uncover their reading practices and strategies:

- From the title, what do you think you are going to read? Answer before you read. Give an opinion.

- Write the first line of the first three paragraphs here.

- Read the article. Do not write in the magazine please. Below you can write difficult vocabulary.

- Summarize the article. Do not copy a single word. Use your own English and write in the present tense what the story says. 100 words.

At the end of this assignment, the students were given a second set of questions to have them reflect on what happened during the reading process and what they were thinking while completing the activity:

- What is your opinion of the article?

- What went through your mind while you were reading?

- Did you translate a lot? Why or why not?

- Did you use a dictionary while you were reading? Why or why not?

- Was it difficult to read a real text in English? Why or why not?

The Level 6 students, with their teachers B and C, participated in the writing study. Students were asked to write an opinion essay. This activity also related to the teaching of grammar from their textbooks. While the students worked, each of us observed and took notes on what her students had been doing during the classroom activity.

Once we completed our observations, we were able to evaluate our students' final products. We analyzed the reading assignments with regard to how students responded to the questions. In turn, we analyzed the writing assignments for structure, vocabulary, and content. Then, we compared these results with the comments and curiosities collected during the observation to create interview questions.

The interview process was used for clarification purposes. The teacher researcher returned to the classroom to ask participants some questions regarding the general practices noted in the final products. The interviews were semistructured, held during class time, and involved all participants of each course.

Once all the procedures were completed, we triangulated the information gathered from the initial reflection, the survey, and the classroom study (observations, evaluation of classroom activities, and semistructured interview) to identify any differences between our students' learning and our teaching practices.

Results

Overall, the analyses of our practices (see Appendix B) showed incongruence in our approaches and methodologies to obtain the objectives for Levels 5 and 6. Our students clarified what their previous English learning practices were, if they felt they had been prepared for reading and writing, what their attitudes toward the reading and writing process were, and what reading and writing practices they currently used. The classroom investigation (the observations, the review of final tasks, and the interviews) demonstrated that our students were capable of undertaking reading and writing assignments at their levels, but our study revealed that their practices were not necessarily critically developed.

When we looked at our responses to the research questions about what we were doing, what we felt we were accomplishing, and what we believed needed improvement, we found different teaching practices for each of us. In terms of how we obtained level objectives, we found that we tended to use the reading texts from the book to practice reading strategies, which consisted of identifying main ideas, accessing background information, making predictions, recognizing vocabulary from context, and answering general comprehension questions. Although some of these activities were more critical than others, we did not go any further than the instructions provided in the book to complete each task. Sometimes, we supplemented book activities with readings from magazines, Web sites, or news articles, with little or no reference to what students were actually learning. The writing practices were also consistently based on the textbook, including having students write summaries, letters, opinions, narratives, or group stories. None of us mentioned any other, specifically critical, practices regarding the teaching of reading or writing. We gave similar answers when we looked at what objectives we met. We tended to review the grammar aspects given in the textbook and to cover general reading and writing aspects such as identifying main ideas, expressing and justifying opinions, identifying specific and general information, using deduction, discussing familiar topics, and writing short compositions. However, when we responded to what we felt was weak or needed improvement in our teaching, we indicated that organizational aspects of texts, longer writings, cohesive devices, and vocabulary were not being addressed adequately in our classroom practices. We considered this an interesting and thought-provoking discovery.

When we reviewed the information about students' current reading and writing practices and their attitudes toward these activities in their L1 and L2 (see Table 1), we found that most of our students had been in the university for more than 2 years and that most of their English studies had been with the institute. The data showed that 41.1% of the students felt that they had spent less than 15% of their time in previous English courses practicing reading and writing. Almost all believed that they had been well prepared for reading and writing in

Spanish, commenting on the fact that it was their first language. However, only half of the students felt that they had been well prepared for reading and writing in English.

Most of the students mentioned that they typically approached a reading text in either English or Spanish by looking at the title and subtitle. Their approaches

Table 1. Student Survey Results (*n* = 130)

Questions	Answer	%
1. How many semesters have you been studying English?	a) less than 2	40.0
	b) 3–4	26.2
	c) 5–6	24.7
	d) 7–8	9.1
2. In your previous English courses how much time was dedicated to reading and writing?	a) about 10%	10.3
	b) about 15%	30.8
	c) about 20%	34.8
	d) more than 25%	24.1
3. Would you say you have been well prepared for reading and writing in Spanish?	a) yes	86.5
	b) no	13.4
4. Would you say you have been well prepared for reading and writing in English?	a) yes	51.0
	b) no	49.0
5. Choose the best way you begin a reading assignment in Spanish.	a) I look at the title and subtitles.	65.0
	b) I just start reading.	33.2
	c) I don't read it because I don't understand anything.	1.0
	d) I find a friend who has already read the assignment.	0.8
6. Choose the best way you begin a reading assignment in English.	a) I look at the title and subtitles.	52.1
	b) I just start reading.	25.0
	c) I don't read it because I don't understand anything.	4.0
	d) I translate everything I can.	18.9

(continued on p. 14)

Table 1. Student Survey Results (*n* = 130) *(continued)*

Questions	Answer	%
7. Choose the best way you begin a writing assignment in Spanish.	a) I just start writing.	23.5
	b) I think about what I want to say and make notes.	65.2
	c) I make an outline/map of what I want to say.	7.0
	d) I find a friend who has already written the assignment.	4.3
8. Choose the best way you begin a writing assignment in English.	a) I just start writing.	16.6
	b) I think about what I want to say and make notes.	64.3
	c) I make an outline/map of what I want to say.	9.8
	d) I translate my Spanish into English on a computer.	9.3
9. How many hours a week do you read for FUN (free time) in Spanish?	a) 1–2	44.7
	b) 3–4	20.5
	c) more than 4	22.0
	d) I never read	8.3
10. How many hours a week do you read for FUN (free time) in English?	a) 1–2	43.1
	b) 3–4	9.0
	c) more than 4	6.7
	d) I never read	41.1
11. Do you know what a reading or writing strategy is?	a) yes	23.0
	b) no	77.0
12. How important is reading and writing in Spanish to you?	a) very important	81.1
	b) somewhat important	9.1
	c) rarely important	6.5
	d) not at all important	3.3
13. How important is reading and writing in English to you?	a) very important	77.3
	b) somewhat important	12.9
	c) rarely important	5.0
	d) not at all important	4.8

to writing tasks, however, differed in Spanish and English. They reported that in Spanish they thought about the task or did some sort of planning before they wrote, whereas in English they just started with the actual writing task. Reading for fun in either language was not a common practice. Almost half of the students reported that they read 1–2 hours a day in Spanish; however, almost half of them stated that they never read in English. Most students felt that the writing assignments they were given in either language were not too difficult to accomplish; in fact, they indicated that the tasks might have been simple in terms of content. By contrast, they considered reading assignments a little more difficult. Most of the students agreed that reading and writing in both English and Spanish were very important. The students' information was useful in helping us begin to understand some of their current practices more clearly.

We could then tackle our research objective to observe, take notes, and clarify what strategies the students used and how they were using them in the classroom. Our observations of students while they were participating in class activities presented surprising results. The reading assignment observations (see Table 2) show that not even one third of the students followed the instructions given; they simply started to read their articles. The observations also confirmed a large amount of interaction in Spanish. The students displayed no

Table 2. Results of Reading Analyses (n = 67)

Objective	Common Results
Observations	
Interaction	Students asked questions of each other and teacher.
Language Choices	Students conducted most interactions in Spanish.
Strategy Use	Nobody took notes. Most students just read.
Correction	No revisions were turned in.
Final Product Evaluation	
Predicting	Not more than 15% of participants actually preread the activity.
Expressed Opinion	None provided an opinion.
Thoughts While Reading	Comments included "Visualization couldn't focus," "guessed the entire reading," "felt very stressed," "not much."
Translate	Some translated while reading.
Dictionary Use	No dictionaries were used.
Notable Comments	Why was the opinion omitted? What are they thinking?

Note: Results represent the common factors noted by the two teachers involved in the reading process.

other observable strategies, such as note taking or dictionary use. The written assignment observations had similar notations (see Table 3). Most students asked others questions, looking for confirmation and assistance. The language they used was simple for their level. It appeared, and it was demonstrated by the students' interaction, as if most of them were thinking in Spanish, then translating into English. They used books, dictionaries, and each other to help them through the composing process. They also asked their teacher to provide spellings and translations of certain words. There were no obvious prewriting practices observed other than talking among themselves. The students did not draw on their classmates for help with checking or proofreading the final version of their texts.

Evaluating the final reading and writing tasks helped us obtain a clearer focus for the interviews. In the final written tasks of the reading assignments (see Table 2), most students stated that they were trying to visualize what they were reading, others had serious difficulties understanding the text, and some mentioned that they had guessed vocabulary and meaning from what they did know. There were a few students who did not have difficulties with their chosen articles because they were accustomed to reading in English. Most students could summarize the articles, but they generally copied written information from the articles. All students left the opinion questions unanswered. Also, most of the students admitted to translating the article word for word, and almost all of them indicated that they found the vocabulary from the reading difficult. The final written products were simple in structure, vocabulary, and content (see Table 4). The students chose appropriate wording according to their level and used compound sentences. Adverb and preposition use was weak, as was the grammar used in the activity. An interesting note is that most of the final products seem to suggest some negative transfer from Spanish. This transfer showed up in word choices such as *consecuencies* for *consequences* and *this* for *these* (see Appendix C).

Table 3. Results of Writing Observations (*n* = 63)

Objective	Common Results
Observations	
Interaction	Students asked questions of each other and teacher, such as "How say . . ." for "What is . . . ?" and "How write . . . ?" for "How do you spell . . . ?"
Language Choices	Students had mostly Spanish interactions.
Strategy Use	Nobody prewrote. Most students just began writing.
Correction	No obvious revisions were turned in.

Note: Results represent the common factors noted by the two teachers involved in the writing activity.

Table 4. Overall Usage of Writing Practices in Student Reports (*n* = 63)

Practice	No Usage (%)	Some (%)	Acceptable (%)	Good (%)	Excellent (%)
Preposition Use	62	15	7	8	8
Adverb Use	67	29	4	0	0
Connector Use	14	44	18	12	12
Stated Opinion	55	21	12	12	0
Complex Structures	18	4	29	35	14
Paragraphing (Introduction, Supporting Points, Conclusion)	6	18	37	25	14
Spelling	0	11	7	22	60
Punctuation	5	29	37	22	7

When we returned to the participating classrooms, the final step for the classroom study, we asked questions about our teacher-researcher observations and the final products. Teachers A and B asked their students why most of them had chosen to read the entire article before reading and guessing from the title. In response, the students indicated that it was just easier for them that way; they did what they were used to doing. When asked why they thought they needed to write down the first sentence of the first three paragraphs, not one of them was able to express that usually the first sentence of a paragraph contains the general idea of the paragraph and thus aids in comprehension without the need to read the entire text. When they were asked why they did not answer the opinion question, the students said that they agreed with the author of the article and did not feel the need to write more. Some of them also mentioned that there was not enough time to complete the activity. The students agreed that the assignment was difficult for them. However, they viewed it as good practice because it was "real English" and therefore offered the vocabulary they needed.

The students of teachers B and C said during their interviews (see Table 5) that they knew how to use prewriting strategies and why they existed; however, they did not bother with prewriting because there was not enough time, because they were not interested, or because there were too many language difficulties. The students also said that they did not proofread but were aware of the necessity of proofreading their work. They said they did not revise their work because they were never instructed to do so and because the grade did not seem to be affected by it. They revealed that they did not like to write in English and that when writing in Spanish they felt less confined by the structure and more free

Table 5. Interview Results

Question	Common Responses
Reading (*n* = 67)	
Why did they not predict?	It was easier to read the article. The title was confusing and difficult. They were scared to guess.
Why did they not write opinions?	The article was good. They agreed with the author. There was not time to finish.
Why was the article difficult?	The article was in real English, which they found difficult without a dictionary. The vocabulary was difficult.
Did anyone understand why students had to copy the first three paragraphs?	None understood the purpose.
Writing (*n* = 63)	
Why did they not prewrite?	There was not enough time. It never seemed to affect the final grade. They did not know how.
Why was it difficult?	Writing in Spanish was easier, simpler, less confining.
Why did they not use proofreading or peer correction?	It did not seem necessary. They were never told to do so.

to discuss whatever they wanted, regardless of punctuation, paragraphing, or content focus. All students said that writing was important but was not the most important task for them. Essentially, they made it clear that they did not see the necessity of perfecting their reading or writing at the moment, however necessary they deemed it.

Reflection

This investigation began in response to the concern about the low scores our students had received on the TOEFL ITP. We assumed that the problem occurred primarily because of students' practices and expected that studying classroom practices would support our assumptions. However, the results reflected that the students were not necessarily at fault. We discovered that we were perpetuating common literacy practices in the learning of the L2 and that there was interconnectedness between teacher and learner. This investigation provided an impetus for change.

When we did our reflective analyses of our teaching and of how we met objectives in our Level 5 and 6 courses, we were not paying attention to our own answers. Only after we entered the classrooms from a researcher perspective did we notice that we did not teach our students to be critical participants in their practices. For example, in the results we noticed that students could not explain the general concept behind writing the first sentence of the first three paragraphs of the article they had read. We found that Teachers A and B assumed that the students had general academic preparation for reading in English, and therefore we did not activate or teach the importance and practice of this skill.

We also found that as teachers we have become accustomed to using the textbook as the major component of our teaching and that our students have learned to demonstrate their learning by repeating and reiterating given information. This practice became apparent when we looked at the reading and writing results. For the reading task, Teachers A and B were expecting perfect reading practices set outside the classroom and outside the English class context. Teachers B and C reported in the analysis of the writing activity that students placed more value on form than on content. These observations suggested that we were employing little critical pedagogy in our practices and that we should become more aware of our tendency to teach by instinct. We needed to eliminate our assumptions and implement teaching practices that enabled our students to become more critically literate and interested.

The investigation as a whole was helpful to the pedagogical practices of all three of us, and we expect the results to lead to changes in the institute. The participants in the investigation motivated us to continue studying classroom practices so we can incorporate more meaningful activities for learning. Two of us (Teachers A and B) have begun direct reading strategy teaching in our specific classrooms. We have also added more academic readings as well as extended readings to enhance reading competencies. Two of us (Teachers B and C) have integrated writing skills into daily classroom teaching practices, making these practices part of the course rather than a separate function with a grade. We have all started to talk with our students before any activity begins, explaining, verifying, or explicitly helping them understand what strategies they are using or should be using to complete the activities. We have found this a great approach for establishing rapport in addition to motivating students to use more noticeable reading and writing processes and produce more concise and worthwhile finished products.

Studying strategy use within a classroom and discovering differences is a recommended method for unveiling practices. As Hutchinson and Waters (1987) advised, "if learners, sponsors, and teachers know why the learners need English (and how they are learning it), that awareness will have an influence on what will be accepted as reasonable content in the language courses . . . and what potential can be exploited" (p. 5). We have learned that our students need direct guidance and instruction to carry out critical reading and writing activities with a higher level of accomplishment. This goal will drive us to adjust to the participants we have in front of us as we strive for the institute's expected results for the TOEFL ITP.

Angela Bailey teaches at Universidad del Norte in Barranquilla, Colombia.
Lourdes Rey teaches at Universidad del Norte.
Nayibe Rosado also teaches at Universidad del Norte.

Appendix A: Reading and Writing Questionnaire

The following questionnaire is to evaluate your knowledge, feelings, and understanding of reading and writing in both your Spanish and your English. Please read the questions carefully and answer the questions according to which answer best suits you.

1) How many semesters have you been studying English?

   a) Less than 2 semesters

   b) 3–4 semesters

   c) 5–6 semesters

   d) 7–8 semesters

2) In your previous English courses, how much time was dedicated to reading and writing?

   a) About 10% of the course

   b) About 15% of the course

   c) About 20% of the course

   d) More than 25% of the course

3) Would you say you have been well prepared for reading and writing in Spanish?

   a) Yes

   b) No

4) Would you say you have been well prepared for reading and writing in English?

   a) Yes

   b) No

5) Choose the best way you begin a reading assignment in Spanish.

   a) I look at the title and subtitles.

   b) I just start reading.

   c) I don't read it because I don't understand anything.

   d) I find a friend who has already read the assignment.

6) Choose the best way you begin a reading assignment in English.

   a) I look at the title and subtitles.

   b) I just start reading.

   c) I don't read it because I don't understand anything.

   d) I translate everything I can.

7) Choose the best way you begin a writing assignment in Spanish.

   a) I just start writing.

   b) I think about what I want to say and make notes.

   c) I make an outline/map of what I want to say.

   d) I find a friend who has already written the assignment.

8) Choose the best way you begin a writing assignment in English.

   a) I just start writing.

   b) I think about what I want to say and make notes.

   c) I make an outline/map of what I want to say.

   d) I translate my Spanish into English on a computer.

9) How many hours a week do you read for FUN (free time) in Spanish?

   a) 1–2 hours

   b) 3–4 hours

   c) More than 4 hours

   d) I never read

10) How many hours a week do you read for FUN (free time) in English?

    a) 1–2 hours

    b) 3–4 hours

    c) More than 4 hours

    d) I never read

11) Do you know what a reading or writing strategy is?

    a) Yes

    b) No

12) How important is reading and writing in Spanish to you?

    a) Very important

    b) Somewhat important

    c) Rarely important

    d) Not at all important

13) How important is reading and writing in English to you?

    a) Very important

    b) Somewhat important

    c) Rarely important

    d) Not at all important

Appendix B: Reflection on Teaching Practices

Specific Level 5 reading and writing objectives:

- Identify general and specific information in a given text.

- Deduce words from the context of a reading.

- Write short, coherent essays using connectors.

- Express opinions, likes, and dislikes based on information given by peers using current technological tools.

Specific Level 6 reading and writing objectives:

- Compose personal presentations.

- Identify and use reference elements.

- Use ideas in an organized and coherent fashion in paragraphs.

- Express what they would do in certain situations.

- Express opinions and ideas with respect to themes discussed in class.

- Write a short, argumentative essay (200–250 words).

- Narrate stories that have happened, or mysteries or facts seen or heard.

- Infer ideas in distinct written styles.

- Read analytically and critically.

- Reinforce reading strategies.

What do we do to meet the objectives?

We do short readings, biographies, summaries, predictions, life histories, quizzes, strategies for texts such as identifying main ideas, making deductions, making predictions, analyzing vocabulary from context, skimming, and scanning. We also have them write opinions, narratives, dialogues, reports using direct speech, chats in WebCT, additional reading from the Internet, and mysteries.

What objectives of the levels are met from what we do?

We address a general review of grammar, some lexical knowledge mastery, identifying main ideas, expressing and justifying opinions, identifying specific and general information, and deduction/predictions.

Which objectives of the levels are not met or need improvement?

We do not address organizational aspects of written texts, give explicit help or information for essay writing, help with vocabulary acquisition, or allow for more autonomous behaviors from the students.

Appendix C: Sample Student Writings

SAMPLE 1

In this days, the people enjoy are free, but this liberty is not absolute because the society have a rules that the people should obey.

Sincerely, I think that the people always have the liberty to do things that they enjoy doing, but this things should respect to laws.

Sometimes, the people should do thing that they do not enjoy, because this things could inrespect to other person.

SAMPLE 2

In many cases the people do not like listen to the truth, because in different situation telling the truth is very cruel.

In my personal opinion the people should tell the truth, but I can not tell the truth because it depends of different situations if your truth could destroy families persons etc. you can tell the truth, but you have to analize the consecuencies. In different situations to know this, can help us, because you look for solutions for yourself, sometimes people do not accept and they prefer listen a series of lies.

However, while the people are growing, learn in what situation tell or not the truth. The problem is not tell the truth but how the people accept this in the best way.

CHAPTER 3

Revisiting Peer Review (*Canada*)

Sandra Burger and Catherine Danforth

Issue

In the winter of 2005, two classes at a bilingual Canadian university—one teacher training class, one English as a subsequent language (ESL) writing class—were the subject of an investigation into the influence that direct experience with ESL writing would have on the developing expertise of student teachers. The student teacher participants were enrolled in Teaching Speaking and Writing to ESL Students, a language pedagogy course that was part of an undergraduate program in second language (L2) teaching. This one-semester, 12-week writing pedagogy course is normally taken in the 1st or 2nd year of the program. This class consisted of 27 students, of whom 5 were not native speakers of English. These 5 participated in the exchanges but were not included in the study because it relied on native-speaker reactions to ESL texts. The 25 participating ESL students from 10 different language backgrounds were registered in an undergraduate university credit-bearing course, Advanced Level I Reading to Writing, which met 3 hours per week. The central question of this investigation was: Can prospective writing teachers be trained to provide feedback that leads writers toward successful revision?

The collaboration between the two classes consisted of ESL writers sharing the first drafts of six texts with a designated partner in the teacher training class. The student teachers, with guidance from the instructor in their pedagogy class, commented on photocopies of these drafts as they received them. The original papers, now with comments, went back to their ESL authors. The expectation was that the L2 writers could benefit from native speakers' responses to their drafts. The collaboration with an ESL class of heterogeneous L1 backgrounds provided the student teachers with a range of real writing problems to address. Through these exchanges, we were able to study the development in student teachers of writing response techniques.

THE FIRST ISSUE

In planning this writing pedagogy class, the instructor wished to provide her students with hands-on experience that had more authenticity for them than a bank of anonymous ESL papers. She decided to partner her students with actual ESL writers and have her students respond to the drafts. She wondered whether this would provide adequate experience for her students to implement the theory they were being taught at the same time. She expected that coaching by the instructor would ensure that the ESL students received suitable feedback and avoided the pitfalls noted by Zamel (1985), in particular the treatment of and reaction to grammar errors. With these safeguards in place, we felt comfortable implementing this study and were able to investigate the effectiveness of training prospective teachers in this way.

THE SECOND ISSUE

The ESL classroom teacher hoped her students would gain additional feedback on their writing, beyond the feedback she was able to offer. Because the student teachers were to comment under the supervision of the pedagogy instructor, the ESL instructor anticipated that their comments would be in the main helpful and give her students additional learning opportunities. In the typical peer review scenario, classmates—approximate peers as to writing proficiency—exchange texts and make comments to help their partners improve their drafts. However, in this case the peers were native speakers of the language, students of roughly the same age, with a shared interest in ESL writing but coming from a different perspective. The ESL instructor also anticipated that the exchange would provide the benefits of peer review without some of the difficulties identified by Leki (1990). She hoped that, as a consequence, ESL students would be more discriminating in their revisions because the suggestions would come from peers and not from their teacher, the final evaluator of their assignments.

Background Literature

TRAINING ESL WRITING TEACHERS

Reid (1993) described the roles the ESL writing teacher must assume: "coach, judge, facilitator, evaluator, interested reader, and copy editor" (p. 217). This is a tall order for a beginning teacher. Notwithstanding this broad range of future responsibilities, Leki noted in 1992 that until recently few ESL teachers had received specific training in teaching writing. Even in the past several years, few graduate ESL programs were noted for including separate courses in teaching writing (Crusan, 2005; Garshick, 2002; Matsuda, 2003). In other words, there is a dearth of teacher training programs that actually train teachers to teach writing. Even in the few enlightened programs, training in giving appropriate feedback is often missing. Consequently, the beginning teacher must learn on the job. A comment by Crusan (2005) struck us as typical of one problem that beginning writing teachers face:

> I remember the first time, as a very green teacher right out of a teacher educa-
> tion program at a small western Pennsylvania university, I gave a writing
> assignment to my L1 [first language] developmental writers. When the students
> handed in their work, I was stunned with the realization that I had not the
> slightest idea of how I would assign a grade. Clearly, I was unprepared for
> the task before me. I had established no criteria by which I would assess what
> my students had written. Worse yet, I was not sure where I might find help.
> I quickly realized that I had little expertise in the teaching of writing and
> still less proficiency in the assessment of writing. I felt slighted by my teacher
> preparation courses, especially the testing and measurements course in which
> the professor had spent nearly the entire semester teaching us to write "good"
> multiple-choice questions! (p. 3)

It is important to write good multiple-choice questions, but the art of responding to student writing does not deserve the neglect it often receives. This art is a demanding one.

Although professors of specific content areas appear to be less disturbed by grammar errors than by the perceived lack of maturity of thought and of rhetorical style in L2 students' writing (Leki, 1990), writing teachers generally fall into the trap of attending to surface-level features even in first drafts (Zamel, 1985). This practice gives learners the false impression that these features of writing are more important than meaning-related concerns. Other pitfalls teachers face in providing corrections, as noted by Zamel, include misreading student texts, displaying inconsistent reactions, providing arbitrary corrections, writing contradictory comments, offering vague prescriptions, and rarely making content-specific comments or offering specific strategies for revising the text. Zamel also found that teachers' comments on organization were general and vague.

The more conscientious the teacher is in giving feedback to student writers, the more passive the students seem to become. Ferris (2003) cautioned teachers against appropriating the students' texts by being too directive in written feedback. Reid (1995) spoke of "the tension between appropriation (rewriting the passage for the student) and intervention (describing what the student text seems to say, discussing the linguistic and rhetorical decisions the student has made, and offering alternatives based on the teacher's knowledge of North American audience expectations)" (p. 164). She further described her own experience with student drafts as follows: "The more time I spend with student drafts, the less time students spend on them; that is, once students see how interested I am in making suggestions to improve their drafts, they do their best to transfer all responsibility to me" (p. 165). Sommers (1982) noted that students surrender ownership of their work particularly when teachers identify errors in usage, diction, and style in a first draft and ask students to correct these errors when they revise. Zamel (1985) further noted that if teachers misconstrue the meaning of students' texts, the students are unlikely to point this out to their teachers. Finally, Leki (1990) concluded that appropriation of the students' writing by the teacher is at least to some extent inevitable "because students know very well that whoever gives the grade is the audience" (p. 60).

Three of Ferris's (2003) suggestions for preparing student teachers to respond to student writing stood out for the pedagogy teacher. First, Ferris said, student teachers should read through the text without writing comments. Next, they should write an encouraging endnote with a summary comment. Only then may they proceed to specific marginal comments. In this study, student teachers needed to be especially clear about the purpose of each assignment, so they would know what elements to look for in the text. Student teachers also need to keep in mind that responding to ESL writers' texts should entail individualized communication between the teacher and the writer, as Ferris advised. They should, therefore, also consider the writer's individual strengths, weaknesses, and interlanguage level.

An earlier study by Ferris (1997) provides insights into the kinds of comments writing teachers make. In that study, one experienced teacher graded 800 essays in the context of a freshman creative writing class. Ferris categorized the 1,526 comments. The approach taken in that class was process writing. Ferris found marginal comments to be text specific and end comments to be more general. In her study, the most common marginal comments were those asking for information, and the other comments were spread consistently across her seven remaining types. The most common end comment was positive. There were more requests in statement than in question or imperative form. Few of the comments related to grammar, and most of those were found in end comments.

RESPONDING TO ESL WRITING

The process approach to writing instruction (Zamel, 1982) requires that students write several drafts of their work and submit each draft to the teacher for revision suggestions. Evidence (Freedman, 1987; Ziv, 1984) suggests that teacher intervention during the writing and revising stages results in improvements in final products as compared with intermediate drafts. The teacher must be careful to consider the work as a draft and not as a finished product. The proponents of process writing encourage teachers to focus on content rather than form at the draft stage, that is, on the logical development of ideas rather than on mechanical problems that may disappear in subsequent drafts. Even if teachers do restrict their suggestions to matters of content, student writers may still "unquestioningly alter both the form and the content of their writing, assuming that the native-speaking teacher must know what is required in English writing" (Leki, 1992, p. 123), and thus the possibility of development is lost. Peer review, then, is one way to counteract this tendency of students to abdicate responsibility for their own texts.

This peer review process has advantages and disadvantages. Three benefits of peer review and response noted by Ferris (2003) are as follows: (1) additional feedback from a more diverse audience than their teacher alone, (2) feedback that they will not be afraid to discount if they so wish, and (3) feedback from naïve readers noting when the author's ideas are not clearly expressed. Leki (1990), on the other hand, pointed to some of the difficulties with typical ESL peer responses, suggesting they are "ineffective responding behaviours, making . . . comments that are overly directive, blunt or even unkind, and lack face validity in that ESL writers do not trust their peers' expertise" (p. 108). More precisely, Ferris (2003) identified the following problems: ESL writers have difficulty identifying which writing issues have priority; they are unable to provide specific, helpful feedback; and, from the teacher's point of view, peer review is too time-consuming.

Procedures

Each of the two courses involved in this study had a specific curriculum and textbook. The ESL writing text was *Reading Writing: Skills for ESL* (Dasgupta & Redfern, 1997), which focused primarily on paragraph writing. Four in-class writing assignments were preselected for the study: selective summary, unity paragraph, coherence paragraph, and point-by-point summary. The textbook for the ESL pedagogy course was *Understanding ESL Writers: A Guide for Teachers* (Leki, 1992), and supplementary readings on responding to student writing consisted of *Teaching ESL Writing* (Reid, 1993) and the article "Responding to Student Writing" (Sommers, 1982). Each set of completed assignments was photocopied, with appropriate permission, and delivered to the student teachers at their next class for their feedback. (For the fourth exchange, the pedagogy instructor provided the student teachers with two photocopies of each ESL paper, one for their customary feedback, the other for student teachers to practice giving corrective feedback on grammar and mechanics.)

The interval between production and receipt of commentary was 1 week. The student teachers also received photocopies of the writing checklists that the ESL students used for each task (see Figure 1), as well as the ESL in-class writing assignments (see Figure 2). Each student teacher was required to write commentary and return the text with feedback to an assigned peer partner. Initially two practice assignments (not included in this study) gave the student teachers their first exposure to ESL writing. In line with Ferris's (2003) suggestions, the student

Selective (Biographical) Summary	
• Does your **Topic Sentence** contain	*Author's name?* *Article title?* *Subject (a person)?* *Focus (a life)?*
• Do you have relevant **Supporting Details**	Life details (chronological)?
• Have you written a **Concluding Sentence**	Return to Subject and Focus?
Paragraph Unity (Choice of Three Topics)	
• Is your paragraph **Complete**?	Nothing missing
• Is it **Organized**?	Nothing out of order
• Is it **Whole**?	Nothing irrelevant
• Is only one **Voice** speaking?	No other person intrudes
Paragraph Coherence (Marriage)	
• Have you used **Time Words**?	Ordering ideas
• Have you used **Transition Words**?	Linking Sentences
• Are **Key Ideas** repeated?	*Linking ideas*
Have you used **Pronouns and Indicating Words**?	*Linking nouns + determiners*
Point-by-Point Summary (Business)	
• Topic sentence: Author and title/subject and focus	
• Supporting details: main points	
• Concluding sentence	

Figure 1. ESL writing checklist.

1. **Selective (Biographical) Summary**
   Take notes on the article by Carol Howes.
   Purpose: to write a biographical summary of the life of Alan Whittall.
   Note: author's name and title.
   Identify: biographical information in the article.
   Select: important details about his life.

2. **Unity Paragraph**
   Choose one of the following subjects and write a unified paragraph about it.
   Violence on Television
   English Grammar
   Valentine's Day
   Remember, your paragraph must
   - be **Complete, Ordered,** and **Whole**.
   - have a **Consistent Point of View** and a **Concluding Sentence**.

3. **Coherence Paragraph**
   Write a paragraph of your own about marriage. Your paragraph may describe your picture of the ideal marriage, or your ideal partner. Make sure your paragraph has a clear topic sentence giving the subject and focus, details supporting the main idea in the topic sentence, unity of ideas, and especially coherence.

4. **Point-by-Point Summary**
   Write a one-paragraph point-by-point summary of the article by Debra Black. Be sure to mention the title of the article in your summary's topic sentence.

Figure 2. ESL in-class writing assignments.

teachers each responded to the same partner throughout the exchange whenever possible, so as to be familiar with their peer partner's strengths and weaknesses.

Throughout the exchanges between the classes, the student teachers were instructed to be positive, be specific, and respond to the instructional focus of the assignment. During an initial practice exchange, we had noted that the student teachers tended to correct surface errors. Furthermore, the ESL teacher noted inaccuracies in the "corrections" offered. Thus, thereafter the student teachers were reminded not to correct grammar at the first-draft stage. Guidelines for the task required them to read the entire text before writing any comments; to write an encouraging, general endnote summarizing the main points to revise; and then to write specific marginal suggestions for revision. After each exchange, the annotated texts were photocopied for later tabulation and analysis, then returned to the ESL students. Before the student teachers commented on the next ESL assignment, they received feedback from the pedagogy teacher on their response to the previous one.

A number of questionnaires were distributed to ascertain the reactions of all the participants. To get the ESL learners' impressions of the exchange, an open-ended questionnaire was handed out in class at the completion of the study to be filled out anonymously. Feedback from the student teachers on how useful they considered each exercise was collected through a Likert scale and open-ended questions at the end of the project.

Following the exchanges, we began our analysis of the data. We categorized and counted all student teacher comments. We first counted the number and length of marginal versus end comments. We also took note of whether the comments were general or specific. The analysis of the comment types was based on Ferris's (1997) classification system (see the left-hand column of Table 1). In contrast to the assignments in Ferris's study, however, the writing tasks in this study were more structured. Only Assignments 2 and 3 involved creative writing. We therefore wrote parallel examples (see italicized words in the right-hand column of Table 1) to approximate the type of comment given by the student teachers. For example, Ferris's reference to a thesis statement (Example 2) was not relevant to paragraph writing. The final assignment comments relating to grammar or mechanics (Type 8) were not included in the analysis because the pedagogy teacher had asked the student teachers to comment on this aspect only for her (on a separate photocopy).

Results

Table 2 reflects the count of marginal and end comments. Marginal comments ranged from 247 short ones to 10 very long ones. Endnotes showed the reverse ratio (16 short and 113 very long.) The findings match those of Ferris (1997); marginal comments were shorter than endnotes due to space limitations and the more general nature of endnotes. As anticipated, more of the marginal comments, 334, were text specific, and only 116 were of a general nature; 74 of the end comments were text specific, and 130 were general.

The tabulation of categorized student teacher comments is presented in Table 3. The most frequent comments student teachers made, both in margins and in endnotes, fell into Type 7 (make a positive comment/statement), as shown in Table 3. This reflects their pedagogy teacher's advice that they should be positive in their feedback. Even for the two creative writing assignments, the Unity and Coherence paragraphs, the student teachers did not ask questions that might lead to broadening the content (Type 1) of the ESL text but tended to rely heavily on Type 3 (make a request/statement) and Type 4 (make a request/imperative). Even in the rarely used categories, Type 5 (give information/question) and Type 6 (give information/statement), more comments were Type 6. These results further suggest the student teachers' preferences for comments framed as statements rather than as questions.

A closer look at student teacher comments provided insight into how well

Table 1. Comment Classification Systems and Examples

Comment Types From Ferris (1997) Study	Comment Types From Current Study
1. Ask for information/question Example: *Did you work out this problem with your roommates?*	1. Ask for information/question Example: *Do you think this process really makes a relationship stronger?*
2. Make a request/question Example: *Can you provide a thesis statement here? What did you learn from this?*	2. Make a request/question Example: *Who tried to change it?*
3. Make a request/statement Example: *This paragraph might be better earlier in the essay.*	3. Make a request/statement Example: *You left out some relevant points about Whittall's successes. For example, his book.*
4. Make a request/imperative Example: *Mention what Z says about parental pressure.*	4. Make a request/imperative Example: *This idea should be linked to the previous sentence.*
5. Give information/question Example: *Most states do allow a waiting period before an adoption is final—Do you feel that all such laws are wrong?*	5. Give information/question Example: *What are your thoughts on the type of marriage you want?*
6. Give information/statement Example: *Iowa law favors parental rights. Michigan and California consider the best interests of the child.*	6. Give information/statement Example: *This (→) is your topic sentence.*
7. Make a positive comment, statement, or exclamation Example: *A very nice start to your essay! You've done an impressive job of finding facts and quotes to support your arguments.*	7. Make a positive comment/statement or exclamation Example: *Good example!*
8. Make a grammar/mechanics comment/question, statement, or imperative. Example: *Past or present tense? Your verb tenses are confusing me in this paragraph.*	8. Make a grammar/mechanics comment/question, statement, or imperative. Example: *Reorganize your sentence structure.*

they understood the task of responding to ESL writing. Figures 3 and 4 show samples of appropriate and inappropriate comments made by student teachers. The examples in Figure 3 are evidence that the student teachers, following instructions given in class, could make clear, focused comments on content for their ESL partners. For example, they indicated where they did not understand the text, where the logical coherence was missing, and what information would clarify the message. Unfortunately, however, the student teachers sometimes took

Table 2. Tabulation of Length and Specificity of Comments

Comment Category	Marginal Comments	End Comments
Short (1–5 words)	247	16
Average (6–15 words)	138	30
Long (16–25 words)	55	45
Very Long (26+ words)	10	113
Total	**450**	**204**
Text-Specific Comments	334	74
General Comments	116	130
Total	**450**	**204**

over the text or misinterpreted the intention of the ESL writer (see comments in Figure 4).

In addition to commenting inappropriately on content, when it came to surface features, student teachers sometimes made inaccurate comments. They misidentified the problem, "corrected" where no correction was necessary, or miscorrected. Examples of these problems are shown in Figure 5.

Table 3. Number of Student Teacher Comments by Type and Location

Assignment	Comment Location	Frequency of Comment Type							
		1	2	3	4	5	6	7	8
1. Biography	Margin	1	6	9	9	0	7	29	25
	End	0	1	12	4	1	5	38	2
2. Paragraph unity	Margin	2	12	21	13	0	4	60	16
	End	0	1	9	2	2	8	41	10
3. Paragraph Coherence	Margin	5	5	21	18	2	7	38	25
	End	0	0	6	4	0	6	44	20
4. Point-by-Point Summary	Margin	3	8	4	5	0	14	38	*
	End	0	2	11	1	0	16	29	*

Note: *Comments not tabulated because they were requested and would skew the data. Comment types are 1—Ask for information/question; 2—Make a request/question; 3—Make a request/statement; 4—Make a request/imperative; 5—Give information/question; 6—Give information/statement; 7—Make a positive comment/statement; 8—Make a grammar/mechanics comment.

Are you aware that the Toronto businessman and the old entrepreneur are the same person? The way you introduced it led me to believe that they were two different people. Is that what you wanted?

Your concluding sentence is a little abrupt—can you expand on it a little and briefly say *why* it was revolutionary?

[ESL text excerpt:] *what managers should do . . . besides being a coach* Your concluding sentence was great. It was clear and told readers you were ending your summary. One suggestion here would be to omit the words "besides . . . coach," as Howes was saying how Whittall suggests that a manager's job *is* to be a coach.

In the section where I wrote I did not understand how parenting was related to your idea of common knowledge, I think you were trying to point out that common knowledge is important to have between two people in a relationship together. Thus, when it came down to raising children together they would share common ideas on how to raise them.

Also, you might want to include what Allan Whittall was criticizing (North Americans are addicted to power and control)—it seems to be fairly relevant to the article.

Figure 3. Appropriate comments by student teachers.

The questionnaires that were distributed to the students participating in this exchange project yielded interesting and positive results. Some typical comments by the ESL students in response to the exchange experience are displayed in Figure 6. The ESL students seemed to take their partners' comments seriously

[ESL text excerpt:] *Indeed, in order to escape from the jail, Alan Whittall accepted the choice offered by a judge to participate in a university program research made about street gangs and their success.*
This sentence is a little long. Might I suggest: "In order to escape jail time, Alan Whittall accepted a proposition offered by the judge. This offer involved participating in a university research program about street gangs and their success."

[ESL text excerpt:] *Although I don't have any experience of marriage right now, I have a lovely dream for it in the future.*
You could have used a time word in this section, perhaps to indicate when you would like to be married, instead of just saying "in the future." For example: "I *often* have a lovely dream for it in the future."

I've broken down your paragraph into its components to better illustrate my comments [totaling one and a half pages]
• Introduction: People, especially the young, are affected by television violence.
• Viewers are not aware that what they see is choreographed.
• Supporting details: Due to their natural curiosity, people *learn* from television.
• They learn to imitate what they see.
• They learn that heroes do not die, nor do they get punished.

Figure 4. Inappropriate comments by student teachers.

[ESL text excerpt:] *someone who works to be self-employed have to follow* Needs proper tense → should be "has."
[ESL text excerpt:] *they found out that the seller desired to retire* Needs different verb complement, e.g., "wanted."
[ESL text excerpt:] *The first steps before buying were to acquire ... and to have* Should be in present tense → is.
[ESL text excerpt:] *As a gang leader, he encourages risk-taking and trusts people.* (Correct!) to trust. The 'to' has to go there in order to get the meaning of what you were trying to say.
[ESL text excerpt:] *because of many kinds of difficulties* "due to"
[ESL text excerpt:] for *a much lower price than proposed* "than the one" to make it parallel
[ESL text excerpt:] *Because marriage is forever, it is primordial to find the right partner.* Try not to start your sentence with "because." You could use "since" instead.

Figure 5. Miscorrections of mechanics by student teachers.

and to appreciate receiving personalized feedback from "someone other than their teacher." They indicated that they felt they had learned from the student teachers' comments.

The tabulation of student teachers' Likert responses is shown in Table 4. Almost all the student teachers found the experience useful, if not very or extremely useful, in learning to respond to ESL writing. The table below reflects how, over time, the student teachers responded more and more positively to the practice they were getting.

In addition to the Likert responses, student teachers commented on the exchange overall. They also wrote detailed comments on each assignment. They further recommended changes that might be made in future exchanges. Typical comments are displayed in Table 5. The student teachers realized with the first task that assessing and critiquing ESL texts is a daunting task. Their firsthand look at ESL writing showed them the difficulties involved in providing instructive feedback. Among other things, they learned that summary writing requires a careful reading of the source text, some thought beforehand about what to expect in the summary, and a careful reading of the student's text to ensure that they understand what the student is trying to say. They expressed uncertainty about performing the ESL tasks themselves. They noted the necessity of maintaining an objective distance to avoid appropriating or wrongly judging student writing, and the challenge of evaluating a piece of student writing that does not follow the instructions. The comment about real "teacher" writing showed the

1. Biographical Summary
• I learned which details were needed in the biographical summary.

2. Paragraph Unity (Three Topics)
- I learned how to make the details more relate to the topic sentence.
- It made my paragraph connected to each other.
- I should stick with the topic rather than getting off the track.

3. Paragraph Coherence (Marriage)
- I learned how to link paragraphy well in the essay.
- I learned the use of both transition words and subordinating conjunctions.
- I learned how to recognize a coherent paragraph.

4. Point-by-Point Summary (Business)
- I learned to write the article and author's name in the summary.
- I learned to use a few sentence to summarize the whole article which includes all the information.

5. Overall
- I could get comments for my writing from different people besides my teacher. It's helpful.
- The writing exchange was very useful.
- Sincerely, I enjoyed reading the comments and that they were pointing out some good mistakes.
- It's interesting to have another point of view about our work; and other pieces of advice.

Figure 6. Comments from ESL students.

usefulness of having an experienced teacher to guide them while learning to give students helpful feedback. In their recommendations for changes, the student teachers exhibited increased awareness of the preparation required to become a writing teacher.

Table 4. Student Teacher Likert Responses

Task	Response				
	Not Useful	Somewhat Useful	Useful	Very Useful	Extremely Useful
Biographical Summary		1	10	8	4
Paragraph Unity		1	8	11	5
Paragraph Coherence		4	6	11	3
Point-by-Point Summary			7	15	3
Overall	1		6	7	9

Table 5. Student Teacher Comments

Assignment	Comments
Biographical Summary	• How difficult it is to pick out the main points and write a summary. This activity really showed me the importance for teachers to feel competent in their own abilities. • Something that is difficult to do. I had to refrain myself from adding too many details.
Paragraph Unity	• A different point of view from mine should not hinder my reading it. • This writing piece gave us a chance to use real "teacher" comments. Sandy's comments helped me see what is appropriate to write and what is not. • Again, well written but off-topic. I had to find a way of positively encouraging the good writing but at the same time saying "You're not writing about the topic!"
Paragraph Coherence (Marriage)	• I started to look in the books of how to evaluate that which I think is useful. • You can't expect second language learners to know all techniques that native speakers do.
Point-by-Point Summary (Small Businesses)	• I think my student didn't try very hard to read the article and summarize it so I learned you have to read the work carefully to make sure it makes sense and they did the task. • Sometimes it's really hard to think of anything positive to say at all.
Overall	• Enjoyable activity! We usually know when the ESL student makes a mistake, but don't know how to go about correcting it. • Marking is harder than I thought because there are lots of exceptions to rules and you have to reread the work a lot to make sure you understand. • Hard to correct every mistake, give it a name, and actually notice them all. • Good for practice. I needed to see that students don't always follow instructions or give 100% but [we] still need to give feedback. • Correcting ESL work was beneficial to give us an idea of how marking is done. • Difficulty of focusing on one aspect of correction.
Recommended Changes	• None. It was great! • Meeting students at the beginning. • Even though it's difficult to do, try to make sure students always have the same partners. • Provide an example before each exchange that shows what we're supposed to look for in the assignments. • Possibly a lesson in grammar would help. • If we could have done more practice with marking things beforehand, we could have done a better job. • More detailed directions with examples of correction.

Reflection

The study taught the pedagogy teacher the value of giving student teachers direct experience with authentic ESL writing. It became clear to her and to the student teachers that providing appropriate comments on student papers requires practice. Moreover, she learned that a pedagogy teacher's careful attention is needed to discourage student teachers from appropriating an ESL student's writing and from prematurely correcting surface errors. In addition, the work with student teachers reminded us that teachers need to have a clear idea of what revisions they intend for their comments to inspire in the minds of ESL writers. We found it interesting that the student teachers tended to use Type 3 (make a request/statement) comments, thereby focusing on a fairly narrow view of the text. Rather than regarding the ESL student text as a whole, they seemed to address the text as a sequence of subsidiary tasks that, when complete, would respond to the larger task set by the assignment. Finally, it was gratifying to see that through careful supervision student teachers could learn to tailor their comments for their ESL partners. Their success was demonstrated by the appreciative responses on the ESL questionnaire (as shown in Figure 6).

The ESL teacher, for her part, had the rare opportunity to learn how her students reacted to "teacher" comments on their papers. She was also led to think more critically than before about the categories of comments teachers make on student papers and to evaluate her own practice in this light.

From this first exchange we have also learned to be prepared for complications. Absences may disrupt the rapport the student teachers have established with their ESL partners. Sufficient turnaround time between exchanges is important. Photocopies may not be legible. We have also learned that it would be beneficial to educate the ESL writers and the student teachers concerning the ultimate purpose of giving and receiving comments on writing assignments. We expect to repeat this project in an upcoming university session and track the revisions ESL students make to their texts as a result of the feedback from the student teachers. We hope to learn whether the exchange is indeed as beneficial as the ESL students and the student teachers have perceived it to be.

Sandra Burger teaches at the University of Ottawa, Canada.
Catherine Danforth also teaches at the University of Ottawa.

Acknowledgment

We wish to thank our ESL and TESL students for their cooperation and helpful comments, which made this study possible. As well, we are grateful to our editors for their helpful comments, patience, and encouragement.

CHAPTER 4

Film in the ESL Classroom:
Hearing the Student's Voice (*Canada*)

Andy Curtis

Issue

The use of commercially produced films or movies in the language classroom has been discussed in the literature for more than 20 years now (Lonergan, 1984) and for nearly as long in the English language classroom (Allan, 1985). A brief review of the literature shows that teachers of English and of other languages have been imaginative and innovative in their use of film to enable students to develop their linguistic and cultural competence. However, in spite of the many publications on the use of film in the language classroom, there appears to be a serious lack of data from the students themselves. Consequently, although many teachers extol the benefits and advantages of the use of film, in most reports the voice of the students is conspicuous by its absence.

This lack of attention appears to be an oversight in any system of education that claims to be student-centered. It is, therefore, desirable to gather student data to find out if students share teachers' enthusiasm for the use of film, especially in relation to what the students find engaging and motivating or disengaging and demotivating about the films used in a course. Beyond motivation-demotivation and engagement-disengagement, few if any classroom studies appear to have reported on what the students believe they are learning by watching the movies. The purpose of this study, then, was to attempt to explore aspects of student motivation, engagement, and student perceptions of how they might be benefiting from the use of film in their English language classes at a Canadian university.

As part of a major curriculum redesign in the School of English, students at the higher proficiency levels were offered a choice of two electives: Drama or Language, Film, and Culture. In the winter semester of 2005 (January to April) 13 students (see Table 1) elected to take the Language, Film, and Culture course, which was offered for the first time. The course was designed to help students develop their oral and aural English language skills through studying aspects of film, language, and culture.

As Table 1 shows, of the 13 course participants, 10 were returning to the school, with 3 students attending their first semester at the school. Eight of the students were female and 5 were male. At the time of the study, the students' three main home countries were China, Korea, and Japan, which was reflected in the makeup of this group, with six nationalities and five languages represented. Not all of the students indicated their age range on the data sheets, but of the 12 who did, 6 were in the 21–24 age range, 3 were in the 17–20 range, and 3 were in the 30–34 range.

The films shown in the course, although of very different genres, were chosen

Table 1. Students' Background Details (n = 13)

Gender	Age Range	New or Returning Student	Semester	Country of Birth	First Language
Female	17–20	Returning	2nd	Mexico	Spanish
Female	17–20	Returning	2nd	Mexico	Spanish
Female	17–20	Returning	3rd	China	Chinese
Male	30–34	Returning	4th	China	Chinese
Female	30–34	Returning	3rd	Korea	Korean
Female	30–34	Returning	2nd	Japan	Japanese
Female	21–24	New	1st	Taiwan	Chinese
Male	21–24	Returning	2nd	Japan	Japanese
Male	21–24	Returning	3rd	Japan	Japanese
Female	21–24	Returning	2nd	Japan	Japanese
Male	NI	New	1st	Libya	Arabic
Female	21–24	New	1st	Korea	Korean
Male	21–24	Returning	2nd	Japan	Japanese

Note: NI = not indicated.

because they all illustrated some type of "culture clash," or "cultures in collision," as it came to be called by the course participants. The three films chosen were also based on factors such as genre, length of film, and languages and cultures represented. The first film shown was *Long Life, Happiness, and Prosperity* (Shum, Jennings, Garvie, Massey, & Foon, 2002), which is set in Canada and portrays the struggles of a Chinese Canadian family living, working, and studying in Toronto. The second film studied was the most recent remake of *The Last Samurai* (Zwick, 2003), an action-adventure war-love story. The third film shown was *My Big Fat Greek Wedding* (Zwick & Vardalos, 2002), written by Nia Vardalos, a Greek Canadian who also played the lead in this romantic comedy. Throughout the rest of this chapter, I refer to these films as *Prosperity*, *Samurai*, and *Wedding*.

To address the conspicuous absence of students' voices in this area, the goal of this study was to use these films to allow students an opportunity to provide input on the use of films and the way we work with them in the language classroom.

Background Literature

One of the earlier studies I reviewed (Gilbert, 1993) focused on using movies with lower level English students in China, using movie material bought from England. According to Gilbert, her Chinese students "had learned English through a very traditional, book-centred method, and video seemed a stimulating alternative" (p. 29). Gilbert concluded the following:

> For the students it was satisfying to see the pieces they knew fitting together, and the dialogues and vocabulary they had studied gave them helpful pegs on which to hang their understanding. Many of them repeated dialogues and key words aloud as they watched. (p. 31)

However, Gilbert did not appear to have gathered any other feedback from the students on how useful or helpful (or otherwise) they found the film and how they assessed its usefulness. Similarly, Massi and Merino (1996), working with student teachers in Argentina, contended that the "possibilities for using film in the foreign language class are endless. Films present slices of life, and as such, provide a realistic, authentic, and entertaining way of improving the learner's command of the language" (p. 20). As in Gilbert's study, Massi and Merino reported positive results from using film in the English language classroom, but feedback from their students is conspicuous by its absence.

A similar absence is seen in a study described by the teacher researcher as "experiments conducted within the Japanese tertiary sector" (Ryan, 1998, p. 1).

The study was specifically designed to address what Ryan identified as a common situation when using film in the Japanese classroom: "Students will often express an interest in using movies as a medium for language learning, then proceed to sleep through any movie shown" (p. 2). Ryan described a six-step process he used to select and employ films. However, again, the students and their responses to the films shown were not reported.

Tatsuki (1998b) asked her Japanese English as a foreign language students (EFL) to keep a written record of points at which they would press the pause button during a movie, if they had the remote control, and to indicate why they would want to stop or repeat each segment. Tatsuki gathered three years' worth of student logs, made while the students saw two movies, *The Graduate* (Nichols, 1967) and *Indiana Jones and the Raiders of the Lost Ark* (Spielberg, 1981). Based on an analysis of the logs, Tatsuki identified 10 recurring themes within the auditory breakdowns, which she referred to as comprehension hot spots, and she proposed four solutions or strategies for helping students repair the breakdowns. However, she did not indicate how the students responded to the films; what they found more and less helpful or useful in developing their English language skills; or which movies, scenes, or characters they found more or less engaging or enjoyable. In a follow-up paper, Tatsuki (1998a) reported on six aspects of using films, and it is clear that she used movies creatively and probably successfully in her classroom. However, the absence in these papers of any feedback from students is still puzzling and is a cause for concern within a student-centered approach.

The use of film in English language classrooms continues in this millennium (Chapple & Curtis, 2000; Curtis, 2003), and an absence of reporting on student feedback is a recurring issue. For example, in Tatsuki's (2000) paper on developing film study guides, she seemed to make learners' needs a high priority: "One learner constraint involves the defining of learner needs that the course is meant to serve" (p. 1) and asked important learner-centered questions, such as "What general language or other pedagogical needs do the learners as a whole have that this course can address?" (p. 1). However, despite this concern for the learners, their voices are absent.

Liversidge (2000) asked, "What do EFL students see in introductory sequences of movies?" based on his assumption that the "beginning of any movie is the most difficult for learners" (p. 1). Liversidge presented what he described as a "research-based approach to discovering perception patterns" of two movies. Like Tatsuki (1998b), he used *The Graduate* (Nichols, 1967), and he also used *Airplane!* (Zucker & Zucker, 1980). Although Liversidge reached a number of informative conclusions and presented some helpful recommendations (pp. 6–7) based on a thorough analysis of the data, the students' words and voices still were missing.

Writing from a U.S. frame of reference, Donley (2000) took a U.S.-centric perspective, stating that *"American* [italics added] movies and television programs offer an excellent opportunity for intermediate-level students to develop fluency in English" (p. 24). Although Donley seemed unaware of the potential problems of "cultural imposition"—in this case imposing American culture on students in Uzbekistan—she was positive and enthusiastic about the use of film in the English language classroom. Again, nothing was reported about her students and how they responded to the films she showed, although her enthusiastic conclusion was that "American films and television shows are a tremendous resource for teachers of intermediate-level students" (p. 29).

The interest in the use of movies in the English language classroom has continued with the impact of new technologies, such as the Internet (Stempleski & Tomalin, 2001). For example, Gebhardt (2004) reported on the use of movie trailers available on the Internet in a computer-aided English language learning course. Similarly, Heffernan (2005) reported on watching movie trailers with English as a subsequent language (ESL) students using an Internet site. Heffernan observed his "students regularly reporting their enjoyment" (p. 4) through student feedback about watching the movie trailers online. Although there is no reason to disbelieve Heffernan or the other teachers who summarized and paraphrased their students' responses to film, the question arising from report after report is what the students would say about the films they saw in the English language classroom—if they had a voice.

Procedures

There were three main steps or phases in the study. First, I collected background data from the course participants. Based on these background details, I selected three different films for use in class during the course to help the students develop their oral and aural English language skills. Then I collected and analyzed data on the students' responses to the films.

At the beginning of the course, each student was asked to complete a background information form, and I have summarized that data in Table 1. I also asked course participants their favorite type of movie (e.g., action, comedy, romantic), their favorite actors, and which movies they had seen recently. One of the potentially most important questions asked was whether the students had attended a course like this before. Most of the students, 11 of the 13, replied that they had not previously taken part in such a course. Therefore, their responses indicated that this was the first time most of the students had used film in this way—not mainly as entertainment or a leisure activity, but as a tool for learning about language and culture and for improving their oral and aural English language skills.

The typical teaching schedule for the English for academic purposes program in the School of English was 3 hours of oral-aural lessons twice a week, divided into two 90-minute lessons. This pattern was changed to accommodate my relatively inflexible administrative schedule, and I was scheduled to meet with my students for a single 3-hour lesson each week. I therefore decided to collect anonymous written feedback from the students at the end of every lesson, for all 12 of our lessons together, which I might not have done at the end of every 90-minute lesson. The written feedback students were asked to provide covered four aspects of what we were doing in the lessons: effectiveness, interest, enjoyment, and usefulness. In each category, they were to select one of four possible ratings: *very, some, a little,* and *none.* For example, the first statement on the feedback sheet was "Please indicate how effective (interesting, enjoyable, and useful in the other three statements) this lesson has been in helping you develop your English language listening and speaking skills." Although *effective* and *useful* may have been difficult for the students to distinguish, I asked for both ratings to confirm that each student's answers were consistent and that the student found the lesson and the course beneficial.

After the first three lessons (9 hours of the course), I started to ask the students for written feedback, always given anonymously at the end of each of the 3-hour lessons, on more specific aspects of the course, such as particular tasks and activities. An example is "Please rate the dictation exercises in terms of how useful they are in helping you develop your focused, selective (close) listening skills." The response ratings again were *very, some, a little,* and *none.* I also asked students to comment on the level of difficulty of the different films by circling one option on a feedback form: *too easy, about the right level,* or *too difficult.* In addition to response ratings, students were asked to give ideas for tasks and activities, for example, "Can you think of other exercises we could do with film that would help you develop your listening and speaking skills?" I used this more detailed written feedback to help me align the course to the needs of the students in terms of task type, level of difficulty, how much of each movie was covered in each lesson, and in what depth and detail we covered each movie.

In addition to this weekly anonymous written feedback from students, one of the most important sets of questions was put to the students in the penultimate week of the course (Week 11), after 33 hours of in-class time. I used the same type of written feedback form that students were now familiar with, which asked students to select a response from a limited range of choices and provided space for details about their choices. The form, which included the six questions that follow, asked students to compare and contrast the three films we had worked with in relation to enjoyment, helpfulness, and difficulty/challenge.

1. Which of the three movies did you enjoy the *most* and why?

2. Which of the three movies did you enjoy the *least* and why?

3. Which of the three movies was *most helpful* in developing your English language listening and speaking skills? Why?

4. Which of the three movies was *least helpful* in developing your English language listening and speaking skills? Why?

5. Which of the three movies was *most difficult/challenging*? What made this the most difficult/challenging movie?

6. Which of the three movies was *least difficult/challenging*? What made this the least difficult/challenging movie?

Results

THE STUDENTS' RATINGS

The results are discussed in two parts. The first part focuses on quantitative responses; however, I want to note that the database of 11 sets of responses is too small to generate statistically useful results. In the second part, I focus on the students' comments, especially because lack of student voice emerged as a recurring theme in my literature review. A summary of student responses to the six questions previously noted appears in Table 2. The data show that there is sometimes a relatively straightforward one-to-one relationship between the students' responses and choices. For example, *Prosperity* was named most often (six times) as *least enjoyable* and was not listed at all for *most enjoyable*, which supports a one-to-one relationship.

However, as Tables 3 and 4 show, the majority of the students' responses and choices do not follow this pattern. For example, the responses show that most students who made a choice chose *Samurai* as the movie they most enjoyed and *Prosperity* as the movie they least enjoyed. In terms of helping the students develop their English language listening and speaking skills, students equally chose *Wedding* and *Samurai* as the most helpful and chose *Prosperity* as the least helpful. The students' selections for most/least enjoyed and most/least helpful show that the relationship is more complex than some previous studies indicated. In other words, students do not necessarily rate the most enjoyable film as the most useful and vice versa. It is possible that students are able to evaluate the different benefits and limitations of films used for language learning and that they can appreciate the strengths while being aware of the weaknesses of some films.

In terms of the agreement between enjoyment and difficulty, an interesting relationship transpired that might contradict a teacher's expectation that the more difficult a task, the less enjoyable it is and vice versa. Specifically, *Samurai* was ranked as the most difficult but also the most enjoyable of the movies

Table 2. Student Responses to Questions on Films Seen (*n* = 11)

Student	Response					
	Most Enjoyable	**Least Enjoyable**	**Most Helpful**	**Least Helpful**	**Most Difficult**	**Least Difficult**
1	*Wedding*	*Samurai*	*Wedding*	*Samurai*	*Samurai*	*Wedding*
2	*Samurai*	*Wedding*	*Samurai*	*Wedding*	*Samurai*	*Wedding*
3	*Samurai*	All good[a]	*Wedding*	All great[b]	*Samurai*	*Wedding*
4	*Samurai*	*Prosperity*	*Samurai*	*Prosperity*	*Wedding*	*Samurai*
5	*Wedding*	*Samurai*	*Wedding*	*Prosperity*	*Samurai*	*Wedding*
6	*Samurai*	*Prosperity*	*Wedding*	*Prosperity*	*Samurai*	*Prosperity*
7	*Wedding*	*Prosperity*	*Samurai*	*Prosperity*	*Samurai*	*Wedding*
8	*Samurai*	*Prosperity*	*Samurai*	*Prosperity*	*Samurai*	*Wedding*
9	*Samurai*	*Prosperity*	*Wedding*	*Prosperity*	*Samurai*	*Prosperity*
10	*Samurai*	*Prosperity*	All three[c]	*Samurai*	*Wedding*	*Prosperity*
11	*Wedding*	*Samurai*	*Samurai*	*Samurai*	*Wedding*	*Samurai*

[a]All good = "All movies were very good." [b]All great = "All movies are really great for me." [c]All three = "All three of them because they present different levels of language."

shown. This potentially important finding supports the notion that students want to be challenged, recognizing intuitively that an essential part of any learning process is the struggle to understand and make sense of challenging and difficult material.

I want to acknowledge that with only three films to choose from, the difference between *most* and *least* in any category is small. Even so, the lack of a simple one-to-one relationship may indicate that teachers should be wary of relying on students' verbal and nonverbal responses during the lesson as the only feedback. The lack of agreement on ratings for a film may also indicate that the students are making more complex decisions about the ways the films engage and entertain them, compared with the ways these films help them develop linguistic and cultural knowledge.

THE STUDENTS' VOICES

Although the data in these three tables shed light on student responses to the use of film in their ESL classrooms, the comments from the students may be of more interest to language teachers. Also, knowing which film the students judged to be most or least useful, for example, is perhaps less important than knowing *why*

Table 3. Summary of Student Responses to Questions on Films Seen ($n = 11$)

	Response					
Film	**Most Enjoyable**	**Least Enjoyable**	**Most Helpful**	**Least Helpful**	**Most Difficult**	**Least Difficult**
Prosperity	0	6	0	6	0	3
Samurai	7	3	5	3	8	2
Wedding	4	1	5	1	3	6

Note: For three categories—*Least Enjoyable, Most Helpful,* and *Least Helpful*—only 10 students made a choice.

they rated the film this way. In other words, teachers would benefit from knowing the basis for students' evaluations of a film as more or less useful, and that could aid in helping students develop their linguistic and cultural knowledge.

The first question was "Which of the three movies did you enjoy the most and why?" As indicated in Table 3, the majority of the students chose *Samurai* as the most enjoyable movie. The reasons they gave included references to the importance of Japanese language and culture in the film in relation to their own first language (L1) or culture: "Because I am Japanese, I can understand the characters' mind or behaviour" (Student 9 [S9]), and "It is very good to understand Japanese old culture" (S4). Other responses reflected what the students had learned about the narrative aspects of film: "because I learn to appreciate the scenes and the meaning of the story" (S10), and "because you [the teacher] taught us the background, cultural differences, and plot most carefully" (S6). In contrast, the reasons for choosing *Wedding* were more related to the level of language and the fun aspects of comedic movies: "fun to watch with your friends" (S7) and "interesting and easy to understand" (S5).

The second question asked the opposite of the first: "Which of the three movies did you enjoy the least and why?" *Prosperity* was selected most often (by 6 of the 10 students who made a selection), and again some of the reasons related to the non-English language portions of the movie: "It was OK . . . but too

Table 4. Rank-Order Summary of Student Responses to Questions on Films Seen ($n = 11$)

Most Enjoyable	Least Enjoyable	Most Helpful	Least Helpful	Most Difficult	Least Difficult
Samurai	*Prosperity*	*Samurai* and *Wedding*	*Prosperity*	*Samurai*	*Wedding*
Wedding	*Samurai*		*Samurai*	*Wedding*	*Prosperity*
Prosperity	*Wedding*	*Prosperity*	*Wedding*	*Prosperity*	*Samurai*

much Chinese" (S9). The students were not asked to indicate their nationality on the questionnaires, partly because giving features such as L1, gender, or similar distinctions might have easily identified some of the students, thus taking away the anonymity necessary for respondents to feel safe in giving full and complete answers. Because the course had an oral-aural focus, the students submitted very little written work. Consequently, their handwriting on the questionnaires did not identify them, so their anonymity was preserved. It was not possible to know whether, for example, the comment about "too much Chinese" was made by a Chinese or non-Chinese student. Also, because *Prosperity* did not have the dramatic impact of *Samurai* or the obvious comedic appeal of *Wedding,* some of the reasons relate to the relative pace of the film, as reflected in the comments "kind of slow and sometimes boring" (S7) and "a little bit boring" (S8). However, it was encouraging to see that some students found it difficult to make a choice because they appreciated all three of the movies. For example, they responded, "Nothing. All movies are very good" (S3), and "I enjoy [*Prosperity*] and I like it, but I had to choose one, but I enjoy them all" (S10).

The third question was "Which of the three movies was most helpful in developing your English language listening and speaking skills? Why?" Students equally chose *Samurai* and *Wedding*. Some of their reasons for choosing *Wedding* related to the type of language and speed of production: "many interesting expressions in the film" (S6) and "because everybody speaks very fast" (S11). Some of the responses made explicit reference to the cultural as well as the linguistic aspects of the film: "We can learn common conversational English as well as learn about other cultures" (S3). They commented on the relative amounts of English and other languages used in the movie: "There is no Japanese and much English" (S9). Again, some of the students were unable to make a choice. However, they were able to give thoughtful reasons for this inability: "the three of them because they show different levels of language" (S10), and "*The Last Samurai* is most helpful for my listening, because it is difficult, and *My Big Fat Greek Wedding* is most helpful for my speaking" (S8). The theme of wanting to be challenged and choosing a film because it was difficult appeared again here: "because Tom Cruise spoke really quietly sometimes, so it was more challenging to hear what he was saying" (S7).

As with the first pair of questions, the fourth asked the opposite of the third: "Which of the three movies was least helpful in developing your English language listening and speaking skills? Why?" As mentioned previously, *Prosperity* was chosen by six students as the least enjoyable film as well as by six students as the least helpful film. However, it is worth noting that the two sets of six responses were not given by the same six students. The reasons given for selecting *Prosperity* as least helpful were similar to those given for its selection as least enjoyable, including pace, impact, and the relative proportions of English and Chinese: "a little bit boring" (S5), "a little bit dull" (S8), "it included a lot of Chinese" (S7), and "there are few native speakers in this film and the plot is unusual" (S6). The reference to plot is noteworthy, partly because there were few such references and because the comment shows that although the *Prosperity* plot was simple—a young Chinese Canadian girl who believes in magic tries to use some traditional Chinese magic to bring good luck to her family—it was less familiar than the themes of the other two films: war and weddings. These responses, then, might indicate a need for more preparatory work with the students before they see this kind of film.

The fifth question asked was "Which of the three movies was most difficult/challenging? What made this the most difficult/challenging movie?" The responses to this question reflected the clearest agreement, with 8 of the 11 respondents selecting *Samurai*, but many also nominated it as the film they enjoyed most (however, not all the same students did so). Important individual differences emerged on closer examination. Many of the reasons given for choosing *Samurai* as the most difficult and challenging related to vocabulary and the ways in which the words were said: "Some actors didn't speak very clearly and use difficult words" (S5), "They use very difficult words" (S8), "Some characters speak very fast and sometimes they use special words" (S6), and "some difficult vocabulary and various accents" (S3).

The following brief passage, presented in *Samurai* in the form of a voice-over accompanying flashbacks being experienced by the Tom Cruise character, Captain Nathan Algren, shows some of the difficulties of the vocabulary used in this film:

> There is some comfort in the emptiness of the sea. No past, no future. And then at once, I am confronted by the hard truth of present circumstances. I have been hired to suppress the rebellion of yet another tribal leader. Apparently this is the only job for which I am suited. I am beset by the ironies of my life. (Zwick, 2003)

Words, phrases, and structures such as "then at once," "the hard truth of present circumstances," and "beset by the ironies of my life" would challenge some native speakers of English. Therefore, the students most likely needed more preparation before encountering such language.

The last question to which the students responded was "Which of the three movies was least difficult/challenging? What made this the least difficult/challenging movie?" *Wedding* was chosen by the majority of students as the least difficult/challenging movie of the three. Their responses may indicate that, although many of the students clearly wanted to be challenged by the films they worked with, they also responded well to films that were in some ways more accessible, such as comedies. Their written responses provide examples: "it's a comedy, so they have to use understandable language" (S7) and "easy words and interesting story" (S5). Some of the comments related to the level of language in relation to particular skills: "they use easy words" (S8) and "because my listening skills improved ☺" (S3). Three of the students chose *Prosperity*, and two chose *Samurai*. They referred to a number of themes, some of which reiterated aspects highlighted earlier, such as accent, frequency of viewing, and multiple selections: "because I have seen this movie twice" (S10), and "because some of their accents are similar to mine" (S4), both referring to *Samurai*, and "I think they were all challenging" (S10), with reference to *Prosperity*.

A note on the use of emoticons is appropriate here because a number of students' written responses included a smiley face. This tendency might be another sign that the students were pleased to be asked for their feedback and happy to give it, and their positive responses support the idea that this kind of classroom-based research should give prominence to the student's voice.

Reflection

Based on the results from this study, I will make a number of changes the next time I teach this course. First, I will not plan the complete course in advance but rather will show clips from several different films to the students at the beginning of the course. Then, based on anonymous written feedback from the students, I will decide which films to use in more detail and study in greater depth. This is not, of course, as convenient for the teacher as having the whole course prepared in advance. However, the above data reinforce the fact that every student is unique, so every group of students is different. Therefore, to make the most of film use in the classroom, I should do more previewing and piloting of the films.

In relation to selecting and preparing the films used in the future, as a result of this study I will be more careful to gather details about how many times the students have seen a movie we plan to use in class. I learned that although it is helpful for them to be familiar with a movie, some of the students' responses support an adaptation of the old adage that "familiarity breeds contempt." In this case, for some students, too much familiarity with a movie led to some discontent. In the future, if some students have already seen a film we plan to use in class, I will ask them about the linguistic and cultural context in which they saw it. For example, seeing a Hollywood movie dubbed in Chinese at a movie theatre in Shanghai or Beijing is a much different experience from seeing the same film in English in a movie theatre in Toronto or Montreal.

In terms of how to use the films based on the data I gathered, I have also learned a lesson. If the films we decide to use represent the languages and cultures of some of the students in the group, I will start by asking those students if they know about that aspect in their own culture and L1. For example, I would ask Japanese students what they know about the stories and legends of samurai in Japan, or I would ask Greek students if they have been to family weddings.

As a result of the findings of this study, before and after viewing a film I will devise and carry out more discussions about the issues raised by the film, regardless of whether it is a lighthearted comedy or a serious social drama. For example, although *Wedding* is a light and predictable comedy of errors, viewing it resulted in much serious in-class discussion (in English) of mixed-race marriages and the roles that the families of the bride and the groom should or should not play in a young couple's life.

One of the practices I will not change is the use of films in which languages other than English are spoken. For example, *Prosperity* has some Chinese, *Samurai* has some Japanese, and *Wedding* has some Greek. This practice goes against the English-only rule at the School of English where I collected the data for this study. Although this is a controversial requirement, students at the school enter in a quasilegal contract, signing and dating a pledge countersigned by a witness, usually their teacher, in which the student promises to try to use only English at all times, especially in class, during the semester. For me to be allowed to show films that used languages other than English, the students were required to sign a special pledge. The students' responses to these films showed that they clearly appreciated multilingual films that showed intercultural challenges. They did not believe that films that used non-English languages and cultures interfered with their learning of English. Indeed, as one Japanese student put it, commenting on *Samurai,* "Because I am Japanese, I can understand the characters' mind or behaviour" (S9).

Andy Curtis teaches at the Chinese University of Hong Kong.

CHAPTER 5

ESL Students as Ethnographers: Examining Academic Interactions (*United States*)

Maria Dantas-Whitney

Issue

After teaching ESL for more than 12 years in an intensive English program at a large public university in the United States, I had become acquainted with many of the international students on campus. During my walks to class and my visits to the coffee shop or the library, I often ran into former students who, after completing English as a subsequent language (ESL) course work, told me about the struggles of their new academic lives. Even though many of them felt their English language skills were adequate, they still had difficulty establishing meaningful academic relationships with classmates and professors. As a listening and speaking teacher at the advanced level, I felt frustrated by these comments. In my ESL classes, I exposed my students to practical academic experiences: I invited guest speakers to my classes, and I assigned tasks requiring my students to communicate with university faculty, staff, and students. I also planned numerous discussions, debates, and presentations in class for oral skill development, which resembled the activities my students were likely to encounter in their mainstream university classes. Still, I knew that the sheltered community of the intensive English program was somewhat artificial for my students, because teachers and classmates were unusually tolerant of communication difficulties and sensitized to sociocultural factors that affect interactions.

When communicating with their teachers and fellow students within the university community, ESL students are often expected to behave according to rules of conduct that may not have been made explicit to them. People they interact with may expect them to be familiar with the communicative practices of the academic community, in other words, the taken-for-granted "way of doing things that is sanctioned by the social collective" (Lindlof, 1995, p. 16). As Johnson (1995) pointed out, students must use "social, cognitive, cultural, linguistic, and paralinguistic knowledge of the new language" in order to communicate effectively. "Paradoxically, to acquire this knowledge they must participate in interactions in the language, but without this knowledge, their chances for such interactions remain limited" (p. 52). The academic success of ESL students depends on how well they can overcome this difficult dilemma.

I soon realized that my students needed a structure to observe, analyze, and reflect critically on interactions within the academic context of the university. With this purpose in mind, I designed a study, the Language Research Project, which would guide them to identify research questions, learn techniques for ethnographic data collection and analysis, gather data, and discuss implications and actions resulting from their findings.

Background Literature

In focusing on the interrelationship between the individual and the larger cultural setting, this study draws on current sociocultural theory. Instead of looking at language acquisition as a psychological process that starts in the minds of individuals and moves toward socialization into the community, sociocultural theorists argue that the process begins in social practices before it is internalized by individual minds. Derived from the works of Vygotsky (1978) and his followers, sociocultural theory has provided the foundation for the social constructivist movement in education (Nyikos & Hashimoto, 1997; Wells, 2000, 2001). One of the main areas of sociocultural inquiry focuses on how language serves as a psychological tool that mediates mental activity. Lantolf and Appel (1994) compared language to other psychological tools or artifacts, such as algebraic symbols, diagrams, and schemes that people use to facilitate their performance of tasks. Language not only mediates mental activity, but it also may "qualitatively change the nature of the activity and it may change the subsequent outcome" (Swain & Lapkin, 1998, p. 321). This relationship is similar to a word processor's role in changing the way a writer composes an essay, for example. "Constructing language is a cognitive function for communicating our thoughts to others and, at the same time, language is a tool for constructing more thoughts" (Wink & Putney, 2002, p. 42).

Several educators have recently described class activities designed to build students' awareness of features of oral interactions (Basturkmen, 2002; Burton, 2000; Celce-Murcia & Olshtain, 2000; Clennell, 1999; Riggenbach, 1999). Classroom projects that encourage second language learners to act as ethnographers have been recommended by Norton (2000; Norton Peirce, 1995) and Hall (1993; 1999). Still, the few research studies that have examined such instructional approaches have been conducted outside of the United States (e.g., Roberts, Bryam, Barro, Jordan, & Street, 2001).

The students and I engaged simultaneously in the ethnography of communication and action research techniques. Ethnography of communication (Hymes, 1972) seeks to analyze uses, patterns, and functions of language in an attempt to construct "a descriptive theory of speaking as a cultural system in a particular society" (Bauman & Sherzer, 1974, cited in Anton, 1996, p. 552). In action research, the researcher is not an outside expert who comes to the research scene with a predetermined agenda, but a coworker who engages in inquiries and investigations with others "to improve practice rather than to produce knowledge" (Elliott, 1991, p. 49). Data collection and analysis in ethnographic and action research follow a cyclical and funneling process. The students and I collected and analyzed data in cycles, which enabled us to explore themes collaboratively as they emerged throughout the study.

Procedures

A total of 23 students participated in this study (Dantas-Whitney, 2003). Table 1 provides information on each participant.

The first phase of the study was conducted during the term of enrollment in my ESL class. During this phase, as teacher researcher I examined students' learning processes and personal perspectives while they observed, analyzed, and reflected on oral discourse used in and out of the classroom. The second phase was conducted during two subsequent quarters. Ten of the 23 students participated in this second phase, which consisted of 18 follow-up interviews. These interviews focused on students' reflections and self-assessments concerning their oral interactions in the university community as they transitioned into full-time academic study in their fields.

STUDENTS' RESEARCH PROCESSES

The Language Research Project was organized around several tasks (e.g., reflections, observations, discussions) that were designed to build on each other progressively. At the center of the project were the students' ethnographic observations conducted in academic settings such as classes, workshops, and advising meetings. Table 2 presents a summary of the main tasks comprising the Language Research Project.

Table 1. List of Participants

Name	Gender	Country	Academic Status	Academic Major	End-of-Term TOEFL Score
*Akiko	F	Japan	G	English	487
Ali	M	Saudi Arabia	U	Finance	543
*Amy	F	Taiwan	G	Zoology	547
*Budi	M	Indonesia	U	Food science	507
Chia Ling	F	Taiwan	U	Undecided	447
Edgar	M	Mexico	G	Rangeland resources	537
Eun Hee	F	South Korea	U	Communication	467
Hiroko	F	Japan	G	English literature	510
*Hong	F	Thailand	G	Nutrition	560
*Jae	M	South Korea	G	Civil engineering	483
Jin Young	F	S. Korea	U	Crop science	493
Katie	F	S. Korea	U	Clothing & textiles	500
*Keon Ho	M	S. Korea	G	Accounting	[a]
Khaled	M	UAE	U	Computer engineering	477
*Kim	F	S. Korea	U	English literature	533
*Liana	F	France	G	Biochemistry	547
*Mark	M	Taiwan	G	Fisheries & wildlife	583
Ming Ju	F	Taiwan	U	Undecided	480
Natsuki	F	Japan	U	Sociology	503
Porntipa	F	Thailand	G	Journalism	510
Toby	M	S. Korea	U	Electrical engineering	[a]
Yoon	M	S. Korea	U	Mechanical engineering	487
*Yutaka	M	Japan	U	Mechanical engineering	463

F = female; M = male; U = undergraduate student; G = graduate student. *Denotes students who participated in Phase 2 follow-up interviews. [a]Did not take the end-of-term TOEFL.

Table 2. Language Research Project Tasks

Task	Sample Questions/Prompts
Self-Observation Log	Record details of all interactions with English speakers in the community for two days. Reflect on difficulties, feelings.
Web Discussion 1	What types of conversations and discussions in English do you usually participate in? Which types are most/least comfortable? Strategies used? Compare/contrast interactions in English to interactions in native language. Set goals for future learning.
Audio Journal 1; Formulation of Research Question	Reflect on themes of web discussion. Identify topics to explore further. Choose a speech situation. Formulate a research question.
Nonparticipant Observation; Participant Observation	Note details of interactions. Use SPEAKING framework for description. Reflect on research question, using data to support statements.
Web Discussion 2	Write a summary of your findings. Describe and compare all three observations. Reflect on research question. Reflect on personal experiences during observations. State conclusions, using data to support claims.
Audio Journal 2; Discussion of Implications for Action	Discuss and assess the project as a whole. Reflect on your experiences during observations. Discuss plans for future action.

At the beginning of the term, in order to generate ideas for meaningful research questions, the students worked on self-observation logs. This assignment required that students record the details of all their interactions with English speakers in the community for 2 full days, writing down information about the settings, the purposes of the conversations, and the languages used. Then, the students used a Web discussion board (Nicenet, 1998) to reflect on and assess their own participation in interactions in English. They discussed with each other questions such as "How do you feel when you participate in discussions with other English speakers in the university setting?" I read their reflections and replied with further questions and comments.

The students were then ready to make plans for their individual Language Research Projects. They prepared an audiotaped journal in which they reflected on the questions and responses posted on the Web board, identified themes they would like to explore further, and formulated their research questions. I listened to these journals and recorded my feedback to the students on the same audio-cassette, thus creating a type of asynchronous dialogue with the students.

To practice data collection techniques, I brought a movie clip to be analyzed in class. Students took field notes and analyzed the types of contributions by different discussion participants in the video. During this activity, I introduced the students to Hymes's (1972) SPEAKING framework as a system for analysis and observation. This framework is intended to guide the description of a particular speech event by focusing on eight components: situation (setting and scene); participants (age, roles, gender, ethnicity); ends (goals and outcomes); act sequence (message form and message content); key (tone, manner, spirit of the communication); instrumentalities (channels and forms of communication); norms (of interaction and of interpretation); and genre (type of event). This framework was then used as a heuristic to help students focus on concrete features of communication when collecting data during their own observations. The Appendix shows a sample worksheet for data collection.

After the students practiced analyzing a videotaped discussion in class, they were ready to begin fieldwork. They conducted two types of observations: a nonparticipant observation and a participant observation. Most of the students collected their data through written field notes; however, a few of them chose to audiotape and transcribe some interactions. After each observation, the students examined the data they had collected and wrote short observation reports, reflecting on their experiences and trying to answer their research questions. We discussed in class their preliminary findings and exchanged ideas about possible interpretations of the data, following a process of analysis similar to the one used with the videotaped discussion we had examined.

Based on the analysis of their observations, the students used the Web board again (Nicenet, 1998) to share insights about their findings. They compared and contrasted the interactions they had observed, trying to answer their research questions. They also revisited their own self-reflexive comments previously posted on the Web and revised them. Again, they responded to each other's comments with further questions and reflections. I also contributed to the Web discussion by providing feedback on the students' comments and by posing questions for further reflection.

At the end of the course the students prepared a final reflection on an audio-taped journal, in which they evaluated the project as a whole. They used information from their data collection sheets, observation reports, audio journals, and Web discussions to reflect on what they had learned. They also discussed what surprised them and compared what they had observed to similar situations in their countries. Finally, they made plans for actions they could take to improve their own participation in interactions in the future. I listened to the journals and again provided feedback. Throughout the term, the students and I engaged in numerous class discussions about the different activities involved in the Language Research Project. The purpose of these discussions was to sharpen the students' ethnographic and discourse analysis skills.

TEACHER RESEARCHER'S RESEARCH PROCESS

As both the classroom instructor and the researcher for this study, my role was that of participant observer. I used multiple sources of data: (a) class materials (student data collection worksheets, Web discussion entries, audiotaped journals, and lesson plans); (b) transcripts of selected class sessions; (c) a teacher researcher's journal; (d) midterm interviews conducted with 21 students; and (e) follow-up interviews conducted with 10 students for two consecutive terms after completion of the course. I used the constant comparative method (Strauss & Corbin, 1990) for data analysis, which involves sorting, coding, prioritizing, and connecting pieces of data according to recurring patterns and themes.

Results

The Language Research Project provided students with a variety of opportunities to grasp the complexities of communicative practices in the university discourse community. Perhaps the most important characteristic of the project was that it promoted a gradual and cumulative process of knowledge construction among the group. Designed in a progressive sequence, the tasks enabled students to build on their prior (and collective) experiences to further their inquiry endeavors. Amy described her process of critical inquiry:

> From the Language Research Project, what I learned is attitude, I mean, when I face a thing . . . I learned how to think in different aspects or directions, and I learned how to analyze it in different ways or sides. And I also learned how to use different ways, or different methods, different equipments to find out what I want to know. So, I think the attitude is very, very important to me in my life . . . I think in everyone's life because life is a learning . . . process. And . . . the learning will be continued without end. . . . So, the method, the ways, the procedures we use will influence how much we will get. (Audio Journal 2, 11/26/01)

Amy was able to capture the essence of mediated knowledge construction. She recognized that the quality of the learning that took place in this classroom was significantly enhanced by the use of alternative approaches, methods, and equipment.

The students' observations prompted a sophisticated process of theory building about patterns of interactions in English. Porntipa described patterns of interruptions in English:

> I observe that one who has question or wants to express his or her idea always stares or makes eye contact to the speaker first. It shows that he or she is ready to say something. Or sometimes they will move their body a little bit and ready

to raise their hands. . . . In addition, during the discussion, I observe that one who wants to interrupt always make some sounds before speaking such as, umm . . . , urr . . . rr . . . or raise his or her hand. Also, if others agree with that opinion, they usually nod, smile, or say . . . "yes . . . um . . ." for accepting. Besides, if they don't agree, the room is more quiet and one who wants to disagree will move body a little bit and then say something like . . . "umm . . . but I think . . ." in the end of speaker's sentence before the speaker will continue showing the idea. (Porntipa, participant observation report, 11/5/01)

Porntipa's detailed description revealed several interesting features of the interaction. She remarked on the body language (e.g., "makes eye contact," "move their body a little bit," "raise their hands") used to indicate that a person was ready to talk, and the "back-channel responses" (McCarthy, 1991, p. 127) used to signal message acceptance and comprehension, such as "nod, smile, or say . . . 'yes . . . um. . . .'" Porntipa also described expressions used to convey disagreement, such as "umm . . . but I think. . . ."

Akiko described her observations regarding intervals, or pauses in speech, during interactions:

From my observation, the speaker had intervals at least two seconds before they speak important things or move to new topics. Through the interval, speaker could make us pay attention, and it shouldn't be too short or too long. I think it is kind of technique, and it determines whether speaker make people boring or not. I also realized that the intervals are in connection with conjunct word such as "well," "let's see," or "so" so on, and tone of voice. For example, before speaker have interval, speaker always use conjunct word like "well . . . we're going to talk about . . . ," and when speaker talk about important things, their voice gets more louder and higher. (Akiko, Web discussion 2, 11/20/01)

Akiko's careful observation was evident in her description. She noted that the speaker used pauses to emphasize the importance of an upcoming utterance or to change topics. She also observed that the speaker used expressions such as *well* and *let's see,* or raised the tone of voice before a pause. In addition, Akiko determined that the pauses lasted only about "two seconds"; in other words, they were not "too short or too long." She concluded that pauses such as these served to keep the audience's attention.

These excerpts illustrate the quality of the students' ethnographic descriptions and interpretations. The SPEAKING model helped the students to focus not only on the language being used in the academic community, but also on other sociocultural aspects of the context (e.g., intentions of participants, purposes of the interaction) that can affect the outcomes of communication.

At the end of the course, when asked to evaluate the Language Research Project as a whole, the students reflected on the most valuable aspects of the project and described their plans for future language development. Three themes were identified as most salient in the students' evaluative comments: (1) the value of observation, (2) language awareness, and (3) self-awareness and confidence.

THE VALUE OF OBSERVATION

Many students reflected on the value of the participant observation techniques they learned throughout the course. Acquiring these observational skills, in their opinion, was one of the most beneficial aspects of the Language Research Project. Akiko reflected on the value of observation for language learning:

> Throughout the term I learned so many things I've never known. For example, in class, through the Language Research Project, I realized that how important observation is. It gave me great effect because I've known how to observe and analyze. Observing and analyzing help me improving English so much. . . . Through this project, I think . . . my expression improved well. . . . I tried to pay attention more detailed things every time. For example, from daily conversations with native speakers, TV programs, movies, so on. I can pay attention everything, and I can learn from everywhere. I learn how to improve language. I wish I knew this way from the beginning. From now on, I try to talk to native speakers as much as I can with using my gestures and facial expressions, and at the same time, I can observe how they react by use their gestures, too. (Akiko, Audio Journal 2, 11/26/01)

Akiko displayed a great deal of self-direction and autonomy. She was able to evaluate her own language improvement and to transfer the skills she learned in the ESL classroom to other present and future language learning contexts.

Similarly, Liana remarked that participant observation skills helped her adopt an open-minded approach:

> Now I don't see life as I did before. I think that what I will use in the future is more my open mind than the differences I observed. (Liana, Audio Journal 2, 11/26/01)

Like Akiko, Liana plans to continue to use the skills of observation and critical analysis learned through the Language Research Project in the future.

LANGUAGE AWARENESS

Many students reflected that the project served to increase their awareness of English communicative practices. Both Hiroko and Hong had chosen the topic of body language as the focus of their projects. They reflected on an increased sense of awareness about the use of body language in English interactions:

> Through this research, I could learn the importance of gesture, eye contact, and smiling. So, I want to practice those things and use them in my speech. (Hiroko, Audio Journal 2, 11/26/01)

I think this research question made to learn more the new thing of American. I feel . . . when I talk to my friends, especially American friends, I observe their body language . . . when I see Americans talk to each other, . . . I found that most of them always use their hands, their heads, and use eye contact. . . . And I realize that body language can help people to understand each other. (Hong, Audio Journal 2, 11/26/01)

These excerpts illustrate the types of comments made by most students. Through their observations, reflections, and analysis of data, the students learned a great deal about language use in social and academic interactions.

SELF-AWARENESS AND CONFIDENCE

Another important benefit of the Language Research Project was that it helped students gain greater self-awareness and confidence. Amy reflected that the project helped her develop a deeper sense of her own abilities:

What I got from observing myself is just the data from my . . . results, but it helps me to know myself more. . . . So, in the future I hope I can just be myself in the English environment. Because sometimes I need to hide my feelings, my opinions, my thoughts, just because I don't have enough language to share them with other people. (Amy, Audio Journal 2, 11/26/01)

Amy's ethnographic observations and fieldwork gave her the means to understand herself better. Her understanding of her own difficulties and challenges did not make her paralyzed or pessimistic about the future. On the contrary, her awareness of her own knowledge and experiences motivated her to seek personal growth.

Other students also expressed a renewed sense of confidence in their abilities to interact in English:

I believe that what I did and what I got from all of my observation is very useful for my future. In the past I felt nervous when I spoke with someone using English language, but now I can handle it and feel more comfortable because during the observations I have participated myself to be more confident, self-confidence when I speak with people using English language, although there are mistakes in my pronunciation. (Budi, Audio Journal 2, 11/26/01)

I think that my research project showed me that I can explain my opinion in English and by this way I made a lot of progress. . . . Now I'm more comfortable to talk to Americans even if I know that my English is not perfect. (Liana, Audio Journal 2, 11/26/01)

Budi's and Liana's reflections are representative of many other comments found in the data. These students concluded that the project helped them to feel less

---

anxious when communicating with English speakers. Similar to Amy's reflection, Budi's and Liana's comments revealed their ability to come to terms with their own limitations. Rather than trying to reach an idealized nativelike level of language competency, Budi and Liana expressed confidence in their not-so-perfect capacity to communicate in English.

As the students reflected on their newly developed observation skills, they recognized that these skills could be transferred to different learning contexts and used for future language development. The students also reflected that the project helped to enhance their awareness of English discourse practices, particularly within academic contexts. Another important benefit of the project was that it helped students gain greater self-awareness and confidence. As the students examined their own performance in interactions with others in the community, they became aware of their own skills and limitations and more confident about their ability to communicate.

Reflection

This study has informed my classroom practice in several important ways. Through my process of data analysis, in particular through the analysis of my researcher's journal, I became aware of the importance of collaboration and risk taking within my classroom. I learned that collaboration was the factor that contributed mostly to the group's process of constructing knowledge. Although I felt pleased with my students' active engagement in my class, I struggled to encourage them to take risks and to participate in academic interactions within the larger university community.

In the following journal entry, I reflected on my conversation with Eun Hee during her midterm interview:

Eun Hee says she never participates in [her mainstream] class, even though it is a small class and participation is encouraged. "It is too hard to do," she says. The most remarkable thing for me is that Eun Hee says she has a lot of American friends and she has no trouble talking to them in informal settings. Her American friends are friendly to her and include her in social activities. (She says, "Social activities are not for a grade. They have nothing to lose!") But in class she doesn't feel comfortable talking. She says most international students she knows feel the same way. They choose large lecture-style classes in which participation is not required and where they can be "invisible." I tried to encourage her to do her participant observation in the university class, to try to push her to participate in a context that doesn't feel totally comfortable for her, but she says it is too difficult. In her plans for the participant observation, she had written down another social conversation in the dining hall. (researcher's journal, 11/14/01)

It was clear from my conversation with Eun Hee that she felt extremely hesitant about speaking up in class and anxious about engaging in academic discussions with American classmates. She was much more comfortable in social settings, where she felt Americans were more friendly and receptive. Eun Hee was disinclined to take on the challenge I had posed to her of conducting her participant observation within her mainstream class. Instead, she chose the safe and familiar setting of the university dinning hall, where she would be conversing with her American friends.

I was initially frustrated and disappointed by the students' unwillingness to take risks; however, I finally concluded that I could not push my students to take risks that they were not ready to take. I could only encourage them to reflect on the conditions that were preventing them from taking these risks and hope that their reflections would pave the way for their future engagement in academic interactions. As I continue to implement the project with future students, I plan to modify slightly the sequence of tasks so students move gradually from observations in social settings (i.e., interactions with friends) to observations in academic settings (i.e., interactions with classmates and professors).

Through my students' observations and reflections, I was able to gain a better understanding of their experiences outside my classroom. As I reflected on my students' experiences, I gained important insights about the obstacles they faced in mainstream classes at the university. The students' perception of the mainstream university classroom as a site of tension comes in sharp contrast to their description of my ESL classroom—a place where they trusted and encouraged each other, felt safe to express ideas, and worked collaboratively to construct knowledge. Mark's comments described his changing self-image in each setting:

> In the [ESL class] I'm . . . outgoing . . . I'm comfortable in that situation because everyone is . . . international student and . . . everyone is very patient. . . . But I think in my department I'm kind of shy . . . I feel . . . embarrassed because I cannot explain myself very well, and I cannot understand the Americans very well. (follow-up interview, 5/22/02)

As Mark reflected, he went through an intense identity-shifting process as he left the ESL context and stepped into the classrooms of his academic department. In my ESL class, he considered himself to be outgoing, but in his department he became shy and embarrassed.

This contrast represented for me a troubling paradox: Although I felt rewarded by my students' accomplishments in my classroom, I was also left with a sense of distress. After all, my mission as an ESL instructor in higher education is precisely *to prepare* language learners to succeed in mainstream academic settings. Certainly, I do not believe that I should replicate the harsh realities of mainstream classes to prepare my students to succeed in them. However, the insights gained through this study have opened my eyes to further critical work that needs to be done in my own classroom.

Benesch (2001) urged those of us who teach ESL for academic purposes to adopt a critical pedagogical approach. Rather than regarding our mission as a "service enterprise" (p. 35) whose purpose is "to prepare students unquestioningly for institutional and faculty expectations" (p. 23), she envisioned our task as a transformative activity. In a similar vein, Zamel (1997) proposed a "transculturation model" (p. 341) of ESL instruction, which recognizes that learning another language does not simply involve imitating and reproducing the norms of the dominant culture. On the contrary, it involves a process of adaptation that is "dynamic, involving active engagement and resistance" (p. 350).

The Language Research Project proved to be a powerful curricular innovation, which in many respects conformed to Benesch's (2001) definition of a transformative activity and Zamel's (1997) transculturation model. Through the project, my students were able to explore crucial issues related to their own and others' use of language in the university community. The students sharpened their observation skills, gained awareness of academic discourse practices, and developed confidence in their own language abilities. However, I realize that the project offered further opportunities for critical language analysis which were left somewhat unexplored. As I continue to implement the Language Research Project in my classes, I must encourage my students to become more critical about the power dynamics that operate within their communicative interactions in English, both with their peers and with their professors. I must also engage with them in dialogue about their changing social identities and the transformative power of their own actions. In sum, as an ESL teacher I must do more than simply focus on issues related to the use of English in academic contexts. I must address questions of power and access related to language use in an open and direct way. As Norton (2000) argued, although it is important for language learners to study the rules of the target language, it is also important for them "to explore whose interests these rules serve" (p. 15).

Maria Dantas-Whitney teaches at Western Oregon University in the United States.

Appendix: Sample Data Collection Worksheet

Research Question: _____**?**

Date of observation: _____ Duration: _____

Location of observation: _____ Number of participants: _____

1. Note as many details as you can about the following components of the scene. Use the **SPEAKING framework** to guide your analysis.

S **Situation** (Description of the place. Seating arrangements, size of room, objects, etc. Good idea to draw a map.)	
P **Participants** (Description of the people. Gender, age, educational level, role, ethnic background, native country, etc.)	
E **Ends** (Purpose of the event. Goals and motivations of each participant.)	
A **Act sequence** (Sequence of speech acts and topics of conversation.)	
K **Key** (Tone or spirit of communication. Serious? Formal? Informal?)	
I **Instrumentalities** (Written language? Oral language?)	
N **Norms of interaction** (Rules for participation)	
G **Genre** (Type of activity. Class? Meeting? Seminar?)	

2. Now it is time for you to **reflect on your research question.** Try to provide answers based on your observation notes. Give several examples from your data in order to support your statements.

CHAPTER 6

Studying Classroom Practices and Learner Perceptions to Improve Test Quality (*Canada*)

Wendy Fraser and Janna Fox

Issue

Why do some of our students who perform so well in our English for academic purposes (EAP) classes fail miserably on language tests? Over the years, we have frequently asked this question and at times adjusted our practice to prepare our students better to take such tests. Thus we do not need to be convinced that washback exists. Evidence from our own experience suggests that tests affect our teaching and our students' learning. Indeed, much has been written in the literature about the complex washback phenomena (see particularly Alderson & Wall, 1993; Bailey, 1996). This research has focussed mainly on teachers' perceptions of washback (Alderson & Hamp-Lyons, 1996; Wall & Alderson, 1993). More recently, however, there has been an increasing emphasis on students' and test takers' perceptions of washback (Cheng, 1998; McDonald & Boud, 2003) and the interactions between teaching, testing, and learning in our own EAP program (Fox, 2003). This literature helped us to frame the issues that this chapter explores and reconsider washback from yet another perspective.

We know that what we learn from our students about tests and testing influences how we as teachers develop our own internal classroom tests. But this learning can (and should) influence external tests as well. By examining the potential of classroom practice and learner perceptions to shape and change external tests, we are suggesting a kind of bidirectional washback, in which recognitions about tests and testing that arise as a result of classroom experience influence test development, use, and interpretation. The exploratory study reported in this chapter examines the washback potential of classroom practice and learner perceptions in informing external test development in an EAP learning context.

CONTEXT

Our EAP classes, situated in a large Canadian university, attempt to provide second language students with the language skills and academic strategies necessary to engage in university study. The course material is presented within a framework of topic-based or thematic units in which content selected from a variety of academic sources forms the basis of EAP tasks. The format of the EAP units developed over the 12-week term is similar to the format of the internal end-of-course achievement tests and the external placement/admissions test. These tests are high stakes in that they have significant consequences for our students. The tests differ, however, in that the internal test score is averaged along with other course work undertaken throughout the term in determining a final mark, but the score on the external test stands alone. In the next section, we provide additional detail about these tests and analyze why they prove so challenging for our students.

THE EXTERNAL TEST

The score on the external placement/admissions test, the Canadian Academic English Language (CAEL) Assessment, either grants students admission to the university or requires them to take English language support. If they are placed in a required EAP course, they may also take a limited number of discipline-specific courses and begin their academic program, albeit in a limited way. The test is also used to identify students whose English language ability is such that they are not ready for any type of academic study and need intensive ESL classes.

More specifically, the CAEL Assessment is criterion referenced with criteria defining nine band levels, ranging from 10 to 90. Bands are tied directly to course placements in the language support program, with Bands 40 to 60 allowing students to take courses within their disciplines along with required EAP support (i.e., concurrent study). Students with scores below Band 40 are limited to registration in language courses only; students with scores above 60 enrol in full-time university programs without language support. Thus, when evaluating the differences in scores, although shifts within the band are important, it is shifts from one band to a higher or lower one that have the greatest impact on the test taker.

The test purports to measure English in use for academic purposes, specifically, as it is used in a Canadian university classroom at the first-year undergraduate level. The developers (see particularly Fox, 2000) argue that in academic study, the gathering of information is approached with a specific question or line of questioning in mind. Academic readers have a frame of reference, which allows them to make judgments concerning the relevance of information, concepts, and ideas. Therefore, test takers are asked to consider the prompt of the final writing task at the beginning of the test to encourage focused reading and listening. Questions on the readings and the lecture (i.e., reading and listening subtests) provide the test takers with scaffolding (i.e., language and content support) for the final writing task. In this way, the activities the test takers are asked to perform attempt to represent the types of activities they will be required to accomplish in the EAP program and the university. In addition to the reading, listening, and writing subtests in the CAEL Assessment (which are fully integrated and topic based), a separate test of speaking (the Oral Language Test) and a cloze test are administered to CAEL test takers. The reading, listening, writing, and speaking subtests are averaged for the final overall test score. The cloze test is used for research purposes only.

INTERNAL (CLASSROOM) TESTS

Within the context of the EAP classroom, students are guided to reflect critically on the significance and relevance of academic texts and lectures. Using a variety of techniques, we encourage students to find relationships among the ideas presented in the texts and the lectures, to identify the significance and complexities of the issues, and to evaluate the logic of the arguments presented. Through classroom engagement, a context for deeper and broader understanding is constructed, and this richness of thought is apparent in the language that students produce while performing the unit tasks, whether written or spoken. The final test for each of the levels in the EAP program is a condensed version of the unit tasks they engaged in during the course. One key difference between the class units, the in-class test, and the external test (i.e., the CAEL Assessment), however, is time. The EAP units typically take place over 2 or 3 weeks, the internal in-class final test occurs over 2 or 3 days, and the external test takes 2 hours. Another difference is the opportunity provided for discussion with the teacher and other classmates. This interaction is encouraged across university disciplines and in the EAP units, but is limited during the internal in-class test and absent from the external test.

A problem, then, is encountered when students are required to perform complex academic tasks in a limited amount of time and without interaction. Without the interaction of the guided classroom activities, language performance on the in-class test tends to lack the complexity and richness that students have successfully demonstrated throughout the course and can result in disappointing grades and placement. This may explain in part why we, and our EAP colleagues, have often commented that students' responses on tests are "superficial." As one EAP teacher put it, "Students who excel in my class are often unable to recognize the complexities of the issues and actively explore them on the tests, as they have done so often during class discussions."

So the question becomes, what exactly is it in the classroom context that enables these students to understand the nature of the tasks and to respond appropriately to them? And can whatever *it* is be included somehow in the testing context? When faced with a test of any sort, whether an internal or external test, many of our students seem to revert to their ingrained habits of copying and superficial manipulation. They seem to forget about the questions they have been asked (or have come up with themselves) that encouraged reflection on how texts are related to one another and the relevance of information or ideas to the tasks. This tendency may undermine the validity of the inferences we draw from our tests, as Lindquist (1951, cited in Linn, Baker, & Dunbar, 1991) pointed out: "The most important consideration is that the test questions require the examinee to do the *same* things, *however complex*, that he is required to do in the criterion situations" (p. 154). Thus, in order to see if we could improve our students' performance on the internal and external tests and enhance test validity, we decided to experiment with adding tasks within the testing context that would encourage students to engage in reflection. At this point, we examined the literature.

Background Literature

Moffett (1968) was one of the first to theorize about the role of reflection in student writing, describing discourse as "(a) reflective and relational . . . and (b) rhetorical" (p. 18). Later, Britton (1970) suggested that there are three stages in this response process—conception, incubation, and production—and that these processes are constantly interacting with each other.

> First the new experience—the reading or the experimenting—has to be fitted into the whole hierarchical complex of what the student already knows and what he thinks and feels about what he already knows. Then . . . he has to apply it to the writing assignment, which makes new demands on him. (p. 22)

Elbow (1991) identified *reasoning* as key to the genre of academic discourse across disciplines and "being clear about claims and assertions" (p. 32). Thus, as Britton, Moffett, and Elbow suggested, an effective academic response must reflect the student's ability to abstract, choose relevant information, and reorganize ideas to support claims. These activities may be said to define the act of reflection as it is integrated into the process of responding in an academic setting.

Further, "writing is inherently social" (Thralls, 1992, p. 64). The writing produced in a testing context is no exception. In fact, we would argue that testing is an intensely social interaction. In the case of our EAP students, testing is the process by which established members of the academic community evaluate each student's language and academic readiness to participate in the disciplinary activities of the academy. Within our EAP classes, the final test evaluates the development of a student's ability to use English for academic purposes. As the culminating activity of the course, test performance is supported by the previous activities, discussions, and feedback that have occurred throughout the term, all of which provide a kind of "covert collaboration" (Parks & Maguire, 1999, p. 143) that supports the student's performance on the test. Further, the in-class test is structured to occur over two or more classes, which allows students the time to reflect on their performance. The external test should also be considered intensely social. In a fully integrated test such as the CAEL Assessment, the questions are intended not only to test students' listening and reading comprehension, but also to guide the test takers through the listening and reading texts in order to support the student's final written responses. The tasks implicitly indicate what is relevant and what may be ignored, mimicking, in a sense, a teaching situation and providing covert collaboration. The responses of the test takers are an indication of their readiness to engage in this collaboration.

In a testing situation in which academic writing is evaluated, then, it is important that writers be encouraged or guided to reflect on meaning because "written examinations discourage extensive premeditation of the writing. . . . It takes courage, or despair, to sit in an exam room just thinking" (Britton, Burgess, Martin, McLeod, & Rosen, 1975, p. 25). Thus, if teachers recognize the importance of reflection in academic writing and the ways in which stress, time limitations, and the absence of interaction constrain this essential activity during tests, then they should consider ways to directly support reflection during tests—just as they do in classroom activities. In fact, tasks that were specifically designed to encourage reflection during a test might make the difference between "bombing" and performing successfully.

In sum, the literature suggests that the act of reflection is at the heart of constructing meaning in written discourse and particularly in academic writing. In tests of academic writing, the pressure of time constraints and the absence of interaction may distort the natural writing process unless opportunities for reflection are built into the testing procedure. If writing is distorted during the testing process, it cannot be considered representative of the abilities of the test takers, and thus inferences drawn from test results will not be valid. It was on the basis of these assumptions that three reflective tasks were developed to encourage and support reflection on an internal and external test. Aligned with that effort, our study addressed the following research questions:

- Can tasks promote useful reflection during testing?

- Do test takers recognize the activity of reflection as inherently different from information gathering (e.g., skimming, scanning, identifying key words)?

- Do reflective tasks aid the test taker in understanding the requirements of a writing task?

- Do reflective tasks have a positive effect on scores on external tests?

Procedures

Our study took place over two phases. In Phase 1, we explored the potential of reflective tasks as part of tests. Specifically, we included reflective tasks in an internal, in-class test and then examined student perceptions about how useful those reflective tasks were in helping them respond to the test's final writing task. Subsequently, in Phase 2, we compared the scores of test takers who wrote the external test (the CAEL Assessment) under two conditions: with and without reflective tasks.

PARTICIPANTS

Phase 1 involved 23 students from one of our intermediate-level EAP classes. Eighteen were Asian and spoke Mandarin Chinese as a first language (L1), 2 spoke Tamil, 2 spoke Arabic, and 1 spoke Spanish. The age range was 18 to 27, and there were 9 females and 14 males. Phase 2 examined the test performances of 116 test takers who took the CAEL Assessment at our university. In general, people who take this test require assessment of their English language proficiency in order to study in an English-medium academic institution or for accreditation from a professional institution. They are typically international students who wish to complete a degree at a Canadian university, permanent residents who have been in Canada for less than 3 years, high school students wishing to continue their education, or adults returning to upgrade their education. The group considered in this study consisted of 40 female and 76 male test takers with an age range of 18 to 29. In terms of language, 71 test takers spoke Mandarin Chinese as their L1, with small numbers of Arabic, Tamil, and Spanish speakers. The characteristics of the test takers in Phase 2 are representative of those in the overall CAEL Assessment test-taking population (Fox, 2000) as well as the EAP classes in which we teach.

INSTRUMENTS

We used two test instruments. In Phase 1, we developed and administered an in-class, internal test. In Phase 2, we adapted a version of the external test, the CAEL Assessment, to include reflective tasks. In addition, we administered two posttest questionnaires (one in each phase) to elicit test taker responses to the tests.

In Phase 1, the design of the internal test was based on typical end-of-course tests and CAEL Assessment specifications, except that three reflective tasks were added to the first reading. The test was fully integrated and topic based, consisting of two readings, a lecture (with comprehension questions), and a short essay. The students were given the essay prompt before listening and reading about the topic. The test was timed in the same manner as the CAEL Assessment and took 2 hours to administer. Students were allowed 10 minutes for the three reflective tasks, which asked students to take time to respond to three questions (see Table 1) after completing the first reading.

The posttest questionnaire administered immediately after the in-class test aimed to discover if students perceived the reflective tasks as useful in forming their responses to the essay question. We also wanted to see if they recognized that the strategies needed to complete these reflective tasks were different from the strategies needed to process information at a more superficial level during information gathering (e.g., identifying main ideas, locating examples).

In Phase 2, one form of the CAEL Assessment was extended by 10 minutes to allow for two different sets of tasks at the end of the first reading. Three reflective tasks (see Table 1) were added to the end of the first reading in the reflective version, and a nonreflective task (i.e., a multiple-choice vocabulary matching task)[1] was added to the end of the first reading in the nonreflective version.

Table 1. Reflective Tasks

Task	How Does the Task Encourage Reflection?
What is the most important information in Reading 1?	Encourages test takers to step back from the activity of detail gathering and examine the article as a whole to establish its purpose.
Based on Reading 1 do you agree or disagree that . . . [the essay prompt of the final writing task is inserted here, in the form of a yes or no question].	Reminds test takers that the reading is linked to the final essay task; encourages test takers to take a position based on new information gathered in Reading 1.
How will the information in Reading 1 help you to write the essay at the end of the test?	Encourages test takers to begin thinking about essay organization. Answers to this question might include *define, give examples, give background to the problem.*

The posttest questionnaire, administered at the end of the test, was designed to ascertain if the test takers identified the version of Reading 1 with reflective tasks as being useful in completing the writing task.

PHASES

Prior to beginning the study, we sought and obtained ethics approval from the university's ethics review board. In Phase 1, we administered the internal, in-class test during class time, and then two EAP teachers marked the tests. This test had high stakes for the students because it was part of the final, end-of-course testing activity that occurred over 2 days. After the test, students were asked to review their test responses as they answered questions on the posttest questionnaire. The questionnaire asked specific questions about the reflective tasks to elicit student perceptions about the nature and usefulness of these tasks in writing their essay responses. Students responded to the questionnaire in writing, and we analyzed their answers.

In Phase 2, the CAEL Assessment was administered according to the established testing protocol. This phase of the study used a split half design (Hatch & Lazaraton, 1991) in which the two test versions (reflective and nonreflective) were distributed to even- or odd-numbered test takers in the same room. Test takers were not aware that they had different versions of the same test. We allowed 10 more minutes at the end of the first reading task to accommodate the extra tasks. Because of the administration protocol, test takers were not able to retain the test and review their responses while filling out the posttest questionnaire. Thus the questionnaire was more general, focusing on the subtest sections (i.e., Readings 1 and 2, Listening) that the test takers found most useful, rather than on the specific tasks (as in the internal, in-class test in Phase 1).

Trained raters marked all the tests (see Fox, 2000, for an explanation of marking procedures). Because this was an official administration of the CAEL Assessment for which test takers would receive official scores, the raters of the reading section were instructed to ignore the reflective and nonreflective tasks, and these were not considered in the final scores compiled for the test. Therefore, the scores received on the added tasks were not calculated into the raw score that test takers received for the reading section. Raters were not informed of the research study, in order to avoid affecting the essay evaluation in any way.

ANALYSIS

As discussed previously, Phase 1 was designed to explore students' perceptions of the reflective tasks on the in-class, internal test. Therefore, we analyzed the written responses to the posttest questionnaire for indications of the students' perceptions about the reflective tasks. Through an iterative process of analytic induction (Creswell, 1994; Lincoln & Guba, 1985), we categorized the responses on the basis of recurring themes and patterns.

In Phase 2, we compared the means, standard deviations, and overall distributions of scores from our study sample of 116 test takers with those from CAEL test takers between the years 2000 and 2004 (i.e., the overall test population). Next, we undertook a between-group analysis of the sample of 116 by comparing means and standard deviations of the overall test scores and subtest scores (i.e., reading, listening, writing, speaking, cloze) of the reflective and nonreflective groups to identify any group differences of interest. Subsequently, we analyzed the posttest questionnaires for indications that the reflective tasks were useful in responding to the final essay. As a result, a subgroup of 11 test takers was identified for further analysis because they indicated that Reading 1 with the reflective tasks was useful in helping them write the final essay. We then compared this group of 11 test takers in terms of overall and subtest performance with the other groups considered in the study.

Results

PHASE 1: THE INTERNAL TEST

Our analysis of the questionnaires identified four main themes, which accounted for the recurring responses of the 23 students who commented on the end-of-term internal classroom test. These themes were (1) recognizing the difference between reflection and information gathering, (2) clarifying the task, (3) formulating an initial stance in relation to the final writing task, and (4) finding a personal voice. The following sections discuss these themes in relation to the research questions that framed the study.

Can Reflective Tasks Promote Useful Reflection During a Test?

Given the time constraints, some students mentioned that they did not have an overall understanding of the first article when they finished answering the informational questions. As Student 4 remarked, "We had not enough time to think deeply. The only way was to skim the article in order to find the answer." The reflective tasks seemed to encourage review of the article as a whole, by directing students to discover the purpose of the article and how it related to the essay response at the end of the test. As Student 11 commented, "It makes me thinking about what's the main idea and the purpose of the article."

Did Students Recognize Reflective Activity as Somehow Different From Information Gathering?

It seemed that students did perceive reflective tasks as different in kind from informational ones. Some students commented that skimming the article for key words or getting the answer "directly from the article" (Student 10) differed from "concluding the answer from the reading rather than just copying it" (Student 7). As one test taker noted, "They make you think" (Student 8). We would argue (with the support of Britton, 1970; Elbow, 1991; Moffett, 1968) that such thinking is a necessary part of producing academic writing. The students' remarks suggest in some cases that the reflective tasks may have supported their recognitions of previous assumptions, which they modified according to the new information provided in the test. Student 12 alluded to this process when she noted, "I thought that probably I was being too radical when I supported" the position taken in the text. This comment suggests that she is aware of a change in her stance. Although only some of the students remarked that this process was more difficult than simply skimming and copying key words or phrases, a number of students commented that they appreciated the opportunity to refocus on the meaning of the whole text in relation to the final essay question, to begin the process of finding original relationships among the ideas in the text and the language to express them. Several students made comments such as the following: "I realized how understanding the theory could help me" (Student 12); the reflective tasks "helped me because it's difficult to answer in my own words" (Student 14); "I needed to think harder here" (Student 11); "it was a chance to express my own opinion" (Student 15); and "I realized there's no answer in the text" (Student 8).

It is important to note, however, that most of the test takers did not recognize that they were involved in a different activity during reflection than during information gathering. Rather, they identified the reflective tasks as more difficult. However, students may not need to notice that they are engaged in reflecting in order for it to be useful.

Did Reflective Tasks Aid the Test Takers in Clarifying the Final Writing Task?

Did the reflective questions help the test takers understand who the audience was or, more specifically, what the raters (their teachers) were expecting? It seems from the students' remarks that the reflective tasks did refocus their attention on the essay question at the end of the test. As Student 15 pointed out, the reflective tasks "helped in writing the essay because I knew I had to use the readings in writing the essay." The reflective tasks may also have helped clarify for the students that academic writing is partly about taking a position (Giltrow, 2002) on others' discussions—in this case, other texts. In other words, to succeed on this test, it was essential for the test taker to use the readings and the lecture as research or background to support and elaborate his or her ideas. One test taker showed how she understood this element in the following comment: "People have done some researches, and it can help me to have more suggestions of writing the essay" (Student 10). It is possible that for some students the reflective tasks helped to clarify the dimensions of the writing task and the audience expectations of the final essay response.

In sum, Phase 1 of the study suggested that reflective tasks could in fact influence the testing process for some students. In Phase 2, we turned to an examination of test performance overall in addressing the final research question: Do reflective tasks have a positive effect on scores on external tests?

PHASE 2: THE EXTERNAL TEST

In Phase 2, we first compared the means, standard deviations, and overall distributions of the test scores of the 116 test takers considered in our study with CAEL test takers between the years 2000 and 2004 (i.e., the overall test population). The means of the sample and target populations were 35.6 and 35.8, respectively, with standard deviations of 14.82 and 13.02. Thus, no significant or meaningful differences were identified. Next we compared the scores of the reflective and nonreflective groups. The results were inconclusive. However, two interesting differences emerged from the analysis: (1) there were differences in the distribution of writing scores across the reflective and nonreflective groups, and (2) there were differences in the listening performance between the reflective and nonreflective groups.

Differences in the Distribution of Writing Scores

Comparing the two groups, the overall scores awarded the reflective and nonreflective groups were at the same band level (30), with the nonreflective group having a slightly higher mean (36.38) than the reflective group (34.74). It was interesting to note that although the writing score means of the reflective and nonreflective groups were almost the same (36.84 and 36.72, respectively) the standard deviations were quite different (17.3 and 14.7, respectively). Figure 1 shows how the writing scores were distributed across the band levels in the two groups. To investigate these differences in distribution, we examined the posttest questionnaire responses.

Looking at listening performance, we began by examining the mean and band scores of both groups (reflective and nonreflective) in relation to whether the test takers responded on the posttest questionnaire (Question 1) that they had

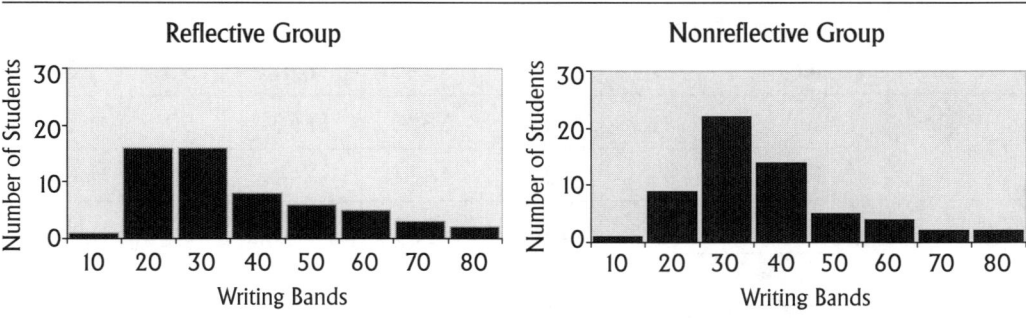

Figure 1. Reflective and nonreflective distribution of writing band scores.

found Reading 1 useful. Posttest Question 1 specifically asked the following: Can you remember any questions that helped you decide what you would say in the essay? Of those test takers who responded *yes* to indicate that Reading 1 was useful, 8 were from the reflective group and 10 were from the nonreflective group. The remainder of the test takers (50 for the reflective group and 48 for the nonreflective group) responded *no* to the question. Our analysis of Question 1 showed that most respondents did not indicate that Reading 1 was more useful than other subtest sections of the test. However, the data presented a slightly different picture with regard to Question 2 (see Table 2).

The results for Question 2 on the posttest questionnaire showed that those test takers in the reflective group who identified Reading 1 as useful and felt less confused about writing the essay at the end of the test ($n = 11$) performed better than any other group. Did this mean that their use of the reflective tasks at the end of Reading 1 positively affected their test performance, or were they simply a group with a higher level of proficiency? Our ability to answer these

Table 2. Test Performance Compared With Answers on Posttest Question 2

Question: Did you think about the essay question at the end of Reading 1?
If yes, how did you feel about the essay question after Reading 1?
More confused, less confused, or no change? ($n = 116$)

Test Section	Question 2 Answer	N		Mean		Band	
		R	NR	R	NR	R	NR
Overall	Yes	11	19	41.82	35.79	40	30
	No	47	39	32.95	36.67	30	30
Reading	Yes	11	19	40.00	37.37	40	30
	No	47	39	35.00	38.97	30	30
Listening	Yes	11	19	47.27	37.89	40	30
	No	47	39	35.23	42.31	30	40
Writing	Yes	11	19	41.82	37.37	40	30
	No	47	39	35.45	36.41	30	30
Oral	Yes	11	19	58.18	51.58	50	50
	No	47	39	46.36	47.44	40	40
Cloze	Yes	11	19	17.45	15.42	N/A	N/A
	No	47	39	13.61	13.44	N/A	N/A

Note: R = reflective group; NR = nonreflective group; Yes = Reading 1 "more useful," and test takers indicated they were "less confused."

questions using the data in this exploratory study is limited by the small number of cases we are considering here. What is important to note is that the group of test takers who had the reflective tasks (i.e., the reflective group), and who responded *yes*, indicating that they did think about the essay question at the end of Reading 1 (i.e., they stopped to reflect), performed at a significantly higher level than those test takers who responded *no* or did not have the reflective tasks to support their performance. Whether this outcome was an artefact of higher levels of language proficiency or the result of the task differences in the test is impossible to determine.

The subtests of reading, listening, and writing were derived from one integrated measure of language performance, but the oral subtest and cloze represented independent measures of language and thus allowed for another window on proficiency—outside the reflective or nonreflective frame. Although the group of 11's scores on the cloze test were marginally higher, their band level on the oral subtest was the same as that of the nonreflective group that answered the same way on Posttest Question 2 ($n = 19$). Given that a score on the oral subtest depends as much on listening ability as on speaking, the following question arose: If reflective and nonreflective groups performed at the same level on the oral language test, why did the group of 11 perform at a higher level on the listening subtest of the integrated test? Considering that the listening subtest is situated immediately after Reading 1 (and the reflective tasks), could the reflective tasks have positively contributed to higher performance on their listening subtests? In exploring this question, we discovered an interesting pattern in the relationship between the listening band score and the overall band score in the different groups, with the reflective group showing the highest correlation between listening and the overall band score (.83) and the nonreflective group showing the lowest correlation (.76). In the reflective and nonreflective groups the correlation between reading and writing was low but still statistically significant ($p < .01$). In the reflective group of 11, however, the correlation between the reading and writing was much lower (.37) and not statistically significant. These results suggested that the reflective tasks may in some way have affected test takers' performance in listening, which, in turn, may have affected the distribution differences we observed in their writing performance. However, due to the very small samples, without further investigation the results remain inconclusive.

Reflection

Our study was an initial exploration of the potential that reflective tasks might have to support student performance on internal and external EAP tests. Any conclusions we might draw, however, are only tentative. The samples were small, and the design did not allow for generalization. Our exploration did suggest that this line of inquiry may be fruitful, and there may be reason to incorporate more reflective tasks on integrated EAP tests in internal and external testing contexts.

One outcome of the study at the program level was an increase in the development of reflective test tasks by our EAP colleagues and by CAEL test developers, who continue to investigate their use. This study illustrates the potential that recognitions arising from classroom practice and student perceptions can have to improve the quality of tests and the testing process. Such recognitions should inform tests so that they elicit from test takers the same types of responses and interactions as are elicited from students engaged in classroom learning activities. This is particularly important for the students who are now in our EAP program. Many of them have considerable experience in test-driven cultures in which superficial strategies and memorization have earned them high scores. When confronted with our internal or external EAP tests, therefore, they are likely to respond in the same manner that they have in the past—unless the tests themselves encourage the same types of reflection as we have encouraged in our classrooms. Knowing the importance of reflection in their learning, we must also support its use in our tests. Some students may bomb not because they cannot perform on tests, but rather because the tests do not engage them in activities that allow them to show what they know and can do. This study has reconsidered the potential bidirectionality of washback—in this case, from the classroom to the test. We suggest that teachers and students—the key stakeholders in learning (and testing)—can and should influence high-stakes tests.

Another lasting outcome of this experience at the personal level has been to reinforce the value of research arising from our classroom practice. If our students bomb in the future, we will not just discuss it in the staff room. We now realize that we can funnel our day-to-day intuitions and questions into research. We have learned firsthand the power of research to inform, support change, and improve the quality of testing, teaching, and learning. What is key is that this is our own teacher-led research. When we as teachers move beyond anecdotal exchanges of information about learning and use research as a tool, we validate, inform, and improve our classroom activity.

Wendy Fraser teaches at the College of the North Atlantic–Qatar in Doha, Qatar. Janna Fox teaches at the School of Linguistics and Applied Language Studies at Carleton University in Ottawa, Ontario, Canada.

Note

1. The nonreflective task had been piloted with intermediate-level EAP students. The results of this pilot showed that the strategies needed to complete this task were skimming and scanning the text for discrete items rather than engaging in deeper processing of text for meaning.

CHAPTER 7

Listening to Text and ESL Students: Facilitating Low-Frequency Vocabulary Acquisition Incidentally (*United States*)

Jami Gurkin

Issue

Moving to the United States is a major transition for a child. Mourning the loss of everything familiar and at the same time adjusting to a new home, a new school, a new culture, and a new language is an overwhelming task. What would be a daunting situation for the most confident adult can be a terrifying and confusing time for an English as a subsequent language (ESL) student left alone in a school, unable to communicate with his teachers or classmates.

Although many schools with a small ESL population offer just 30 minutes of ESL daily, the majority of the children acquire the common social vocabulary of English fairly quickly. In less than 1 academic year, most of my ESL students can comfortably discuss the weather; follow simple directions such as *trace, circle, cut,* and *underline*; play with new friends; watch TV; and order ice cream at the neighborhood ice cream shop. By the end of the school year, I receive many compliments from ESL parents and classroom teachers. Everyone decides that I must be a wizard because of how quickly the children have learned English. Clearly, they have learned a lot, but my job is far from finished. The ESL students need to learn English as quickly as possible for academic as well as social purposes. Great demands are placed on the ESL students in the affluent suburban community in which I teach ESL. The school curriculum is a rigorous one to satisfy the high expectations of the parents, faculty, and administration for student achievement. In 2003, 99% of students in the school passed the New Jersey Assessment of Skills and Knowledge (NJ ASK) for Language Arts Literacy, a cumulative progress indicator of the New Jersey Core Curriculum, compared to the county average of 86% and the state average of 77%.

Learning vocabulary is essential to language learning; therefore, facilitating vocabulary acquisition, especially difficult or low-frequency vocabulary, needs to be a main focus in ESL classrooms. No input is comprehensible unless there is an understanding of at least some of its vocabulary. An insufficient subsequent language (L2) vocabulary is a major handicap to ESL students. Young L2 learners need to develop language and literacy skills simultaneously, and for many this is their first formal experience with reading and writing. They need to use language for challenging academic work in the mainstream classroom, and they have a limited amount of time to catch up to and keep up with their English-speaking peers. For academic success, ESL students need to acquire language quickly and efficiently.

Listening to stories read aloud with explanations of new words is considered to be an effective way for elementary school L2 learners to gain word knowledge incidentally. However, this method may not sufficiently address the needs of these students. Many researchers have studied vocabulary learning from listening to stories read aloud when a brief explanation of the meaning of each target word was given as each word was encountered (Brett, Rothlein, & Hurley, 1996; Elley, 1989). Multiple-choice tests were used in these studies to measure recall of the definition of the words. But researchers did not test to see if the participants were able to use the words. Does listening to stories with explanations of targeted words address the range of skills needed for word use or are instructional activities needed in addition? Can students internalize the new words and use them as part of their written and spoken vocabulary? Will listening to stories provide the learner with enough word knowledge to use the new words, or are instructional activities following the reading session necessary? These questions establish the foundation of my study, which was designed to see if participants were able to use the target words in contextually appropriate ways with and without instructional activities.

Background Literature

In first language (L1) acquisition, vocabulary knowledge has been shown as a strong predictor of academic achievement, reading comprehension, and overall intellectual ability (Sternberg, 1987). Researchers, aiming to enhance vocabulary acquisition, have attempted to determine the most effective method for facilitating the development of word knowledge. Although no one method has been found to be the most effective, some research shows that children learn vocabulary incidentally from context while reading. Advocates of incidental vocabulary acquisition argue that new word meanings are derived and learned through reading, even though the reader's purpose for reading is not the learning of new words (Jenkins, Stein, & Wysocki, 1984; Nagy, Herman, & Anderson, 1985, 1987).

Once termed the *default* argument (Jenkins & Dixon, 1983), incidental vocabulary acquisition is supported by strong evidence in two areas. The first area of support comes from the extensive yearly gains shown to occur in children's vocabularies (Nagy & Anderson, 1984). Average annual vocabulary growth between the 3rd and 12th grades is calculated to be about 3,000 words (Nagy & Herman, 1987). Such substantial growth could not easily result from direct language instruction unless substantial amounts of school time were dedicated solely to vocabulary instruction. Jenkins, Matlock, and Slocum (1989) have estimated that individual word meaning instruction of 15 minutes per day, 5 days per week, is required for students to learn 430 words in a 36-week school year. The second indication of incidental vocabulary acquisition is the assertion by Jenkins et al. (1984) that vocabulary gains are made from reading. Their research shows that students exposed to low-frequency target words in specially constructed passages are able to acquire word meanings incidentally during reading. Also, an increased number of context presentations results in more word learning.

INCIDENTAL VOCABULARY ACQUISITION FOR THE L2 LEARNER

Similar to L1 findings, L2 research indicates that incidental vocabulary learning is also possible for the L2 learner (Elley, 1989; Elley & Mangubhai, 1983; Krashen, 1989). Until recent years, vocabulary instruction in the L2 has not been a main focus in L2 pedagogy. Historically, researchers and teachers have prioritized the phonology and grammar of language, and vocabulary was traditionally given little or no priority. More recently, L2 research studies have linked reading success with vocabulary, and an interest in the role of vocabulary has developed. In particular, extensive reading has a major role to play in the success of L2 vocabulary learning. Krashen found that language learners acquire vocabulary and spelling competence most efficiently by receiving comprehensible input while reading. This is particularly true when the learners are motivated and focused on meaning. High-interest storybooks provided the motivation, and class discussions based on the story and its pictures emphasized the meaning. Thus, stories allow children to learn naturally and are good models of written English. Elley and Mangubhai discovered that after ESL students from rural Fijian schools with very few books in English were exposed to a flood of high-interest books, they performed well above the typical performance of similar students in English, science, social studies, and mathematics.

To test the connection between lexical competency and reading comprehension, Laufer (1989) designed a study to measure the relationship between the number of words understood by a reader in an academic text and the reader's comprehension of the text. He found that adult L2 learners could not read well in the L2 if their vocabulary was below a lexical threshold of the basic 3,000 word families or 5,000 basic lexical items, regardless of academic ability. Laufer concluded that readers need to understand 95% of the words in a text to ensure reasonable reading comprehension.

The dilemma is how to learn enough vocabulary to read well when many words, termed low-frequency vocabulary, are found only in written English and are encountered only through reading. To succeed academically, L2 learners need to learn sufficient vocabulary to read well. Frequently, the vocabulary of the L2 learner is not large enough to allow for good comprehension while reading. For these students, reading becomes a tedious experience, and they lose motivation. Nuttal (1982) proposed that many L2 readers are trapped in a vicious circle that links lack of comprehension, lack of enjoyment when reading, and slow and infrequent reading. Nuttal asserted that the L2 reader can enter the vicious circle at any point and can escape only when one of the links is broken. Effective instructional intervention that results in enjoyment of reading and extensive reading can break the links in the vicious circle.

INCIDENTAL VOCABULARY ACQUISITION FROM LISTENING TO STORIES

Listening to stories instead of reading them has been reported to benefit all students including the poorer reader. According to Elley (1989), listening comprehension is typically stronger than oral and silent reading comprehension for all readers. Listening to stories provides the student with the opportunity to enjoy literature rather than attempting to struggle through the text alone.

A further benefit from listening to stories is vocabulary acquisition. Research indicates that incidental learning of new words from context does occur when students listen to stories. In 1989, Elley conducted two similar studies with 7- and 8-year-old students in New Zealand to assess their ability to acquire vocabulary from listening to stories. In both studies Elley found that the students gained vocabulary. Their gains ranged from 15% for reading aloud without teacher explanation to 40% for reading aloud with teacher explanation. Elley's study suggested that students with the lowest vocabulary scores on the pretest gained at least as much vocabulary as the students with larger vocabularies, but that students with larger vocabularies also made vocabulary gains. In addition, incidental L2 vocabulary learning from listening to stories is also possible, Elley found during a series of three read-aloud pilot projects with 9- to 11-year-old participants learning ESL.

SCAFFOLDING

The term *scaffolding* is used to describe a teacher providing a student with assistance in some form or another as a temporary means to aid performance at a level above what the student has achieved independently. Scaffolding helps the student operate within the zone of proximal development (Vygotsky, 1962), which is a highly motivating and challenging skill level. Boyle and Peregoy (1990) have used the term *literacy scaffolds* to describe the ways teachers help students gain immediate access to the meaning of text. Through the use of scaffolds, the ESL teacher can increase the student's ability to make sense of a text, exceeding the individual's current unassisted capability. By making the text of a read-aloud passage comprehensible for the student, the ESL teacher can facilitate vocabulary acquisition. Replicating Elley's 1989 study, Lambert (as cited in Ulanoff & Pucci, 1999, p. 411) found that L2 learners were able to listen to stories and make gains in vocabulary acquisition similar to those made by L1 speakers when the teacher helped the children understand the story.

PROBLEMS WITH INCIDENTAL VOCABULARY ACQUISITION

Although incidental vocabulary acquisition does lead to increased word knowledge, problems exist. One problem is that vocabulary acquisition from reading is unpredictable. It is impossible to determine which words a student will acquire and how well the words will be learned. A second problem occurs when the context provides rich or redundant information to the reader and the reader is able to guess the word's meaning. In this situation, the reader easily disregards the unknown but correctly guessed word because the text is understood. For vocabulary learning to take place, learners must attend to the unknown word. A third problem is time constraints. Incidental vocabulary learning may not be the best type of learning for L2 learners who need to learn the language quickly. Some form of explicit instruction or instruction-enhanced reading may be needed to get many ESL students over the 3,000-word-family threshold (Zahar, Cobb, & Spada, 2001).

One way to increase the chances that students learn vocabulary incidentally is for the teacher to provide explanations for unknown target words. The second part of Elley's (1989) study showed that teacher explanations of unknown words as they occurred more than doubled the vocabulary gains children made without explanations. In addition, results on a delayed posttest showed that the new vocabulary learning was relatively permanent.

A study by Brett, Rothlein, and Hurley (1996) also demonstrated that reading aloud to children and providing explanations of unknown vocabulary as the words were encountered was an effective way to help children learn the meaning of new words. Their findings suggested that repeated readings of a story might not be necessary if new vocabulary was explained as students encountered the new words. Appel and Vermeer (1998) designed a program that sped up the acquisition of vocabulary by migrant children learning Dutch in the Netherlands during their first four grades of primary school. Lessons were designed around a certain story. First, background knowledge was activated, and then the teacher, who also explained the meaning of the target words during the lesson, read the story. Follow-up lessons focused on the target words.

LEXICAL COMPETENCE AND DEEP PROCESSING OF VOCABULARY

Lexical competence involves knowing the linguistic, psycholinguistic, and socio-linguistic elements of a word, not simply being able to define a word. Learners gain lexical competence gradually through a complex process that occurs during their exposure to a word in meaningful contexts. L2 research points to the need for rich, deep processing of word knowledge for word retention and word retrieval. Hulstijn and Laufer (2001) investigated the effect of involvement load on the retention of 10 low-frequency English words by six groups of advanced university learners of English as a foreign language in an incidental learning setting. They determined that greater involvement with target vocabulary facilitated greater retention of the words.

Meaningful instructional intervention combined with reading enhances incidental vocabulary learning. In a study designed to determine if a reading-plus-vocabulary-instruction treatment would produce greater vocabulary gains than a reading-only treatment, given the same amount of time for each treatment, Paribakht and Wesche (1993) found that both treatments produced highly significant gains for all types of target words. The reading-plus group, however, achieved significantly greater gains and reached higher levels of word knowledge for the targeted vocabulary than the reading-only group.

Procedures

PARTICIPANTS

In my study of vocabulary acquisition, which started with a pilot study, 16 ESL students took part. For purposes of analysis, participants were divided into four groups, even though the testing was done on different occasions. The participants were grouped according to proficiency level except for the kindergarten students, who were grouped by grade level. All of the participants were elementary school age. The participants in the pilot study group were older than the other participants and ranged in age from 9 to 12 years old.

The 3 participants in Group 1 had low English proficiency. These participants had been in an ESL group for new English language learners for approximately 6 months and were making steady progress acquiring English. The 3 participants in Group 2 were very proficient in English. Each had passed the language proficiency assessment instrument called the MACaulitis II Test for their grade level the June prior to the study, but they continued in ESL because of the tremendous vocabulary demands of the school's curriculum. One of the participants in this group had been evaluated by the school child study team and speech team, which determined that this child was language handicapped. This participant's scores were not counted along with those of the other members of Group 2 in this study. The participants in Group 3 were 5 kindergarten boys. Four of them had attended an American preschool the year before kindergarten. The fifth boy had lived in the United States for a year before kindergarten but did not attend preschool. He had spent most of his time in the United States at home with his mother, a limited English speaker.

MATERIALS AND PROCEDURES

The book selected for this study, *Billie the Hippo* (Malane, 2001), is an informational text, chosen because it is an enjoyable book about an animal. The photographs in the book are clear and simple and match the text well. Although the book is easy to understand, it contains at least 15 words determined to be unfamiliar to the study population.

The study was conducted over a 2-day time period. In Lesson 1, I read the first two chapters of the book aloud to the participants. Prior to reading *Billie the Hippo*, I showed the cover of the book, read the title, discussed the cover photograph, and led an initial discussion about hippos to activate the students' prior knowledge.

Fifteen words or phrases were selected as the study's target words. I categorized seven as nouns: *barrel, tusks, toenails, nostrils, wild animal, breaths,* and *muzzle;* five as verbs: *control, weighs, graze, equal,* and *poking out;* and three as adjectives: *huge, thick,* and *sunburned.* I gave explanations of the targeted words or showed photographs depicting the words during the first day of the study. I gave a brief demonstration for *breaths* and *poking out.* During the reading, when I came to a target word in the book, I stopped and read the definition, showed the photograph, or gave the brief demonstration. I gave no further explanations of the target words.

Following the reading, I asked the participants to discuss what they had learned about hippos. Each participant gave at least one piece of information learned from the text. Then I gave a two-part test of vocabulary knowledge to the students. The first part (Test 1A) was a 15-item vocabulary test to check the knowledge of difficult and unknown words from the story. The items were pictorial multiple choice. For each item, I asked the participants to circle the picture that showed the target word. The second part (Test 1B) consisted of eight fill-in-the-blank sentences. Participants were instructed to choose the correct answer from the word box at the top of the page. Only one correct answer was possible for each sentence. Each word had to be used. There were no distracters.

Kindergarten participants completed the second part of the test individually with me, and I read the sentences aloud to them.

For Lesson 2 of the study, I wrote 7 of the 15 targeted words on the blackboard, leaving ample space between them for information to be added later. These seven words or phrases, *poking out, wild animal, graze, tusks, nostrils, thick,* and *muzzle,* are referred to as *supertargeted* words. I then reread chapters 1 and 2 of *Billie the Hippo,* offering the same brief definitions, photographs, or demonstrations for the 15 targeted words as I had done in Lesson 1. After rereading the two chapters, I provided instructional activities for the supertargeted words.

To enhance the benefits of reading aloud, I adapted Text Talk—a project designed by Beck and McKeown (2001)—for my ESL students. I first used a word in its role in the story and then asked the participants to repeat the word. Next, I explained the word using a definition that was ESL student friendly, wrote at least one example on the board showing how and when the word might be used, and drew illustrations to facilitate understanding. Finally, I asked participants to use the supertargeted word. For each example given by a participant, I asked another participant to explain what the first one had said.

Following the vocabulary instruction, I directed the students to return to their seats, and I erased the writing on the board. For Test 2, I gave each student a piece of 12-inch-by-18-inch manila drawing paper with 15 boxes. I wrote the 15 target words (which included the 7 supertargeted words) on the board and added directions. I read the directions, which instructed the students to write a sentence for each word and to draw a picture to illustrate each sentence, and I made sure that all the students understood the assignment. The kindergarten participants dictated sentences to me individually. From previous work with these participants, I knew that they were able to create sentences and present them orally but that their literacy prevented them from writing the sentences easily. Fifteen sentences would have been an overwhelming task for them.

Results

Unlike other studies previously mentioned (Brett et al., 1996; Elley, 1989) that tested for recall of word definitions, this study was designed to see if participants were able to use target words in contextually appropriate ways. Similar to other studies' tests, Test 1A was designed to see if the participants were able to choose a pictorial representation of the definition of each target word. Test 1B, however, was a fill-in-the-blank test that required participants to use the target words to complete sentences. The test was designed to show if the participants had gained enough word knowledge of the target words from the first lesson to place each word in its correct context. Jenkins et al. (1984) found that more than two encounters with a word were necessary to noticeably affect vocabulary learning. Test 2 was designed to see if after two encounters with brief explanations of the target words the participants were able to use each word in a sentence. The instructional activity part of Lesson 2 provided the participants with greater information for 7 of the 15 target words, the supertargeted words, and the contexts in which they could be used. I used Test 2 to discover whether the participants had gained enough word knowledge to use the words in contextually appropriate sentences. Moreover, Test 2 was intended to provide evidence about the necessity of instructional activities, such as those used in Lesson 2, if the results showed that more supertargeted words were used appropriately than target words were.

Following the 2-day testing session, I compared the scores from Test 1A, Test 1B, and Test 2. I examined each participant's correct and incorrect items. First, the scores of Test 1A (pictorial multiple choice) and Test 1B (fill-in-the-blank from a word bank) were compared to see if the participants were able to choose the correct picture and choose the correct corresponding word in the fill-in-the-blank sentences after listening to the text once. From this comparison, I found that a combined 17 words identified correctly by the participants on the pictorial multiple choice were not used appropriately in the fill-in-the-blank sentences. These results indicate that students could choose the picture depicting the meaning of the word correctly but did not have enough word knowledge to use the word correctly in a fill-in-the-blank sentence. Next, I looked at the words answered correctly on Test 1A (pictorial multiple choice) and checked to see which ones were used incorrectly on Test 2 (forming sentences with the words). This comparison showed that a combined total of 26 words correctly chosen by the participants on Test 1A were not used correctly on Test 2.

Finally, I determined which words were used correctly in sentences on Test 2 but not matched with the correct pictorial definitions on Test 1A. I considered these words to have been learned by the participants. Each incorrect item on Test 1A was checked, participant by participant, to see if it was used correctly on Test 2. Results showed that a combined total of 41 words were learned from listening to the text two times with teacher explanation of the target words. Approximately two words per participant were acquired from listening to the text read aloud.

To analyze the test results further, I compared the mean number of words acquired per subject to see which group had acquired the greatest number of words. Table 1 shows that the mean number of words acquired by the most proficient group and the least proficient group were roughly the same. In comparison, Elley's (1989) study found that vocabulary gains for the low-ability group were at least as much as the gains for the higher groups. Robbins and Ehri (1994), however, found during their study that gains were greater among children with larger vocabularies.

Table 1. Words Acquired per Subject Group (*n* = 15)

Group	Words Learned	Students in Group	Mean Number of Words per Subject
Pilot Group	19	5	3.8
Group 1, Low Proficiency	7	3	2.3
Group 2, Advanced Proficiency	5	2	2.5
Group 3, Kindergarten	10	5	2.0

In my study, the pilot group learned the most words per participant. The participants in this group, made up of the oldest participants in the study, learned almost four words each. Many studies (Asher & Price, 1967; Genesee, 1987; Krashen, Long, & Scarcella, 1979; Stern, Burstall, & Harley, 1975) have concluded that older children were better L2 learners than were younger children. The information gathered in this study supports these findings.

Finally, to see if more supertargeted words than targeted words were acquired by participants, I compared the mean number of supertargeted words acquired by each group with the mean number of targeted words acquired by each group. Words that were not known by the participants on Test 1A but were known by the participants on Test 2 were considered to be acquired. Table 2 shows that the participants acquired 57.64% of the supertargeted words and 39.85% of the targeted words. Clearly, then, this study found that participants acquired more supertargeted words than targeted words.

The findings of this study have implications for improving the instruction of

Table 2. Means of Supertargeted and Targeted Words Acquired by Group (*n* = 15)

Group	Supertargeted Words		Targeted Words	
	Not Known on Test 1A	Acquired (*N* = 7)	Not Known on Test 1A	Acquired (*N* = 8)
Pilot Group (*N* = 5)	4.8	3.2	2.4	0.6
Group 1 (*N* = 3)	3.3	1	3	1.3
Group 2 (*N* = 2)	2	2	0.5	0.5
Group 3 (*N* = 5)	3.4	1.6	1.2	0.4
Mean for All Groups Combined	3.4	2.0	1.8	0.7
% of Words Learned	57.64		39.85	

ESL. They indicate that reading aloud to L2 learners and providing the meaning of target words contributes to their vocabulary acquisition and that less proficient and more proficient ESL learners make gains. This supports the finding of previous research (Brett et al., 1996; Elley, 1989; Robbins & Ehri, 1994) and the recommendations that teachers and parents should read aloud to children to facilitate vocabulary acquisition. Important to note is that for the read-aloud sessions to benefit the more proficient students' vocabularies, the books chosen should contain several words unfamiliar to the students. In addition, instructional activities can enhance students' capacity to internalize word knowledge and improve their ability to use the words.

Reflection

I began this study to determine if what I did in the classroom every day was benefiting my students. When I was a new teacher, the curriculum I designed for my students developed more from my instincts and less from what I had learned about ESL instruction in college. When I began my first job as an ESL teacher, I was given one box of materials including three much-worn ESL instruction books. The lessons in these books seemed more like those I had encountered as a student learning French as a foreign language. They just did not seem suitable for ESL learners. Having no budget to purchase any materials, I went to the library and searched for simple books that I could use for my lessons. Merely reading aloud to the students and using literacy scaffolding did not seem to be enough. I knew the words needed to be more meaningful for my students to own them. I followed read-aloud sessions with short instructional activities like the ones I saw regular education classroom teachers use, but I adapted them for ESL students' limited language. Gradually, my lessons became more sophisticated, and my list of read-alouds grew as my students gained language fluency. Soon after, I returned to graduate school and was introduced to Elley's studies (Elley, 1989; Elley & Mangubhai, 1983) involving students' vocabulary acquisition during read-alouds.

It is important to note that language instruction in the ESL classroom is very different from foreign language instruction because of the needs of the students. For the past 10 years I have read authentic literature aloud to all of my students, from the beginner to the more advanced, starting on the first day of instruction. Initially, the books for the beginners are very simple to understand. Illustrations are colorful and fun and closely reflect the text. Literacy scaffolding, including my own simple artwork, aids comprehension, too. Instructional vocabulary activities, based on drawing pictures and using items found in picture dictionaries, follow the read-aloud sessions. As the students' fluency grows, I target words in the text that are beyond the basic social vocabulary of English. Various instructional activities surrounding the vocabulary—such as brainstorming activities, using the words in sentences, and illustrations—help to increase word knowledge.

As a result of my findings, I have much more confidence in my teaching method. I know my students are learning because of the lessons I design for them. Typically, I target three to five words per story. The targeted vocabulary may not actually be a word used in the text. Stories that are comprehensible for beginning ESL students, even when literacy scaffolding is utilized, are fairly simplistic ones, but the vocabulary targeted does not have to be. As my students progress, I target more sophisticated vocabulary that is related to the story. Sometimes the targeted word is part of the story's theme. In *Harriet's Halloween Candy* (Carlson, 1984), one of the words I target is *selfish* even though the author never uses that word in her story. But Harriet acts selfishly, and after reading the story aloud to the children, I use the word *selfish* to describe Harriet's behavior. Then I invite the children to share times when someone they know has behaved in a selfish way. I also target the word *sharing,* which does appear in the story. Later the children make illustrations showing someone who was being selfish and someone who was sharing. Then they write sentences explaining the illustrations, or I write the sentences they dictate to me.

Other times, the targeted vocabulary is shown in a story's illustration. In *Kitten's First Full Moon* (Henkes, 2004), one illustration shows the moon reflected in a pond. Among other words that I target for this story, I target the *reflect* word family using *reflect, reflected,* and *reflection* to discuss the illustration. When the story has ended, I give each child a hand mirror to view his or her reflection. After studying their reflections, the children draw themselves. The following day, we look into a glass door in our classroom to see what is reflected in the shiny glass. We list all the things we see and then make illustrations.

The most rewarding part of this study has been seeing that the curriculum I have developed to use in my classroom every day is valuable to my students. ESL students are under tremendous pressure to acquire English fast and succeed academically. My job is to facilitate this process. By targeting specific vocabulary and following read-aloud sessions with instructional activities, my lessons help my students to acquire the language skills they need quickly and efficiently.

*Jami Gurkin teaches at Mount Prospect Elementary School,
Basking Ridge, New Jersey, in the United States.*

CHAPTER 8

Promoting Innovative Practices Through Reflective Collaboration (*Brazil*)

Andrea Jesus, Heliana Mello, and Deise Dutra

Issue

Speaking a foreign language in Brazil, especially English, is a highly valued asset. In addition, foreign language teaching in junior high and high schools is mandatory. Some teachers face the reality of a lack of resources, overcrowded classrooms, and insufficient pedagogical and linguistic preparation. Many English as a foreign language (EFL) teachers in Brazil are caught in a seemingly never-ending cycle of powerlessness and low self-esteem. Considering these challenges, we hope that our collaborative pedagogical experience may be relevant to these teachers and to those in other countries in South America and elsewhere. Our experience tells us that through collaborative research groups teachers can achieve professional development and innovation in their EFL classes.

The grade level at which foreign language teaching is compulsory or recommended varies in South American countries; for example, it is Grade 1 in Colombia and Grade 10 in Paraguay (Abello-Contesse, 2005). However, the teaching conditions may not be so different, and English is the most commonly taught foreign language in most of these countries. In Brazil, compulsory foreign language teaching begins at Grade 5. Although any foreign language can be chosen by the school and its community, English is the most commonly taught foreign language in public and private junior high and high schools.

We have been involved with EFL teaching in Brazil for many years, and in this chapter we are reporting on a collaborative effort to implement a communicative project in one of our classes. Andrea Jesus carried out our plans in her classes for almost an entire school year. She is a public school teacher who has looked for professional improvement by taking part in courses promoted by the state education secretary, attending conferences and a continuing education program, and becoming a member of a research group. Heliana Mello and Deise Dutra are university teachers who have carried out research with preservice and in-service teachers and who also coordinate a continuing education program for foreign language public school teachers.

At the time the research project was developed, Jesus worked in two large public schools with about 2,200 students each. One of the schools was on the outskirts of a big city in Brazil; the other was located in a suburban area in the same city. The students came from low-income families and did not attend private English language institutes, as many other children from middle- and upper-class families in Brazil do. The two classes Jesus identified for the research were sixth-grade classes with 38 and 37 students that met twice a week for 50-minute English classes. Jesus chose one of the classes because the achievement of the students in English was low yet they were doing well in other subjects. This made her eager to understand what was going on. The other class was chosen because it was also a sixth-grade class and matched the research needs for the study. Neither of the schools provided textbooks, and Jesus was responsible for the definition of the course syllabus and the selection of the material.

In this context, our research aimed to establish a collaborative environment for pedagogical exchange and solve a specific pedagogical challenge set by Jesus: the development of students' writing as well as their linguistic and communicative abilities. To achieve these objectives, we all emphasized the reflective collaborative partnership we wanted to develop. Jesus had a central role in the research dealings related to her pedagogical actions, and her work was supported by the other group members through systematic reflection.

Background Literature

This section offers a brief review of readings on issues such as reflection, critical pedagogy, action research, and collaboration, which are the basis of our work together.

The research on English as a subsequent language and EFL teaching, based on a process-product paradigm (Freeman & Johnson, 1998), focused for a long time on what would lead to efficient teaching and, consequently, students' learning. In the 1990s, this research area witnessed a focus on the teacher, on opportunities that reflective practice could offer to engage teachers (Gebhard & Oprandy, 1999; Richards, 1998; Richards & Lockhart, 1994), and on the positive effects of action research on professional development (Burns, 1999; Wallace, 1998). Yet many of the principles that underlie reflective teaching and action research were discussed 80 years earlier by Dewey (1910/1997). One of these principles is that reflective thought is different from the daydreaming type of thinking. Reflective thinking is not random thinking, but a meaningful sequence of ideas. Although reflection may, at first, be seen as a personal characteristic, we believe that reflection is a useful skill that can be developed as long as the person is actively engaged in a systematic process that aims to develop reflective behavior. This process of reflection consists of the following:

> (i) a felt difficulty; (ii) its location and definition; (iii) suggestion or possible solution; (iv) development by reasoning of the bearings of the suggestion; (v) further observation and experiment leading to its acceptance or rejection. (Dewey, 1910/1997, p. 72)

The idea that structured reflection can foster a better understanding of the professional environment and therefore improve individuals professionally has been further expanded in publications on action research (Burns, 1999; Wallace, 1998). Although it is not the focus of this chapter to discuss action research, we mention that the research we conducted was a collaborative action research project that led us through a process of reflection.

Various research studies have focused on collaborative work that helps create appropriate environments for professional development (Edge, 2005; McCotter, 2001; Smith, 2005). Group support can make a difference in a craft such as teaching, yet it does not substitute the personal motivation to learn more about oneself, the teaching context, the students, and ultimately the will to change one's practice if it seems to be a necessary condition to improve students' learning. Therefore, if deep professional development is to occur, there must be a combination of self-motivation (Dutra & Mello, 2001) and group collaboration.

The involvement in group collaboration advances the implementation of research, and this experience can lead to critical reflection. Teaching centered on research, situated in the appropriate social and academic context, and based on insights provided by reflection can give the learner a chance to create knowledge and therefore can positively interfere with the student's reality. Freire (1996) emphasized the importance of research to continuing teacher education:

> There is no teaching without research and there is no research without teaching. . . . While I teach, I continue my search, researching. I teach because I search, because I asked and I ask myself. I research to find out, finding out I intervene, intervening I educate and I educate myself. I research to know what I still do not know. (p. 32)

Based on these theoretical principles, we started and conducted our research. In the beginning of our partnership, we had no research agenda. The discovery of a perceived difficulty was primarily up to the classroom teacher, Jesus, with the support of the research group. The role of the group was to foster reflective action through collaboration.

Procedures

During the research period, Jesus regularly had a classroom research assistant sit in on the whole class and take careful notes on the interactions between teacher and students and among students. Furthermore, notes were taken regarding methodology and procedures followed in each class. Later, Jesus reviewed these notes and shared them with the research team. The group then proceeded to a collaborative session, looking into understanding the classroom events that had been noteworthy from Jesus's point of view, her strategies for dealing with them, and her actions to solve any issue that needed attention.

The research group supported the following activities:

Preproject Phase

- Observation, reflection, and assessment
- Definition of the problem

Project Phase

- Raising students' awareness of cultural differences
- Choosing pen pals
- Development of reading strategies (skimming and scanning)
- Production of a descriptive paragraph
- Genre analysis (personal letter)
- Letter writing
- Peer editing
- Letter exchange

Supplemental Activities

- Vacation diaries
- Teacher feedback on the diaries

PREPROJECT PHASE

We started our research project with a period of observation and reflection to arrive at a needs analysis that focused on areas Jesus had chosen from her two classrooms. This led to the detection of a problem and its definition. After the observations, we held a collaborative session to discuss the classes, which had focused on grammatical aspects. According to Jesus's views and evaluation of needs, grammar should not be the sole focus of her classes. She thought it necessary to develop her students' writing skills. Although she believed it was a difficult task, it seemed feasible to work with writing, given the size of her classes. Jesus then, in association with the research team, started a process of selecting writing projects. After brainstorming possibilities that seemed conducive to student engagement, Jesus opted for a correspondence project through which students from the two different schools would regularly write to each other. She chose this project because she had detected students' interest in writing about their town to other students their own age. This decision showed Jesus's commitment to the communicative approach.

PROJECT PHASE

An essential part of the project phase was Jesus's initiative to raise her students' awareness about the existence of different cultures. After accomplishing that, she had the students do some drawings of their town to represent their local cultural world. First, Jesus suggested a theme: different places, different people. She took a world map to class and posed the following types of questions: Do you know anything about the countries you have pointed out on the map? What do people who live in this country look like? How do they live typically? What is their life like? Through this process, Jesus was able to engage her students in the right mode for questioning their own lifestyle, their culture, and their place in the world. As a next step, Jesus led activities in class that required students to fill in gaps and provide missing information in sentences referring to cultural habits of people of different nationalities. Besides doing the fill-in-the-gap activity, students produced short paragraphs about the nationalities explored.

Taking advantage of the previous writing task, Jesus had students write about themselves and their habits. To keep her teaching methodology coherent, Jesus provided the students with a textual model that used cues for grammatical structures, collocations, and vocabulary associated with the topic being developed. Later, Jesus mediated a discussion about the characteristics of the town where the school is located and the tourism sites there. Then the students were invited to participate in a class discussion about their town, expressing their own views about specific places and their perceptions of familiar locations and ones they did not know well. Although one of the schools is located in a well-known historical area, many students had never had the opportunity to visit the important sites in town. After the discussion, they drew pictures illustrating the sightseeing areas in town, monuments, and so on. Jesus arranged an exchange of drawings made by students from the two schools, and they chose their pen pals based on their preference of drawings.

The next step was the introduction of a letter model to help students develop reading strategies and have examples for their own writing. Several strategic activities were presented to students at this point. They practiced skimming and scanning activities as well as paragraph writing. Students learned to describe themselves so that they could productively exchange this kind of information with their pen pals. Jesus prompted them with the following types of questions: What do you look like? What is your height? How much do you weigh? What is your hair color? As a conclusion to this stage, students wrote a self-descriptive paragraph.

Only after helping students develop skills related to skimming, scanning, and paragraph writing did Jesus introduce the letter as a genre. She used models in class that illustrated what a letter looks like, focusing on the format, heading, body, and final greetings; when to use capital letters; and what kind of vocabulary to employ in salutations. After giving students in-class practice and introducing vocabulary and grammatical structures that catered to students' needs, Jesus started working with writing.

After this preparation stage of the project phase, students wrote letters, peer edited them in class, and sent them to their peers in the other school. Writing letters throughout the school year, students eventually wrote about the tourism places in their area and illustrated their letters, thus creating attractive art pieces with illustrations of churches, theaters, lakes, and other local sights (see Appendix A).

After writing a letter to their pen pals as a homework assignment, students participated in a series of in-class activities focusing on peer editing. Jesus developed peer editing as a way for students to further their perception of writing accuracy and genre recognition. She used the process to guide her students into suggested topics, according to their emerging communicative needs. This made students aware of how grammatical structures are needed to express specific meanings and how coherence should be maintained in written texts. In this way, Jesus addressed structures, such as the *simple past* for the students to report to their pen pals what they had done over the weekend, or the *future* in their plans for vacations. From this point on, students exhibited an increasing degree of autonomy and demonstrated this through their writing of other letters (see Appendix B), exploring their own interests, and effectively developing a communicative process with their pen pals. Our research team noticed that students increasingly used markers in their text to create coherence, such as using pronouns and possessive adjectives, organizing ideas into separate paragraphs, and using greeting and closing remarks typical of personal letters. During this part of the project, Jesus acted as facilitator and guide, encouraging her students to write more and helping them with their questions and peer corrections.

SUPPLEMENTAL ACTIVITIES

As the winter break arrived, Jesus had to envision a way to keep students writing in a meaningful way. She chose to ask students to write diaries (see Appendix C) reporting their daily routine over the school break, so they would not forget about their experiences and could report them to their pen pals as school resumed after the break. When school was in session again, students brought in their diaries. Jesus gave them feedback on their writing and encouraged them to start a new letter cycle, in which they reported their vacation experiences to their pen pals. The procedures she adopted at that time were similar to those she had chosen for the first half of the school year: students exchanged letters after class discussion and did peer corrections in class.

COLLABORATIVE SESSIONS

Throughout the development of the letter project, Jesus welcomed the research assistant into her classes and regularly met with the research group. We want to emphasize that the meetings had no preplanned agenda, instead they were designed to suit Jesus's needs. The research group's role was to encourage reflection through questions and support Jesus as she tried new pedagogical strategies. For example, after a class in which Jesus felt disappointed with her students' participation and uncertain about having achieved her goals, the research team raised issues to support her reflection and understanding of what had happened. The following excerpt illustrates how the meetings encouraged Jesus's reflection:

> *Mello:* Do you think that what happened today is related to your planning, or is it something that is going on in the group?

Then the research group provided support for Jesus as she dealt with the problems that emerged:

> *Jesus:* It's the previous planning . . . but I wonder whether the "simple present" makes any sense to them and whether they understand auxiliaries and questions.

> *Mello:* I believe that you shouldn't be afraid of that because in a communicative environment we use several strategies at the same time and it's not necessary to make all of them explicit. I think that our traditional way of studying grammatical paradigms separately creates the impression that everything is difficult, hard, and many times that's not so.

In sum, the project involved two parallel work fronts, the actions developed by Jesus in her pedagogical practice and the collaborative work pursued by the whole research group in the collaborative sessions.

Results

During the implementation of the project, we established a collaborative environment for pedagogical exchange. Within this environment, participants' discussions led to the solution of a specific pedagogical problem in Jesus's class, namely, the development of students' writing. These two objectives—collaboration and reflective problem solving—were intertwined. That is, the collaborative work developed in the group sessions fed Jesus's actions in her pedagogical practice, and then she brought her classroom actions back to the group for new reflections and the search for alternative solutions.

The partnership to establish a collaborative environment among the members of the research group led to positive results because it provided important alternatives to Jesus's resolution of classroom problems. The collaboration was evident in the way the members of the group talked about Jesus's class, giving advice and suggestions, identifying positive points of her classroom practice, and never imposing anything on her, as in the following excerpts:

> *Mello:* Later on then, it's a suggestion that I'm giving you, you could work with the letter genre. . . .

> *Luciano:* Don't you think you are too critical about today's class? Because, I think you made the right decisions in class. You elicited from the students a broad situation and . . . later you went back to their reality.

Jesus reported that her increasing ability to deal with classroom dilemmas was a result of the collaborative work that we did. Yet Jesus always made the final decisions about what to do in class because she was the one who knew the teaching contexts best. She made the following comment:

> *Jesus:* I just have learned with you where, when, and how to look for the possible answers to my daily problems.

Jesus found she could gradually achieve the objective of developing her students' writing skills by employing appropriate methodologies to deal with students' needs. She started to incorporate certain procedures, such as elicitation, questioning, gradation of activity difficulty, and provision of correlated vocabulary, to ensure students' understanding of the focus topic. Jesus's new procedures, or teaching techniques, reflected her conscious effort to innovate, to get away from her traditional practice. The following excerpt highlights her wish to create meaningful contexts for the teaching of structures:

> *Jesus:* I have worked in the lesson planning for the next classes, but I still have questions—I know what type of structures should be taught for the writing of a letter, but I'm not sure about the right way to present them.

Mello: It would be interesting if you considered the teaching of the structures through the letters themselves. You should—and it's just a suggestion you don't have to follow it—you should work with different letters with these different structures, you should elicit instead of starting with the structure itself. . . .

Jesus: So I think that all I need is just to wait for the right moment to introduce the necessary structures, giving responses for questions or making a general elicitation about new information.

Based on Mello's suggestion, Jesus was able to change her thinking about how to address students' linguistic needs and provide meaningful solutions to her classroom problems. As a consequence of this collaborative session, her students were exposed to contextualized grammatical presentations emphasizing the linguistic features that had seemed problematic in the process of writing the letters.

Jesus was pleased with the progress shown on the students' writing products overall. The outcomes can be seen in the samples of letters, diaries, and descriptive artwork in the appendixes. The main focus of the project was the writing of letters, and students' letters (see Appendix B) showed the incorporation of an adequate format for the genre (e.g., initial greetings, date, closing remarks). The students were able to express their ideas in the letters and appropriately used several grammatical structures (e.g., the use of *going to* to express future planned vacation activities). The grammar mistakes they made (e.g., lack of subject-verb inversion in some questions) were compatible with their level of language development (basic).

Despite all the difficulties that Jesus still faced in her teaching context, members of the research group agreed that she dealt well with the wide range of variables in her classrooms. The collaborative work enabled her to become more autonomous and self-reliant. In addition, her new practice convinced her that language should be taught by focusing on its use. As a consequence, learning in her classroom became more contextualized and no longer was fragmented into sequences of linguistic structures. The discussions about her classroom practice, developed collaboratively with the research group, helped Jesus reflect on the real meaning of the theories she had been exposed to in her professional development readings. Therefore, ideas that Jesus was familiar with in theory, such as Freire's (1996) argument in favor of a more autonomous pedagogy, could be implemented in her practice. Freire advised that teachers pay particular attention to the role of a progressive curriculum, developed in a way that integrates technical content and students' real-life situations. In this way learners are engaged in knowledge construction and are more readily prepared to intervene in their social reality. Jesus implemented this idea by having students write letters to actual peers while developing their writing skills.

Reflection

This collaborative action research project brought positive results to all participants. On the one hand, the results that Jesus was able to achieve in her large classes in public schools showed us that a lot can be accomplished in such a context, despite the adversities teachers face. On the other hand, Dutra and Mello were able to envision new methodologies to be employed in their professional activities based on the gains the interaction with a public school teacher brought them. This affected the design of activities in the teacher education program they coordinate and in the graduate and undergraduate applied linguistics classes they teach at the university.

Jesus was able to implement a writing project that successfully addressed her students' needs by contextualizing new linguistic structures and helping students learn suitable vocabulary for the letter genre. The research group gave her the support and confidence to reflect on her students' needs and then to take steps to implement a more communicative approach in her teaching context (which is not typically perceived to be an appropriate place for innovation). Although Jesus had been pursuing professional development since her graduation from university and was attending a continuing education program, the collaborative research project gave her the safety and support she needed to try new practices and to give her students more autonomy in their learning process. The research group also gave her opportunities to see her pedagogical practice from different perspectives and to organize her reflections. Jesus felt that the collaborative process contributed positively to her growth as a teacher, as she mentioned while analyzing a class she had just taught:

> I thought it was all very interesting. It is really interesting to see and analyze my class after it has happened. This is the first time I do this. That is, I have a very different idea now about what I did, as opposed to when I planned my lesson.

As part of the process of implementing new practices, Jesus was encouraged by her research group colleagues to organize her reflections and draw on them when elaborating new activities. Jesus started a self-reflection cycle, which involved writing narratives and journals simultaneously. In the excerpt that follows, Jesus mentioned how she was keeping track of what was going on in her practice by writing a journal after each class and keeping a list of the grammatical structures addressed as the students worked on the letter project. These initiatives allowed Jesus to integrate her practical experience with her theoretical knowledge:

> So I wrote the list in my planning notebook and I started to write a journal of these classes, how they were, what I thought about them.

We all learned a great deal about doing collaborative research with a focus on improving language development in large classes in public schools. First, we were able to create an atmosphere conducive to the promotion of professional development based on a relationship of respect and trust (Underhill, 1992). We respected our previous experiences teaching, learning, and doing research, and especially recognized our professional knowledge in different teaching contexts.

The collaborative partnership we established worked so well that Dutra and Mello decided to include collaborative research as part of the continuing education program offered for public school teachers at our university. In this program, besides attending methodology and language classes, teachers are now involved in research, solving a problem they have in their classes. Because the program includes more than 50 teachers, they are grouped according to the problem they want to understand and solve and have research advisors working with them. Jesus, Mello, and Dutra are research advisors and rely on the support of other university professors and graduate students to cater to the needs of the school teachers.

Throughout the research, we discussed the implications of new teaching practices. Yet Jesus realized that new strategies will work only if the teacher perceives them to be relevant to the classroom context. What she chose to implement became part of her professional development and was critically analyzed by all three of us. The findings have shown us that a strictly structured syllabus can be combined with a project that encompasses ideas such as genre in language teaching and learning, students' autonomy, and a focus on form linked to communicative needs, even in a large public school class. We learned to understand more clearly the power of collaborative partnership by providing opportunities for reflection to emerge as systematic thought (Dewey, 1910/1997). Because the research group met regularly to discuss what was going on in Jesus's classes, we assumed that the reflection steps proposed by Dewey would guide us into our objectives. However, we noticed that the steps did not have to be taken in a linear way. For instance, further observation took place at different stages, after we determined the perceived difficulty, located and defined the problem, and implemented pedagogical suggestions. In this way we all had more data to inform our discussions and our systematic reflection.

The teaching difficulties that we dealt with in the research reported here are very typical of the context of EFL classes in public schools in Brazil, and they may be similar to those in other contexts. This experience was enlightening for Mello and Dutra, who have never been public school teachers yet teach applied linguistics classes for undergraduate students seeking degrees to teach English in junior high and high schools. Jesus's success at implementing a writing project that addressed students' needs led her away from focusing on traditional grammatical paradigms, and her students' accomplishments occurred despite the presence of factors that otherwise might have been blamed for any learning failure.

These commonly mentioned factors are large classes (35–40 students) and little or no support from the education system by way of textbooks, foreign language teaching supervision, or syllabi previously determined by school authorities. In spite of all the difficulties that seem inherent in the public school system, our work shows that it is possible to conceptualize teaching based on the communicative functions of linguistic items in such a context. Jesus's positive results drew on a more contemporary view of language (language for communication) and provided her students with opportunities to use the English language for real purposes.

Andrea Jesus teaches at Escola Municipal Gabriela Leite Araújo in Sabara, Brazil. Heliana Mello teaches at the Federal University of Minas Gerais in Belo Horizonte, Brazil. Deise Dutra also teaches at the Federal University of Minas Gerais.

Acknowledgment

We acknowledge the help of Luciano Silva, a research assistant who collected data during this study.

Appendix A: Samples of Student Artwork

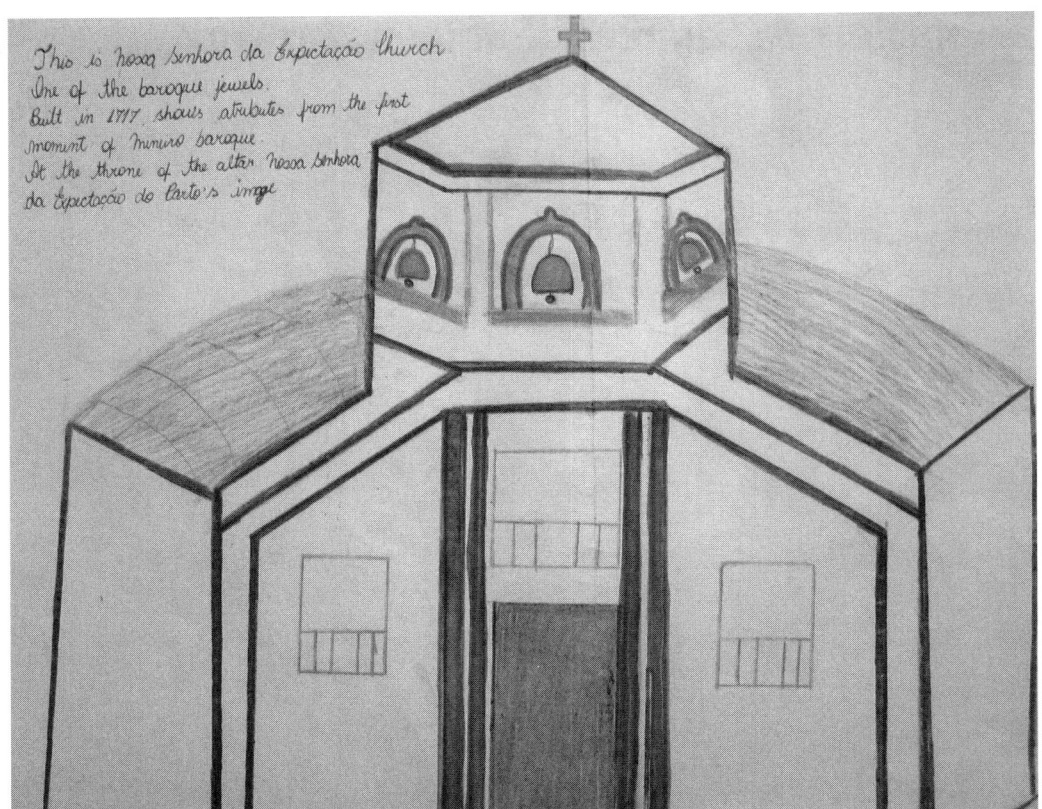

Note: Student work samples used with permission.

Appendix B: Samples of Student Letters

July 9th 2004

dear Gline

how are you? I like you letter very much. My school is big too and full of students. I study in the afternoon but I want to study in the night is more cool, but my mother don't allow.

I have many friends in the class we play and talk, only This. In my free time I like to watch TV, ride my bike and listen to music. My favorite music is Rock and you?

I don't like to study much! english is ok my teacher is good and funy and she like rock too.

In the vacation I'm going to visit my relatives, they live in Bahia. My mother said there is beach and I'm going to swim. And you? What do you do in your vacation?

Please answer me soon. Can you send your telephone number?

Kisses
Rafael

THE BEST OF ROCK N ROll

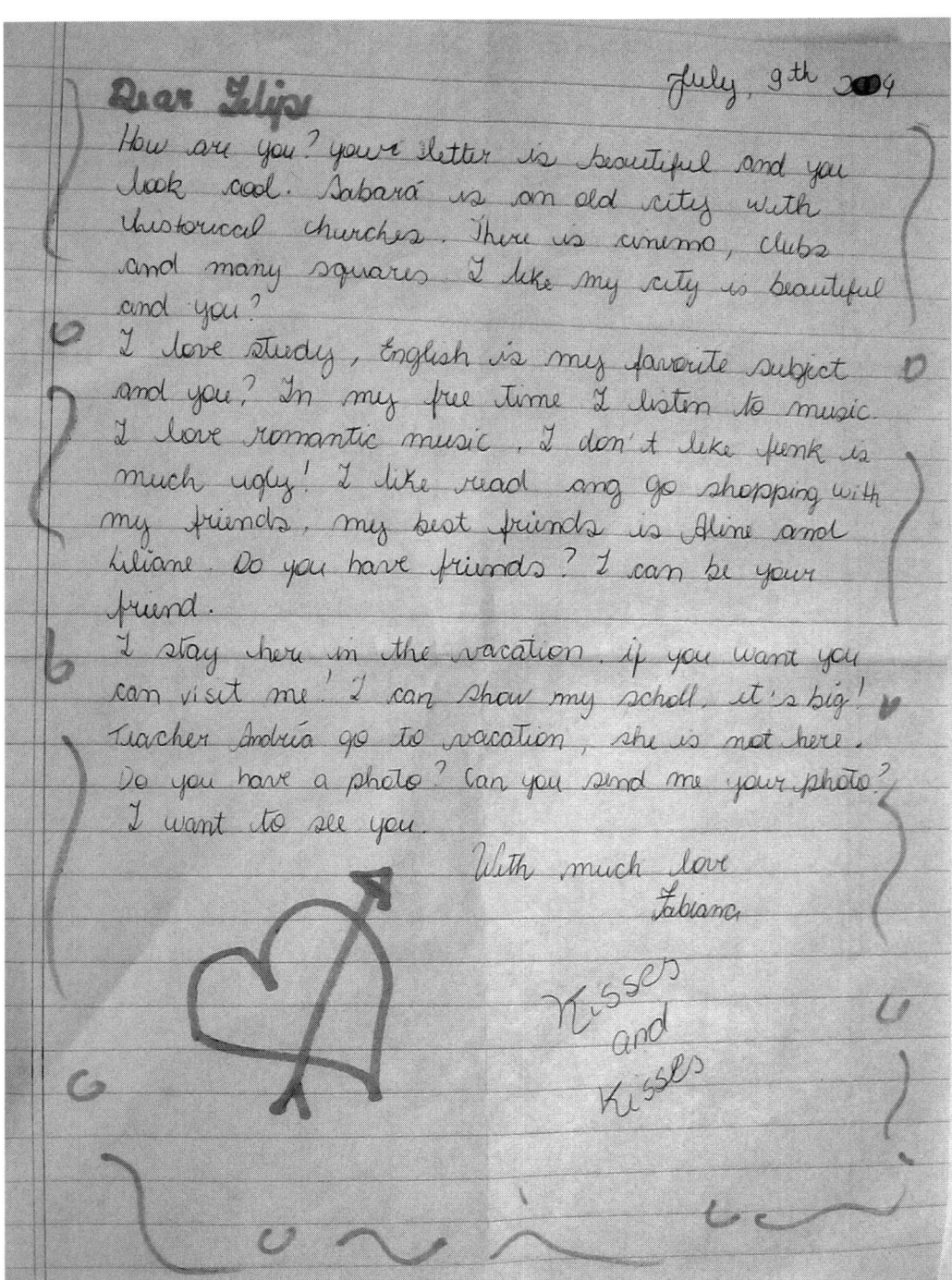

Dear Felipe

July, 9th 2004

How are you? your letter is beautiful and you look cool. Sabará is an old city with historical churches. There is cinema, clubs and many squares. I like my city is beautiful and you?

I love study, English is my favorite subject and you? In my free time I listen to music. I love romantic music, I don't like funk is much ugly! I like read ang go shopping with my friends, my best friends is Aline and Liliane. Do you have friends? I can be your friend.

I stay here in the vacation. if you want you can visit me! I can show my scholl. it's big! Teacher Andria go to vacation, she is not here. Do you have a photo? Can you send me your photo? I want to see you.

With much love
Fabiana.

Kisses and Kisses

Note: Student writing samples used with permission.

Appendix C: Samples of Student Diaries

July 19th 2004

Dear Diary

Today is Monday, I ride my bike, meet my friends, listen to music, I go and see one boy beautiful.

Bye!!!

Stefanie Fernanda

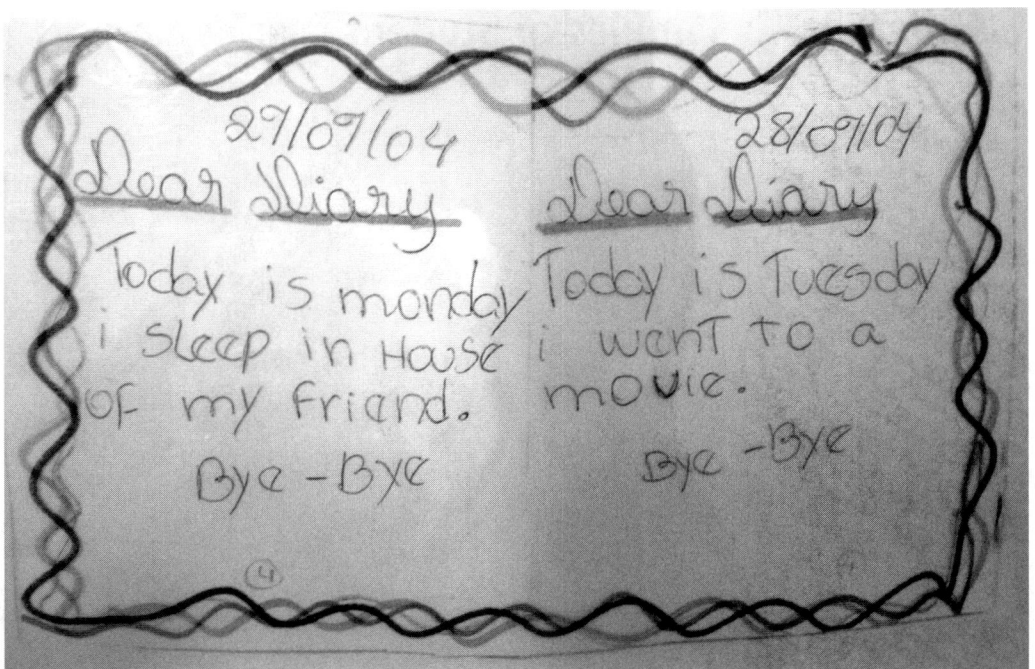

Note: Student writing samples used with permission.

CHAPTER 9

Mi and Myself: Dual Identity in Jamaican Contact Language Speakers (*Jamaica*)

Mary Hills Kuck

Issue

In Jamaica, as in other parts of the Caribbean, an often-neglected linguistic region of the Americas, English speakers also speak a local creole as a contact language along with English. Until recently Jamaican Creole, locally known as Patois, suffered from a negative image. It originated as a combination of African and English grammatical structures and an English-based lexicon with a mix of vocabulary from other languages. When slaves arrived in Jamaica from various parts of Africa, they spoke a variety of languages. They developed the creole to communicate with each other and, to some degree, with their masters. This association of Jamaican Creole with slavery contributed to its negative image, first among the planters and then among its speakers themselves. Until the latter part of the 20th century, English speakers in Jamaica referred to it as *broken English,* and well-educated Jamaicans often claimed not to be able to speak it. Since independence in 1962, however, the status of Jamaican Creole has been rising, particularly among university-educated speakers (Christie, 2003). Its association with slavery has made it an emblem of the courage and resilience of the Jamaican people. Today code-switching from English into Creole is a badge of patriotism that unites a speaker with a Jamaican audience.

In this context, several vocal students in my English language and communications classes announced that they did not like using English anywhere outside the English classroom, and they resisted using it even in the classroom. The students were studying to be teachers in the technical high schools and job-training institutions of Jamaica. They were upwardly mobile, many of them having come to teacher training via the vocational training system Jamaica offers. My class provided their first contact with English language study in our tertiary institution. The students' comments caused me to wonder if negative attitudes toward English were widespread among my students. To address this concern, a colleague and I conducted a survey of attitudes toward English held by the 2002 entering class of vocational/technical trainees (Kuck & Blagrove-Williams, 2002). The decidedly positive attitudes recorded indicated that the students appreciated the pivotal role that English could play in their academic and societal success. Then how could I explain the negative comments and the reluctance of some students to use in their personal spheres the language skills they were gaining in the classroom?

The attitude survey provided a clue. In response to the statement, "I feel as if I have two identities: my English-speaking self and my Creole-speaking self," 69% of respondents agreed or strongly agreed, and 15% were undecided. It seemed possible that shifting identities when switching between the two languages contributed to my students' ambivalence toward using the English they clearly wanted to master. I set out to delineate the nature of the claimed separate Creole and English identities and to examine how the shift from one identity to the other, an integral stage in mastering a subsequent language, influenced what happened in my classroom.

Background Literature

Research relevant to this study focuses first on the nature of identity and its relationship to language. Norton (1997) defined *identity* as "how people understand their relationship to the world, how that relationship is constructed across time and space, and how people understand the possibilities for the future" (p. 410). Norton relied on West (1992) in her assertion that identity relates to the desires for recognition, affiliation, security, and safety, which cannot be separated from the distribution of resources in society. A person's identity ("Who am I?") shifts in a dynamic relationship with changing social and economic forces ("What can I do?") (p. 410). Language learners, according to Norton, are constantly "organizing and reorganizing a sense of who they are and how they relate to the social world. They are, in other words, engaged in identity construction and negotiation" (p. 410). Norton (2000), in her argument that "language is constitutive of and constituted by a speaker's identity" (p. 13), asserted that language encompasses more than words and sentences, that power relationships between speakers influence the learner's investment in the language and the affective filter that may arise during the learning and practicing process.

Lanehart (1998) also discussed the dynamic of language, identity, and power, especially as these relate to language that is low in status:

> Those who use less prestigious ways of speaking or who choose to identify with cultures that are not part of the mainstream are punished by the society, by the educational system, by pedagogical methods, and by the ideologies held in U.S. culture. . . . To punish one's language is to punish the individual. (p. 122)

Lanehart maintained that arguments and ideas expressed in language with low esteem are delegitimized and silenced. She argued that Standard English belongs to those in power, who can determine what is acceptable and what is not. In this sense, the goal of mastering Standard English is political because it can be used for control.

In Jamaica, as in the larger Caribbean, the very existence of creoles testifies that identity is necessarily intertwined with the consequences of slavery and colonialism, which continue to permeate society at every level. Both Nero (1997) and Cliff (1988) asserted that the legacy of colonialism in the Anglophone Caribbean is a split consciousness, which Nero described as a Creole reality masked by an English perception. Nero observed that Caribbean people live and migrate with this dual linguistic identity. Cliff said she writes in both Jamaican Creole and in "the King's English" (pp. 59–60) because she believes it would be just as dishonest to write a novel entirely in Creole as it would be to write it solely in English. Cliff also touched on the relationship of power between speakers when she mentioned "the ancient taboos of the assimilated: don't tell outsiders anything real about yourself. Don't reveal *our* secrets to *them*. Don't make us seem foolish, or oppressed" (p. 62). In situations where one speaker uses the language of hegemony, the speaker using the less esteemed language may conceal truths in order to protect self-esteem.

Scholars agree that language and identity are closely intertwined. Thiong'O (2004) observed that "language is thus inseparable from ourselves as a community of human beings with a specific form and character, a specific history, a specific relationship to the world" (p. 407). Hoffman (1989) discussed the painful transformation of her identity when she began to acquire English:

> This language is beginning to invent another me. . . . My voice is doing funny things. It does not seem to emerge from the same parts of my body as before. . . . It seems that when I write (or, for that matter, think) in English, I am unable to use the word "I." (p. 121)

Hoffman also characterized as rage the feeling that arose when she was dispossessed of her home language because "linguistic dispossession . . . is close to the dispossession of one's self" (p. 124).

Thus it is not surprising that Jamaican speakers of English and Creole should experience a dual sense of identity. It is also to be expected that, along with the sense of dual identity, these speakers of the two contact languages would also sense issues of power, control, conflict, and even rage when shifting from one language (identity) to the other. The question is, how can each of the dual identities in my Jamaican students be characterized, and how do these dual identities and their accompanying issues influence what happens in my English language and communications classroom?

Procedures

To investigate these questions, I organized a focus group. I relied on Pao, Wong, and Teuben-Rowe (1997), who found that the structured nature of focus groups, which employ predetermined questions whose answers can be tabulated, helped to report results. The model I followed also encouraged dynamic group interaction. I thought that discussion within the group could lead to a deeper analysis of cultural influences than could questionnaires. Moreover, most research carried out in our institute had been quantitative, and I wanted to introduce a relatively unfamiliar qualitative method of inquiry. I enhanced the already relaxed focus group setting by avoiding video or audio recordings of the conversation, because I knew they would inhibit free discussion for some of the students. Instead, a colleague and I, as transcribers, recorded as accurately as possible the responses to the questions posed. A respected colleague whom the students knew well facilitated the conversation in the group. We met in our institute's communications theater, seated comfortably around tables. After the discussion, I compared the two records to check the accuracy of my own observations. My observations generally agreed with my colleague's.

For the focus group I chose 9 articulate Jamaican teacher trainees who were in their last year of study for a diploma in technical-vocational education. They all had been in my first-year English language class and had studied English language and communications for 2 further years. Their status as final-year students gave them some perspective on their total English language and communications experience at our institute, as well as confidence in their Standard English skills. The trainees were all older than 21, and more than half were older than 31. The colleague who led the discussion and I sent a letter of invitation to each trainee selected (see Appendix A), explaining the intent of the focus group to explore the idea of having separate English and Jamaican Creole identities.

At the beginning of the session, the students were promised anonymity, as well as an opportunity to see the results of the research. The transcribers, who sat on either side of the room behind the circle of tables, identified the speakers by a number at each student's place rather than by name. Eighteen questions and activities (see Appendix B) led students to talk about their sense of identity as it related to the language (English or Jamaican Creole) they spoke. The tasks included answering questions, such as whether they claimed the dual identity we were investigating, naming and ranking characteristics of audiotaped speakers of English and Creole, and responding to a reading of the Bible in Jamaican Creole. Students described their Jamaican Creole identity and their English identity. Finally, they were asked if having these two identities affected their work in the English language and communications classroom. The leader of the focus group presented the activities in order but allowed the conversation to flow back and forth naturally among the topics. Participants were thanked at the end and given a souvenir pencil for taking part. Later they were invited to a research day for a presentation of the focus group results.

Results

The trainees agreed with the positive responses to the previous survey item (Kuck & Blagrove-Williams, 2002): "I feel as if I have two identities: my English-speaking self and my Creole-speaking self." To get at the nature of the Creole-speaking identity and the English-speaking identity, the discussion leader first asked the trainees about occasions on which they spoke the respective languages.

Table 1 summarizes the responses. Most church services and Bible readings in Jamaica are conducted in English; however, being socialized to worship in English did not inhibit a positive response to an audiotaped portion of scripture read in Jamaican Creole. The students found that the Bible story in Jamaican Creole "painted a picture." They claimed it was forceful; it put into perspective what they had learned in English. The Bible in Creole could be understood by any Jamaican, they maintained. One trainee said that 5 years earlier (before her study at our institute) she had thought that hearing or reading the Bible in Jamaican Creole demeaned God's word. Training and socialization had changed

Table 1. Preferred Language of Trainees

Occasion	English	Jamaican Creole
Prayer	x	Some preference
Bible Reading	x	Openness
Jokes		x
Personal Narrative		x
Anger	x	Some preference
Panic		x

that. "God is not distant," said one trainee. Another asserted, "The language brings God closer to me as a black man."

There was general agreement, however, that prayer ought to be in English in order to express respect and the inculcated way of doing things. Trainees agreed that even those who could not speak English tried to pray in English. Only one respondent asserted that "when you pray, you say what you have to say; God can understand Patois."

Personal narrative and jokes took on much more life for the trainees in Jamaican Creole. One trainee found it impossible to tell a joke in English. Some students said they used English when they were angry because of the dignity it added to their umbrage; a few used Jamaican Creole for its colorful aspect. Panic, however, evoked a Jamaican Creole response in everyone, "whether we like it or not!"

During the discussion, the transcribers noted the positive and negative words trainees used to refer to the respective languages. Table 2 lists some of the most common descriptive terms. The students clearly said that Jamaican Creole was the language that "sounds good." They used it when they were close to someone, when they relaxed, and when they were at home. Nevertheless, as a result of being punished and ridiculed at home and at school for speaking it, they often referred to it in derogatory terms. "Mummy is always correcting you when you speak Patois," was one response. Another trainee expressed embarrassment at her son's use of Jamaican Creole. Some complained that Jamaican Creole was difficult to read, and "raw Patois" was used to describe the Jamaican Creole of those who "don't know anything else."

English, on the other hand, was referred to almost exclusively in positive terms. Trainees recalled being rewarded at school with extra points for speaking English. The only negative references to English related to lack of skill in using it, which sometimes evoked ridicule, especially in school. Trainees mentioned

Table 2. Words Used to Describe Language

Characterization	English	Jamaican Creole
Positive	Best way Dignity Status Straighten up Right	Friendly Relaxing Sounds good
Negative	Lack of skill	Breaking down Slipping Raw Patois Doesn't sound right

the need to think ahead one word at a time to ensure getting the words right. In general, the discussion supported the positive attitudes toward English of the 2002 survey by Kuck and Blagrove-Williams.

In one further probe into the students' responses to English and Jamaican Creole, the trainees listened to tape recordings of speakers of Jamaican Creole and English and assigned rankings to each speaker in the following categories: wealth, intelligence, education, warmth, friendliness, and social status. Table 3 summarizes their rankings, showing which characteristics were more strongly associated with speakers of English or Jamaican Creole.

Here, English was associated with wealth, education, and social status, the assumed goals of upwardly mobile tertiary students. One trainee averred, "I feel I am a cut above the rest when I speak English." Another mentioned, "I get served first if I speak English." However, Jamaican Creole, despite its connection with a lack of education and cultural exposure in such people as laborers and household helpers, was associated with intelligence, warmth, and friendliness, characteristics that enhance human relationships. Students recognized that even English speakers with status, for example, members of Parliament, needed to shift to Jamaican Creole in order to relate effectively to the general population.

Responding to the question "How do you feel when you are asked in the classroom to switch from Patois to English?" participants said that switching from one language to the other definitely affected behavior in the classroom. There was general agreement that a person's control over English determined the response. One trainee avowed that 10 years ago switching would have been uncomfortable but that now, because she had a better mastery of English, she felt all right. Another remarked that answering a question or telling a story in Jamaican Creole was easy. But he added that even though he considered himself an English speaker, he did not control enough English vocabulary to express himself effectively. One trainee reflected the fear of others when she said she was still reluctant to speak in class because of the ridicule her English had evoked

Table 3. Characteristics Most Strongly Attributed to Speakers of English or Creole

Characteristic	English	Jamaican Creole
Wealth	x	
Intelligence		x
Education	x	
Warmth		x
Friendliness		x
Social Status	x	

early in school life. The group agreed that the teacher's attitude toward the Jamaican Creole identity was crucial. If the teacher allowed students to feel that their Jamaican Creole identity was natural and acceptable but that in this particular class the English identity would be emphasized, then switching from one language (identity) to the other was not such a problem. The final comment of a trainee suggested which identity predominated in the group: "We are not English oriented."

Reflection

The trainee responses supported the theoretical underpinnings of Norton's (2000) conceptions of identity: "Language is constitutive of and constituted by a speaker's identity" (p. 5). The students clearly expressed a dichotomy in their concepts of self that seemed based at least in part on which contact language they were speaking. The teacher trainees were indeed eager to learn and use English. However, an adoption of English as the only or even major language of discourse was threatening.

Two fears seemed to lurk behind the trainees' discomfort with Standard English. First was the fear of losing the Creole identity with which they were more comfortable: "Once you learn English, you won't speak good Patois again," according to one respondent. This fear was corroborated in my classroom, where students complained that when they spoke in their home environments the English required in the academic setting, they alienated friends and relatives, who thought they were being "stoosh" (snobbish). This posed a very real threat to the students' well-being as members of a speech community. Second, students feared that their mastery of Standard English was insufficient to place them securely in the privileged group of English speakers. They were moving along a continuum (see Figure 1) that began with an identity strongly associated with Jamaican Creole and ended with a sense of two aspects of a single self that could be expressed in either of the contact languages; however, many were still in the middle of the continuum. When learners are in the middle phase of identity/ language construction, they are most sensitive to criticism of their position in *either* language community.

What did these findings mean for my own teaching? First, they encouraged me to continue in a direction that is still controversial in Jamaica: to use at the tertiary level a bilingual approach to the teaching of English language skills. This meant I had to study grammatical structures of Jamaican Creole, so that I could place side by side the construction of the two languages and show how English and Jamaican Creole differ. I put together a grammar workbook (Kuck, 2004) for our institute that contrasted the structures that caused the most confusion

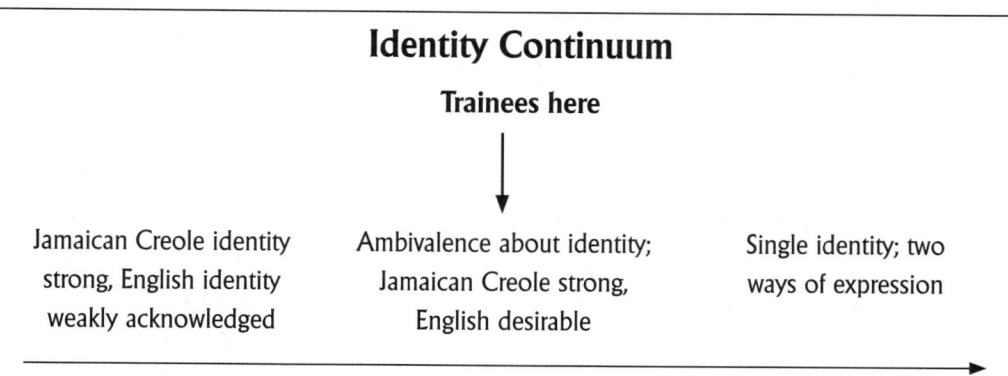

Identity Continuum

Trainees here

Jamaican Creole identity strong, English identity weakly acknowledged

Ambivalence about identity; Jamaican Creole strong, English desirable

Single identity; two ways of expression

Figure 1. Trainees' position on identity continuum.

for our students and presented exercises using vocabulary and content related to the cultural context of Jamaica.

More important, however, I have tried at every available opportunity to highlight the richness, color, and depth of Jamaican Creole, and to demonstrate how students can achieve the same results in English. This is particularly important for me to do, because as a non-Jamaican English teacher, I need to dispel students' apprehension that I might belittle their language in favor of English. Mentioning an appropriate Jamaican Creole proverb or discussing a particularly eloquent Jamaican Creole word lowers the affective filter immediately and leads students to produce comparable expressions in Standard English.

How did the study affect the larger teaching community to which I belong? The focus group generated interest among both the teacher trainees and the colleagues who assisted me. At the time of this research, our technical/vocational institute was just beginning to work toward granting bachelor's degrees in addition to certificates and diplomas. Faculty members were being encouraged to do research, and this project taught us that valuable research could be qualitative as well as quantitative. A faculty research committee sponsored a Research Day not long after I completed the study, and I read a preliminary report there. Colleagues from other disciplines expressed interest not only in the research methodology, but also in the language issues raised.

Finally, the study also clarified that the English language and communications teacher in Jamaica sits on a fence between two worlds: the professed higher status world of Standard English communication and the preferred but lower status community of Jamaican Creole. It takes considerable insight and a talent for flash judgments to know on which side of the fence to land at any moment. It is certain, however, that the English teacher's affirmation of Jamaican Creole and respect for its speakers are important. It enables those who lack confidence in maneuvering not only in the English language but also in the formal, dignified life it represents to speak up in the classroom and venture to improve their skill. Punishment for speaking Jamaican Creole and even rewards for speaking Standard English have the same effect: casting aspersions on the identity Jamaican Creole speakers prefer. Self-esteem, one of the major goals of education, derives from an affirmation of the whole self, which in Jamaica means the Jamaican Creole as well as the English self. This does not mean that students should not be expected to speak, write, and perform in Standard English. Rather, the teacher should relate English to Jamaican Creole consistently while affirming Jamaican Creole as a language just as valid as Standard English in situations outside the classroom. Affirmation of Creole amounts to affirmation of the home identity, which can give learners the self-confidence to venture into the English-speaking world.

Mary Kuck lectures part time at the Vocational Training Development Institute and at the United Theological College of the West Indies in Kingston, Jamaica.

Acknowledgments

I am indebted to Sarah Kuck-Jalbert and Marjorie Blagrove-Williams for their help in structuring the research.

Appendix A: Letter of Invitation to Trainees

Vocational Training Development Institute
Gordon Town Road
Kingston 7, Jamaica
January 2003

Dear Vocational/Technical Education Student:

As a follow-up to research we conducted last year, in which students claimed to have separate identities, one in English and one in Jamaican Creole (Patois), we are preparing a study to find out the nature of these dual identities, and how their existence might affect performance in the English Language and Communications classroom.

With this goal in mind, we are inviting you to participate in a focus group of vocational/technical students to engage in some activities that will lead to a discussion of this issue. We think you will enjoy the process, as well as learn how the focus group method of carrying out research works. The focus group will meet on Wednesday, January 29, from 1–3 p.m. in the Communications Lab. Please let us know immediately if you are unable to attend, as we will need to fill your place with another student.

Thanks in advance for helping us to complete our research.

Sincerely,

Mary Kuck and Marjorie Blagrove-Williams

Appendix B: Questions for Focus Group

Warm-up: two jokes, one in Patois, one in English

1. Do you believe, along with the respondents to the survey, that you have two separate identities, one in English and one in Jamaican Creole? Why?

Play audiotape for the group.

2. List four words that describe this speaker (English speaker on tape). (record on chart)

3. List four words that describe this speaker (Patois speaker on tape). (record on chart)

4. Explain how the words listed relate to the speaker's language.

5. Rank the two speakers in the following categories:

   a. wealth

   b. intelligence

   c. education

   d. warmth

   e. friendliness

   f. social status

6. Would you describe yourself this way when you are speaking English/ Creole? Why?

7. Tell about your holidays in English. Would you tell the same things if you were free to speak Creole? Why?

8. If someone told you to "just be yourself," which language would you use? Why?

9. If you wanted to be sure that another Jamaican trusted you, which language would you use? Why?

10. Which language do you use when you pray? Why?

11. What is your response to this reading? Why? (Play Patois Bible selection.)

12. What is your response to this reading? Why? (Play English Bible selection.)

13. Which language do you use when you are angry? Why?

14. Are jokes in English funny? Why?

15. How do you feel when you are asked to switch to Standard English? Why?

16. Describe the Jamaican Creole identity.

17. Describe the English identity.

18. Do you think that identity switching sometimes affects your work in the English language and communications classroom? How?

CHAPTER 10

Local Cultures, Language Politics, and Service Learning in the TEFL Certificate Course *(Ecuador)*

Kathleen McInerney

Issue

Advertisements for teaching English as a foreign language (TEFL) certificate courses typically assure potential candidates that graduates will be prepared to teach English around the world and in any cultural context. Yet is this the case? Can a one-size-fits-all approach to teaching English adequately address English language learners' cultures? Having team-taught a TEFL certificate course in Ecuador for a number of years, I had become increasingly troubled by the TEFL candidates' apparent apathy about the role of teaching English in the cultures they were entering and their basic knowledge of local current events, economic conditions, and history. Consequently, the lessons they presented, modeled on commercial course books, showed little relevance to the Ecuadorian students' lives and realities.

A further concern was that the TEFL candidates' practice teaching included little experience with English language learners (ELLs) from a range of economic classes. Absent, in particular, were ELLs who did not enroll in English classes at our teaching site because of inadequate resources, such as help with their children and time away from work. Living with middle- and upper-class host families and teaching ELLs from these same families, TEFL candidates had modest, if any, interactions with indigenous or working-class ELLs. Although the TEFL certificate course promises preparation for global teaching, I became increasingly concerned that the TEFL course was not preparing candidates for teaching English to students even within the cultures and class stratifications of our small community in Ecuador.

The TEFL candidates expressed the belief that English is the necessary ticket to upward mobility, and they showed little interest in debating this conviction or its source. In initial journal entries and reflection sessions, TEFL candidates demonstrated a common notion of what Phillipson (1988) termed *linguicism*, "the ideologies and structures which are used to legitimate, effectuate, and reproduce an unequal division of power and resources (both material and nonmaterial) between groups which are defined on the basis of their language (i.e., of their mother tongue)" (p. 339). Indeed, candidates demonstrated resistance to discussing any political aspects of English teaching in developing countries. One student wrote the following:

> As a new TEFL teacher, I know I am more than an English teacher. I am a vehicle for helping people achieve their goals and dreams, whether they be as lofty as using English to work as a doctor or as simple as wanting to take a vacation in Disneyland. I don't agree with, or really understand for that matter, all the political implications of EFL . . . call me unpolitical or a bad citizen, but I don't see the connection.

At the same time, TEFL candidates often voiced surprise and resentment upon discovering that they could not teach in Europe without a European Union passport.

Disturbed by the TEFL candidates' apparently limited interest in examining their future work critically, my teaching colleague and I set out to revise the course to include service learning and reflective activities. We made these course revisions to promote deeper understandings in TEFL candidates of the experiences of Ecuadorian ELLs beyond our classrooms at the language school and, in turn, more awareness of sociocultural aspects of TEFL. Within this context, course revisions were analyzed to (a) identify TEFL candidates' perceptions of the relationships between language learning and culture and (b) determine if TEFL candidates' teaching practices were influenced by their reflections on cultural dimensions of language teaching.

The role of English in Ecuadorian culture in particular highlights the politicized nature of learning English. In the late 1990s, Ecuador experienced an economic crisis that continues to negatively affect, to a great degree, family and community stability, employment, and living standards (Pribilsky, 2001). Although Ecuadorian immigration was extensive prior to 2000, the current migration of Ecuadorian citizens to the United States and Spain for temporary employment is immense. The third largest city of Ecuadorians is not in Ecuador; it is New York (Whitten, 2003). Family life, particularly among rural families, has been decimated; in many villages, one encounters only women, young children, and the elderly. Clearly, Ecuadorians are highly motivated to learn English in order to migrate and become *residentes* in the United States. Ecuadorian teachers I interviewed believed that many secondary students, especially public school students, were motivated to attend school only because they could learn English. English language learning then often becomes the vehicle for procuring a temporary job in the United States that will, after 2 or 3 years of working, allow nationals to pay off the $12,000 to $15,000 debt owed to the *coyote* (or smuggler) who assisted them with entry into the United States. English has become the principal, and most desired, educational commodity supporting migration and transnationalism, and English has becomes the skill that fragments families, communities, and the nation.

Background Literature

Maley (1992) noted, "English language teaching (ELT) has been bedeviled with three perennial problems: the gulf between classroom activities and real life; the separation of ELT from the main stream of educational ideas; the lack of a content as its subject matter" (p. 73). Typical TEFL curricula include little discussion of political and cultural contexts for learning English. H. D. Brown (1994) spoke of the teacher's need to understand local culture, cautioning that "at every turn in our curricula, we must beware of imposing a foreign value system on our learners for the sake of bringing a common language to all" (p. 195). Discussions of the native speaker fallacy as well as an English-only policy in the classroom also address the politicized issues of linguistic advantage—asking whose language and whose culture are privileged in the TEFL profession. Ferguson and Donno (2003) describe the ideological implications of the native speaker as an "anachronistic privileging," born of the "assumption that because native speakers already possess intuitive proficiency in English, they can be certified to teach with a limited amount of explicit language awareness and pedagogical training a one-month course can provide" (p. 29). In her analysis of the English-only policies of ELT, Auerbach (1993) stated, "The rationale used to justify English-only in the classroom is neither conclusive nor pedagogically sound" (p. 9), further underscoring the problematic and politicized history of ELT.

Pennycook (1999) argued that English language teachers need to reflect critically on their work:

> Given the local and global contexts within which English is bound up, all of us involved in TESOL might do well to consider our work not merely according to the reductive meanings attached to labels such as *teaching* and *English*, but rather as located at the very heart of some of the most crucial educational, cultural, and political issues of our time. (p. 346)

Describing his experience of these concerns on a personal level, Ramanathan (2005) outlined the historical practices of teaching a dominant language within the cultural contexts of student learning and considerations for transforming TEFL curricula and practices:

> I have myself begun to probe and cross-examine most aspects of West-based teacher education to include several issues that West-based TESOL typically does not address, including: (a) fronting issues of L1 education by encouraging student teachers to investigate local dynamics between L1 retention and L2 learning practices, policies, and tools; (b) incorporating situated readings regarding English . . . and local languages; (c) drawing on reading and research on heritage language learning and bi/multiculturalism. Although TESOL has generally considered these domains as falling outside of its purview—West-based TESOL has remained remarkably insular—the field can no longer ignore them. (p. 122)

TEFL certificate courses often reveal the problematic elements discussed by Ramanathan (2005), yet they continue to be represented as comprehensive preparation for global teaching. Although traditional TEFL certification requires certain elements of pedagogical and content knowledge, many aspects of teaching and learning common in broader educational discourses—including critical practice and culturally relevant teaching—are absent or truncated. It is also arguable that TEFL certificate courses are driven by tradition rather than research-derived data. Ferguson and Donno (2003), in their critique of TEFL training programs, pointed to this gap: "Considering . . . the relatively large scale of this training activity, the dearth of published research into the phenomena is curious" (p. 26). Because I found little research directly related to my project and concerns, the candidates, the class, and our own reflections became the ground for my fieldwork.

Procedures

The study took place during the 5-week TEFL course in Ecuador, and the participants were 12 TEFL candidates. Although one of the candidates had grown up in the Andes, all candidates were U.S. citizens. Most were or had been traditional students, typically juniors or seniors in college or recent graduates. One student had taught English in Japan for 2 years through a Japanese language teaching program; another student had a few years of experience as a paraprofessional in a Latino preschool in the United States. Course experiences included daily 4-hour class sessions with two professors in the mornings and 2 hours of practice teaching to local residents each evening.

The qualitative measures used in this study of teaching candidates' learning experiences in the TEFL course reflect an ethnographic approach to research methodology. In the role of participant-observer (Spradley, 1980), I employed multiple and triangulated qualitative measures to gather and analyze data about the candidates' understandings of the sociocultural elements of TEFL, their motivations for becoming EFL teachers, as well as their knowledge of subsequent language (L2) acquisition. I collected data from the following sources:

- Pre- and postcourse surveys of TEFL candidates' beliefs about first and subsequent language acquisition, effective teaching and learning, and motivations for becoming EFL teachers.

- Reflective teaching journals.

- Critical incident reports.

- Videotaped classroom discussion sessions.

- Teaching metaphors.

- Reflective writing in portfolios.

Early in the course, candidates filled out questionnaires designed to assess their beliefs about language teaching and learning, their educational backgrounds, degrees earned, and their prior teaching experience. The other data sources provided records of TEFL candidates' reflections, and I analyzed them by employing teacher research approaches to identify relevant data (Cochran-Smith & Lytle, 1992). Most of these artifacts were authentic class assignments in the TEFL course, and these were examined for recurring themes and metaphors (Lightfoot & Davis, 1997). Videotaping of class discussions and debriefing sessions allowed for a more systematic analysis of any revisions in the candidates' questioning and responses. My goal was to mine these artifacts for a better understanding of the candidates' beliefs about their evolving identities as language teachers. I particularly focused on their interpretations of their roles and practices in the classroom in relation to their understanding of teaching in a culture that was not their own.

The reflective writing and discussions of the TEFL candidates in portfolio reflections, in other written artifacts, and in classroom and in postteaching feedback sessions provided a vehicle for them to process their experiences collaboratively. Each candidate was asked, for example, to write for 5 to 10 minutes after each class session he or she taught, before receiving oral and written feedback from the instructor and peers. This practice provided a window into each candidate's complexity of and growth in thinking about lesson planning and implementation. Candidates were also asked, in their portfolio narratives and teaching metaphors, to chart their own development as teachers of English with prompts that asked them to examine their content knowledge as well as their understandings of students, teaching, and learning. I also analyzed the course artifacts produced by candidates for manifestations of conceptual and attitudinal change—for example, candidates' emerging understandings of the local cultures of their students—and then for incorporation of more relevant materials in their classes, using Kolb's (1984) experiential learning model.

In the attitude survey, candidates were asked whether they believed there were any political dimensions to TEFL. Some left the question blank, some begged off as not knowledgeable enough to answer, and some described the necessity of learning English:

> *Elena:* It's quite possible. However, I haven't given it much thought.
>
> *Jennifer:* Sadly, I am very ignorant about politics. I'm sure there are good answers here, but I don't have them.
>
> *Dave:* USA owns the world. People have to learn English if they want to survive.

A second question asked, "How do you expect to benefit personally from gaining a TEFL certificate?" Answers included the following:

> *Simon:* I expect to gain employment because this will make me marketable.
>
> *Jennifer:* Personally, I think it will help me further my education by helping me get into graduate school.
>
> *Alison:* I hope it will give me more chances of getting a job teaching in the U.S.
>
> *Elena:* I can travel the world for the rest of my life and know there will always be a way for me to get by.

The answers to both questions reveal the candidates' beliefs that learning English and teaching English are instruments to achieving economic and personal goals. The TEFL candidates align their purposes for teaching English and their students' purposes for learning English as mirroring each other. In this teaching setting, the teachers perceived little cultural dissonance between the groups and their goals.

An important addition to the TEFL course under discussion included the incorporation of a weekend service project—an effort to broaden candidates' understandings of and experiences with teaching diverse groups, pushing them beyond their comfort zone. The project occurred 2 hours outside our usual site in a small, Ecuadorian village that had suffered greatly in the national economic crisis and subsequent emigration. In preparation for the rural experience, candidates read an anthropological study of the effects of the crisis on rural Ecuadorian families and, in particular, children. The study focused on the province in which our course took place as well as the area from which the majority of Ecuadorian *residentes* in the U.S. emigrate. In the study, Pribilsky

(2001) argued that a condition known as *nervios*—extreme depression in youth—has emerged as a consequence of the transformation of family life from one previously focused on farming and family relationships to one driven by the desire for material goods, influenced by U.S. consumption patterns. In recent years, with the interventions of the World Bank and an increase in transnationalism, Ecuadorians have adopted consumer desires reflecting those in the United States—Gap and Hilfiger clothing, DVD players, and sport utility vehicles. Large homes proliferate in the mountains, built by remittances from fathers and other family members who are working in New York, Miami, and other U.S. cities.

TEFL candidates spent most of their time in the rural village interacting with the local residents by doing interviews, conducting cultural mapping, sharing meals, and teaching English to a group of residents studying to be tour guides. Residents of this village talked not only of the importance of caring for the natural resources of their village and surrounding area, but of the importance of finding alternative methods to create a sustainable community. I analyzed the candidates' written responses to and discussions of their new knowledge about a rural Ecuadorian culture for attitudinal changes in their beliefs about the role of English in such a community. Also, candidates' beliefs about teaching methods and subsequent teaching practices in light of their reflections about the service project were analyzed for evidence of change.

Results

At the beginning of the course, candidates' responses to writing prompts and in-class remarks showed little connection with sociopolitical and cultural aspects of language teaching. As course modifications were implemented to address these issues, however, there was a marked transformation in the candidates' depth of thinking, as seen in their movement from a dualistic certainty about the role of English to a deeper questioning of the implications of English for Ecuadorians as learners within a complex cultural landscape.

The effect of the service experience on candidates' insights into the political and personal meanings of learning English in Ecuador was to contextualize and ground classroom reading with the lived reality of a cultural group different from their own—rural, poor, and suffering from community and family dislocation and fragmentation. In reflection sessions and journal entries, candidates began to express a more elaborated understanding of learning and teaching English and schooling in Ecuador than was previously gained in their practice teaching in the urban language school. A feature of rural Ecuadorian education that particularly stood out to the TEFL candidates concerned the limited quality and quantity of schooling opportunities available to children. At the *primaria*, students have 5-hour school days, but 3 of those hours, typically, are recess time. Because no teachers live in the village, teachers have to travel 2 hours by bus—each way—each day to the school as well as pay for their own bus fare on an extremely limited salary. If a teacher does not come to school, there is no substitute.

Through the experience of the service learning project, TEFL candidates began to critique their own beliefs about the economic and political factors driving English learning for Ecuadorians and the implications for cultural erosion. They also began to think about how these insights fit with their previous experiences and assumptions, recognizing the causes and consequences of emigration. Although the candidates' responses could be seen as romanticizing poverty, the candidates were also at the border—finding themselves in intellectual disequilibrium and beginning to analyze their work as TEFL teachers critically. The following are representative of comments made by many candidates in journal entries and reflection sessions:

> *Elena:* Black and white. Night and day [rural versus urban]. But they [rural residents] don't understand here that if they come to work in the U.S. they will probably have to take crappy jobs. They have this big misconception that all Americans are rich and that if they learn English and move, they too will have a better life.

> *Claire:* They live in one of the most amazing places in the world and they have an amazing culture. I am jealous of what they have and they just want to be like "rich Americans." American culture is not nearly as rich—it's based on material goods and things that to me aren't important at all. So I guess the thing that stuck in my mind the most is how badly these people are striving to be able to be like Americans when, to me, Americans are doing it all wrong.

> *Jennifer:* Personally, I think they [the residents] are doing something right. They have what they need and they get to spend time with their families.

> *Linda:* The children and their families are confronting many of the issues facing their counterparts in the U.S., specifically, the breakdown of family connection through outside influences. In the U.S., parents work more and more with the intent to provide a better life for their children. The result is that children spend little time with their parents . . . the entertainment industry and consumerism are used to fill the emptiness. Depression is rampant—antidepressants are prescribed increasingly for children and young adults. Ecuador's situation, unfortunately, has followed the U.S.'s lead.

Candidates began, during and after the service project, to reflect on their teaching practices within the framework of their new learning. Here, evidence for the third stage in Kolb's (1984) experiential learning model emerged. Kolb formulated the following processes: (a) concrete experience and observation, (b) considered reflection, (c) synthesis and abstract conceptualization, and (d) testing of concepts in new situations. A shift in TEFL candidates' thinking toward more questioning as well as acknowledging a need to understand their students as a critical element of teaching practice became evident:

Meghan: As a TEFL teacher, I need to take into consideration a lot of things. I need to think about the individuals I am teaching and why the students I am teaching want to learn English. Is it so they can migrate to the U.S.? Are they going to ruin their families? Am I okay with that possibility?

Simon: Maybe by teaching English I am causing a rift between them and their friends who are not learning English.

Elena: Symbols of achievement among families come from remittance funds to buy new technology-based gifts, stoves, expensive clothing. These things literally take the place of the fathers. As a TEFL teacher, I have learned how culturally sensitive topics can be.

Dave: English can be a barrier more than it is a gateway for people. This raises some cognitive dissonance in my mind because by being a TEFL teacher, I would be helping to reduce that barrier that exists but I would also be supporting the idea that others need to learn our language in order to thrive.

Linda: As an EFL teacher, I need to be very careful when teaching with the approaches we will use, culturally speaking. We will have to valorize and validate everybody's background and culture.

TEFL candidates also gained insights into a variety of information about literacy practices in school, local cultural knowledge, and avenues of learning (e.g., multiple intelligences) through the service project:

Claire: When I was teaching English in the village, I was totally startled by the incapacity of one student to answer a simple question. . . . The first thing I thought was that I didn't do a good job teaching, but after, discussing my experience with my classmates and colleagues, I realized that this student was doing what he learned to do in school every day—repeat everything the teacher says.

Linda: I realized while I was teaching in the village that traditional classroom learning, whether it be through photos, writing and/or speaking is not necessarily the best form for some people. I showed her [my student] numerous colors and went over words in the classroom, however it was not until I showed her in *nature* that she understood. In the classroom, she couldn't identify a tree, but the moment we stepped outdoors, I noticed it was the first thing she knew when I pointed to it. . . . For the first time, I really saw a difference in the learning techniques away from the way I learn. I know of the theories . . . but through my work with this woman, I finally put a face to the theory. It may be said that this could have happened in the States for me as well, but the fact that it took place in an environment in which I was forced to use alternative methods for teaching makes all the more impact.

The responses are evidence of the candidates' developing sense of dialogic understanding or, as Freire (1970) explained, moving toward a theory of informed teaching practice as cultural action. In the remainder of the course, TEFL candidates continued to critically analyze their practice in light of their new understandings of a culture quite different from their own, now critiquing teaching materials, methodologies, and their own assumptions:

Elena: Blech. That's how I feel about tonight's lesson. Following [a publisher's] lesson plan, I taught "The Twelve Days of Christmas" . . . but teaching students with local realia and developing lexis based on things that are important to them and not me will be helpful in instructing and not simultaneously promoting American ways of life.

One candidate had written early in the course that his only experience with a foreign language was derived from working in a meat-packing plant. In the entry below, the depth of his self-reflection on learning from his time in Ecuador in the TEFL course is evident:

Dave: I was standing out on the deck smoking cigarettes and thinking about things when I thought, "You dumbass. All's you've been doing for the last four years is drinking and screwing around with girls. . . . I think experiencing another culture gave me time to reflect on my life back home. Seeing the way other people live and allowing myself to respect and appreciate that let me realize that there are many ways to live and be happy, especially in places like this village where everyone seemed so happy without having most of the things I think are so great. I don't believe in huge moments of epiphany that change the way I live . . . but I would have never thought anything different if I had not come to South America.

Kolb (1984) described the fourth stage in the cycle of reflection in service learning as being able to apply new understandings to coursework and even one's life. TEFL candidates, by the end of their experience in the course, have accrued information about and practice in teaching English, and also have developed further their abilities to critically analyze not only teaching but their interactions with others and roles within the world.

In examining the TEFL candidates' development as culturally aware, reflective teachers through their journals, videotaped dialogues, and teaching metaphors, I found evidence of engaged reflection through questioning and dialogue about the relationship between the ELLs' cultures and the learning of English. Many candidates began the class with some understandings of these concerns. However, teaching practice in a range of communities, including the rural service project, became the key element in expanding candidates' understanding of teaching, as seen in their reflections. The experience allowed TEFL candidates to reconceptualize their role in the classroom as colearners rather than bankers—or transmitters of knowledge—in Freirian (1970) terms. The analysis of the TEFL course reviewed here suggests that integrating models of experiential or service learning is central in engendering culturally aware and responsive TEFL teachers.

An additional factor to be considered in measuring the project's success is the methodology employed to prepare candidates for the service experience. Using a constructivist experiential teaching methodology, I offered information for candidates to consider in their instructional planning, but I did not provide recipes. Within a constructivist model, learners are seen as self-directed, active participants in their own learning. In this case, the TEFL candidates were given learning resources and then asked to respond to and design their language teaching by first listening to the ELLs.

Curriculum and materials were derived from, rather than imposed upon, the ELLs. In fact, because the English classes in the rural village typically included entire families with children as young as 5, and the class had decided to teach to the families rather than divide students by age and level of English skills, textbooks were not as relevant or appropriate as other, more authentic teaching approaches and activities. TEFL candidates had also read about the local culture and spent time learning about it from the residents themselves in the authentic context of a tour (students were studying to be ecotourism guides). TEFL candidates were encouraged to assume a different role as teachers, specifically by having the tour groups act as teachers for the TEFL candidates during English class time, placing the ELLs in the role of knowledge holders and creators.

By revising teacher and learner roles and rejecting the dominance of publisher-driven instructional materials, TEFL candidates were able to reconceptualize themselves and their learners. Rather than embracing the traditional method of structure-driven direct instruction, they began to see themselves as teachers within a framework of reflective practice and constructivism. In this experience, TEFL candidates' teaching paradigms clearly departed from a model of language learning to Krashen's (2003) model of language acquisition.

Reflection

I have presented the initial insights from an ongoing exploratory study of a TEFL certificate course with a particular focus on enhancing the course through service learning. The experience was designed to increase TEFL candidates' cultural awareness, reflective teaching practice, and professional mindset. As a TEFL course instructor, I find it critical to my own classroom practice to engender in my students a grounded understanding of (a) the complex cultures in which my graduates will teach; (b) formal and informal schooling structures, local literacy practices, and pathways of learning that support or impede language learning in particular communities; and (c) current theory and research from the wider community of L2 professionals. Further investigation of these elements of L2 language teaching would offer valuable insights into the curriculum in EFL teacher preparation.

Based on this research, the TEFL course under discussion continues to be revised in a number of ways, including increased service learning and a focus on students designing culturally relevant thematic units and lessons with a social justice orientation. Candidates are encouraged to analyze their themes critically and to examine, for example, the cultural impact of a lesson based on shopping in the United States or advertisements for Coca-Cola versus a project-based unit on local recycling practices. More local culture is incorporated into classroom materials, including arts, folk literature, and alternative medicine, valorizing the ELLs' cultural assets. Candidates also are introduced to and use more constructivist teaching approaches, for example, learning centers, literacy circles, and other cooperative learning activities (Kagan, 1986). These classroom practices are better aligned with a curriculum demonstrating support for and encouragement of understanding the ELLs in our classrooms and the cultures they represent. Additionally, candidates are required to become familiar with their Ecuadorian students and the cultural and political realities of their lives through interviews, case studies, and cultural mapping as well as extensive reading of work by educational anthropologists about current life in Ecuador. If they did any less in terms of learning about their students, TEFL candidates would gain only a naïve and shallow understanding of their host culture, leading to a complacently simple, if not arrogant, pedagogy. After candidates have gained cultural awareness and practiced reflective teaching, I hope that those moving on to teach in other cultures will bring the same critical habits of mind to their next teaching situations.

With these course changes, I believe it is possible to achieve a primary and necessary course goal—to encourage language teaching candidates to be intellectually, culturally, and professionally knowledgeable about the complexity of language teaching rather than comfortable with unexamined and culturally naïve teaching routines. Foregrounding cultural dimensions in the certificate course places EFL teaching candidates in what Giroux (1994) calls border territory:

> The concept of border suggests something very subversive and unsettling. It means moving into circles of uncertainty. It means crossing into different cultural spheres, it means recognizing the multiple nature of our own identities. . . . Educators have to be more than intellectual tourists. We must move into other spheres where we take up the specificity of different contexts, geographies, different languages, of otherness, and to recognize the otherness in ourselves. (p. 167)

If, through expanding and diversifying the TEFL course field sites, it was possible to enhance and enrich the candidates' concepts of language, culture, and teaching, then it seems clear that, as a TEFL course instructor, I will improve my own teaching and course outcomes by exploring and sharing my own experiences as a teacher within specific cultural contexts as well. By incorporating classroom research approaches and investigating my students' assumptions about language learners, I will more likely succeed in helping TEFL candidates examine their otherness, their cultural beliefs, and their roles and practices as teachers of English. Finally, I will come closer to a deeper understanding of and more informed approach to designing TEFL certificate course curriculum and instruction that will better prepare candidates as socially aware and responsible members of the TESOL profession.

Kathleen McInerney teaches at Chicago State University, in the United States.

Finding and Leveraging Vocabulary Strengths While Addressing Needs (*United States*)

Elizabeth Park

Issue

Daily in my English as a subsequent language (ESL) classes in a New Jersey middle school, I teach English vocabulary as a cornerstone for learning the language. In 8 years of teaching, I have worked with two Mandarin-speaking Chinese students, two Gujarati-speaking South Asian students, and three Albanian-speaking students. In that same period, I have worked with students from Argentina, Chile, Colombia, Costa Rica, the Dominican Republic, Ecuador, El Salvador, Honduras, Mexico, Peru, Puerto Rico, and Uruguay. Speakers of Spanish as a first language (L1) have been in the overwhelming majority of my students, and number over 300. My classroom reflects the composition of the statewide English language learner (ELL) population. According to the New Jersey Department of Education, Spanish-speaking students identified as either native speakers or limited English proficient (LEP) by the state outnumber students who speak other languages by a wide margin (see Tables 1 and 2).

Learning the vocabulary of English is one of the most important tasks facing these ELLs. Vocabulary is at the core of all four language skills: listening, speaking, reading, and writing. As an ESL teacher, I have understood this challenge intuitively and explicitly. I have wrestled with finding the best way to teach English vocabulary to my students. I have watched as my students' eyes glazed and they disengaged from active learning when confronted with vocabulary lists,

Table 1. Languages With Highest LEP Enrollment Statewide in New Jersey, 2005–2006

Language	Native Speakers	LEP Students
Spanish	163,316	39,605
Portuguese	8,430	1,478
Korean	8,918	1,408
Arabic	8,633	1,220
Haitian Creole (French)	3,797	1,004
Gujarati	8,060	972
Mandarin (Chin, Kuoyu, Pekingese, Northern Chinese, Putonghua)	7,209	923
Polish	5,768	892
Urdu	4,598	617
Tagalog (Pilipino, Filipino)	5,436	515
Vietnamese	1,356	387

Source: New Jersey Department of Education (2006b).

lists that were created by so-called experts who presumed to know what ELLs in general, and my ELLs specifically, needed. This happened often enough that I decided it was time to let my students tell me what they needed rather than to continue to dictate their vocabulary needs to them. This became the focus of two related studies I conducted in my classroom over a 3-year period.

Background Literature

The critical nature of vocabulary instruction for ELLs has been addressed by Schleppegrell (2004) and Corson (1997), among others. Scores on standardized reading tests across the United States indicate strongly that ELLs do not have the reading comprehension skills necessary to satisfy federally mandated standards. Abedi (2002) identified a number of studies that addressed the issue of ELL performance on standardized tests and found that the studies clearly indicate that the performance gap between ELLs and non-ELLs largely stems from language factors. The test scores and these studies show that reading comprehension is a major issue for ELLs.

Stefanakis (2004) discussed the need to recognize student strengths so teachers can avoid framing their instructional practices on deficit models. Ignoring

Table 2. Bilingual/ESL Education: New Jersey State Profile of LEP Students, 2005–2006

Category	Number
Language minority students	280,692
LEP students	60,807
Districts serving LEP students	448
Districts with bilingual education programs	66
Districts with only full-time bilingual education	10
Districts with only alternative (part-time) bilingual education	39
Districts with full-time and alternative (part-time) bilingual education programs	17
Districts with ESL-only (including high-intensity ESL) programs	239
Districts with English language services programs	157

Source: New Jersey Department of Education (2006a).

students' needs was certainly not her point, but identifying their strengths in order to gauge their needs accurately was. I found that this concept resonated deeply with what I was seeing in my classroom. One factor in this resonance is the purely practical and logistical issue of time. My classes last for only 42 minutes a day. If I do not carefully identify what should be taught and learned in the classroom, I am wasting those precious moments. If, however, I can identify my students' strengths and teach them to use those strengths as they construct their own learning whenever possible, then I am saving instructional time to devote to the issues with which students truly need my help.

Graves (2006) identified four vocabulary challenges faced by ELLs:

1. A basic vocabulary of the most frequently used English words.

2. A vocabulary of academic English.

3. English idioms.

4. English words that represent new concepts. (pp. 86–87)

The concept of a basic vocabulary can be interpreted as what Beck, McKeown, and Kucan (2002) cited as Tier 1, for example, "clock," "baby," "happy," "walk" (p. 8). In discussing Tier 1, they offered recommendations for classroom practice: "Words in this tier rarely require instructional attention to their meanings in school" (p. 8). This understanding of vocabulary needs is implicit in the way many teachers approach teaching vocabulary, and it proved to be an important part of my findings.

Procedures

FIRST STUDY

The location for both of the studies I conducted is the same: the seventh- and eighth-grade New Jersey middle school where I teach. More than 75% of the students in this school speak Spanish as a home language, and a large percentage of those Spanish-speaking students began their schooling in Latin America or the Caribbean. Along with other teaching duties, a few years ago I spent one period a day teaching literature to an eighth-grade class mostly comprising mainstreamed students who had exited from ESL programs within the previous 3 years. The curriculum for this class closely followed the grade-level volume of the literature textbook series adopted by the school district for eighth-grade students. The book was one of the anthologies provided by major textbook publishers for U.S. schools and, like others of its kind, included vocabulary lists that accompanied each story in the book. I felt that some of the students' vocabulary needs could be satisfied by asking them to translate words from English into their L1.

Seeking a link to students' L1s, I developed a worksheet (see Appendix A) that asked students to list the vocabulary words highlighted in the textbook, identify roots and affixes, and record a definition in English and another definition in their L1. At the time this seemed to be a reasonably productive way to approach the learning of vocabulary. I asked students to complete these worksheets before the story was read in class, expecting the prereading exercises to help establish an understanding of the vocabulary they needed to comprehend and analyze each short story. My intention was also to link that new vocabulary to their home languages.

Results

FIRST STUDY

As I reviewed the worksheets, I saw that the students had frequently filled in the *other language* column with Spanish cognates. As the vocabulary focus, the publishers had chosen Tier 2 words, described by Beck et al. (2002) as "words of high frequency for mature language users . . . found across a variety of domains. Examples include *coincidence, absurd, industrious,* and *fortunate*" (p. 8). This seemed a contradiction. My students were hardly considered mature language users. They were young adolescents, and most of the class members were categorized as basic-skills students, young people who needed more scaffolding than others in order to achieve any level of academic success.

The contradiction lay in the fact that, like *coincidence, absurd, industrious,* and *fortunate,* by far the majority of the Tier 2 words chosen by the textbook publishers had Spanish cognates. Later I learned that "30% to 40% of all words in English have a related word in Spanish. With similar sound, appearance, and meaning, these cognates help students transfer that word knowledge into their second language" (Reading Rockets/Colorín Colorado Project, 2006).

What I learned from those worksheets forced me to reconsider the basis on which to teach vocabulary. My ELLs already knew the meanings for words that most of their teachers, as well as the publishers of the textbooks they used, considered to be vocabulary they did not understand without direct instruction. It also made me ponder why many of the students themselves admitted to me, in informal conversations, that they didn't realize there was a connection between the cognates.

I realized I had often heard students being cautioned to "speak English" and being told that "we don't speak Spanish here." Was it possible, I asked myself, that this contributed to the gap students saw between their knowledge of Spanish and their knowledge of English? How could I convince my students that they could rely on their L1s for a great deal of help with their second language? How could I help students learn to use that rich resource to improve their reading comprehension in English? How could I teach my students to use the formidable lexical tools they already had?

It soon became clear that many students needed encouragement to turn to their L1s for assistance with their second language. They needed to know the immense academic value of their home language, and they needed permission and even direction on how to turn to that language for help. Many students, in my experience, had found that in their school world there was little value placed on the rich linguistic resource they had in their L1. This had led them to separate the two languages with borders in their minds as completely as their two countries were separated by borders on the map.

Fostering those connections was one direction for my questions. Another direction was this: If the students had the means to know Tier 2 words, what was it they did not know in the English lexicon? What was beyond their reach? How could I identify their real vocabulary needs? It was clear that the answers to those questions could come only from the students, and it was up to me to find a way to encourage them to divulge that information.

Procedures

SECOND STUDY

To find the answers to these questions, I constructed a curriculum for an intermediate ESL class that was based on sustained silent reading (SSR). The SSR program was managed with a specific vocabulary goal in mind: to provide data about which English words students did and did not understand. The SSR program consisted of library visits, classroom reading, group discussion, and a game we called Word Work. The program also included assisting the school librarian by shelving books.

Library Visits

Students were free to select books from the school library, and at the beginning of the year, the entire class visited the library once a week to browse the shelves and explore the displays created by the librarian. For many students, these were their first visits to a U.S. library, and it took them a while to learn their way around. When students were comfortable in the library, which I gauged to be after three or four class visits, we stopped going as a class, and students became responsible for making their own visits during lunch or after school.

Classroom Reading

Once students had checked out library books, we started reading in class. Half of each day's session was devoted to reading. I developed a form (see Appendix B) students used to record each book they read. The form included bibliographic information on each book, basic questions about whether the student liked the book or not, and why. It also included—and this was the true research purpose of the form—space for students to list the words they did not know.

Each day, students brought their books with them to class. Of the 42 minutes allotted to each class period, we spent 20 to 25 minutes reading silently. As they read, they recorded the words they did not know. I decided not to ask students to look up definitions. It seemed that the more difficulty there was attached to recording the data, the less likely it would be for them to list all of the words they did not know. Even so, it took encouragement to convince them that they did in fact need to list all unfamiliar words. I read along with the students because I enjoy reading and wanted to model that enjoyment for them. Also, I observed early on that if I was not reading, for example, if I was recording grades or doing anything else, the students had difficulty maintaining focus. When I paid attention to my book, they paid attention to theirs.

Group Discussion

Two times a week, we spent the remaining class time discussing our books. I talked about my book, and the students took turns talking about theirs. Sometimes students interviewed each other about their books; sometimes the format was a round-robin answer to a question such as "What do you like best (or least) about the main character in your book?" or "What experience of your own does the book make you think of?"

Word Work

On the other three days, we played the Word Work game. To win a homework pass, students chose words from the lists they had made and challenged me to define them. If I could not explain a word, the student who had challenged me received a no-homework night. Rules for the game barred any proper nouns or foreign words or phrases. In responding to the challenges, I explained definitions, sometimes adding a bit of linguistic history or pointing out connections to literature. Whenever possible, I referred to the concept of cognates and tried to reinforce the value of the students' L1s.

Assisting the Librarian

This part was focused not so tightly on vocabulary learning but more on a general goal of understanding libraries and the treasures they provide. Judy Klement, our librarian, worked closely with me to develop the library part of the overall program. She and I reasoned that the more at ease students were in the library and the more they learned about its holdings, the more often they would visit on their own and the more books they would read. We decided that once a week a pair of students would report to the library for the class period to shelve books according to her directions. Pairs would rotate through the class roll so that each student had an opportunity to help her. Students thoroughly enjoyed the reading program, but they considered being library assistants a real treat.

Results

SECOND STUDY

Results were consistent across Spanish-speaking students in the class, and across classes for the 2 years I conducted the study. Table 3 provides a representative selection of words identified by students as difficult and shows the etymologies of the words, as traced by Partridge (1959), the *American Heritage Dictionary of the English Language* (2000), and others (Baker, 2003; Harper, 2001).

Most of the words the students did not know were from the Tier 1 group of words. The reason they did not know them, I deduced, was that Tier 1 words come from the Germanic side of English. Tier 1 words are usually considered simple words, often used in baby talk and toddler chatter, and they contribute considerably to the 10,000 English words typical third graders have in their reading vocabulary (Graves, 2006).

Table 3. Etymology of Reading Record Words

Vocabulary Word	Etymology
Nod	Middle English *nodden*
Aim	Middle English *eimen*
Bare	Old Norse *berr*
Beetle	Middle English *bityl*
Blink	Middle English *blenken*
Bliss	Middle English *bletsian*
Bow	Old English *bugan*
Bundle	Old English *byndele*
Cheered	Middle English *chere*
Curl	Middle Danish *crullen*
Daze	Old Norse *dadask*
Deaf	Old English *deaf*
Either	Old English *aegther*
Elder	Old English *eald*
Fade	Middle English *fade*
Fang	Old English *fon*
Feather	Old English *fether*
Grab	Middle Dutch *grabbelen*
Grin	Old English *grennian*
Guns	Middle English *gone*
Huddle	Old English *hydels*
Hug	Old Norse *hugga*
Jiggle	Old Norse *gigia*
Knoll	Old English *knul*
Mischief	Middle English *meschef*
Nap	Old High German *hnaffezen*
Overwhelming	Old English *hwelmian*
Peep	Middle English *pepen*

(continued on p. 147)

Table 3. Etymology of Reading Record Words (continued)

Vocabulary Word	Etymology
Poke	Middle Low German *poken*
Pull	Old English *pullian*
Ragamuffin	*Rag*—Old Norse *rogg*; *muffin*—Middle French *moufflet*
Rub	Middle English *rubben*
Shed	Old English *sceady*
Shove	Old English *scufan*
Shriek	Old Norse *skraekja*
Sideswiped	*Side*—Old Saxon *sida*; *swipe*—Old Norse *sveipa*
Slam	Norwegian *slemma*
Slight	Old Norse *slettr*
Slip	Old High German *slippen*
Snap	Old Norse *snappa*
Squeezed	Old English *cwesan*
Squirm	Middle High German *schirmen*
Such	Old English *swelc*
Tight	Old Norse *thettre*
Tip	Middle Dutch *tep*
Unscathed	*Un*—Old Saxon *un*; *scathed*—Old Norse *skatha*
Uphill	*Up*—Old Norse *upp*; *hill*—Old English *holm*
Wick	Old English *weoc*
Wink	Old English *wincian*

Sources: American Heritage Dictionary of the English Language (2000); Baker (2003); Harper (2001); Partridge (1959).

Reflection

The implications of my findings are enormous for my teaching practice. The words that were unfamiliar to my students are those often assumed to be part of everyone's vocabulary. They are viewed as the easy vocabulary of English. The words tend to have one syllable and are not simple for any intrinsic reason, but they are often considered simple because they are among the first words learned by toddlers who speak English.

In hindsight, it seems obvious that words of Germanic origin would be difficult for these students, at least without direct instruction. However, the implications are even broader than for my Spanish-speaking students and me. These words are out of reach for many other students as well. They are not likely to be part of the basic vocabulary brought to school by students whose primary language is any of the following: Portuguese, Korean, French Creole, Gujarati, Arabic, Polish, Urdu, Tagalog, Vietnamese, Mandarin, Cantonese, or any of the other Chinese languages. These are the languages that the New Jersey Department of Education (2006b) has identified as the L1s of most ELLs in the state (see Table 1). In light of this relationship, the implications of this study could be felt in many other classrooms.

There is also an important sociological component to this concept. The words in question, the short words of the nursery, are also those that make up a much-prized variety of English known in the United States as *plain speaking*. This variety is considered to communicate a stronger, more intense message than those varieties that rely on a large number of English words with Romance roots (and, coincidentally, Spanish cognates). For example, in his essay "The Case for Short Words," Richard Lederer (as cited in Bowler et al., 1994) wrote the following:

> When you speak and write, there is no law that says you have to use big words. Short words are as good as long ones, and short, old words—like sun and grass and home—are best of all. A lot of small words, more than you might think, can meet your needs with a strength, grace, and charm that large words do not have.
>
> Big words can make the way dark, for those who read what you write and hear what you say. Small words cast their light on big things—night and day, love and hate, war and peace, and life and death. Big words at times seem strange to the eye and the ear and the mind and the heart. Small words are the ones we seem to have known from the time we were born, like the heart fire that warms the home. (p. 401)

Lederer writes for an audience of English speakers. Were he writing for an audience of readers whose L1 was Spanish, he would need to reverse his position. For this audience, it would be the small words that would "make the way dark." It would be the big words that would "cast their light on big things." To my ELLs, small words "at times seem strange to the eye and the ear and the mind and the heart." My students could say that the big words are the ones "we seem to have known from the time we were born, like the heart fire that warms the home." This creates almost a mirror-image relationship between the small words and the big words and their affective meaning for audiences of English speakers and audiences of Spanish speakers. And although Lederer's advice is for writing, the piece has a connection to reading and to instructing ELLs in American literature. Carl Sandburg's (1919) poems, for example, are commonly

Table 4. Etymology of Words in the Poem "Fog"

Vocabulary Word	Etymology
fog	Danish *fog*
comes	Old English *cumin*
little	Old English *lyt*
it	Old English *hit*
look	Old English *locian*
over	Old English *ofer*
harbor	Middle English *herberwe*
and	Old English *end*
haunches	Middle English *haunche*
then	Old English *thanne*

Sources: American Heritage Dictionary of the English Language (2000); Partridge (1959).

considered to be powerful and evocative of the mythic hard-working Americans of social realism. Much of the perceived power of his poems comes from the use of short words, words that as Lederer says "cast their light on big things." An example is Sandburg's poem "Fog":

"Fog"

The <u>fog comes</u>
on <u>little</u> cat feet.

<u>It</u> sits <u>look</u>ing
<u>over harbor and</u> city
on silent <u>haunches</u>
<u>and then</u> moves on. (Sandburg, 1919)

To begin to construct a simulation of the way in which a member of my class might respond to this poem, the history of the words used by the poet can be examined. The underlined words are words with a Germanic background (see Table 4).

There are only 18 different words in this poem, yet 9 of them have a lineage that is not of the Romance language family. They are all part of the Tier 1 word group, Lederer's small words, and are widely considered easy words. Eliminating these Tier 1 words, so that the script includes words a newly arrived student from a Spanish-speaking background might understand, results in the following:

"___"

The ___ _____
on _____ cat feet.

__ sits _____
____ _____ ___ city
on silent _____
___ ____ moves on.

For the Spanish-speaking students, half of the words are missing; there is little or no meaning that they can construe. However, rephrasing the poem in words that are more closely linked to the Spanish that my students speak yields the following adaptation:

"Vapor"

Vapor sits
on minuscule cat feet.

Vapor sits regarding
port and city
silently,
previous to moving.

For Spanish speakers, this version of the poem may well hold much of the strength and powerful meaning the original version holds for native English speakers. These longer words are likely akin to the words of their early childhood. In other words, revising the poem with words of Latin roots imbues it with a florid, rarefied element for those who speak English as their L1, but would most likely connote the opposite for my students.

Understanding the subtexts packed into vocabulary and understanding that these subtexts may seem in some ways oppositional when Spanish and English are compared is not easy. It is counterintuitive from both perspectives. However, to teach ELLs not only the text but the nuances crafted by an author who chooses words carefully, it is necessary to try to understand this complexity. It is, after all, part of the responsibility of a teacher of ESL.

To take this on, I have turned again to Beck et al. (2002). Even though they created a classification system for vocabulary that is not applicable to instruction for most ELLs, the methodology in the book is applicable in any language classroom. If I am introducing the word *grab*, the first step is contextualizing the word, in this case referring to a sentence or a passage in which it was encountered. The second step is grouping pronunciation so that the sound of the word is reinforced. This can be more complex for ELLs than for mainstream students, and more critical. The initial consonant blend *gr* should be emphasized with Spanish speakers. The vowel sound in *grab* is not found in Spanish. Finally, it is rare, if ever, that a Spanish word would end with *b*. The third step is explaining the meaning. With my students, this can work most effectively with showing rather than talking. For example, I demonstrate *grabbing* by reaching quickly for a piece of chalk and holding it tight. Then I ask students to grab their pencils. The fourth step is giving other examples of how to use the word. We talk about *grabbing* bookbags when the bell rings, or *grabbing* a bite to eat. Next, in Beck's sequence, the teacher asks students to talk about something they would be reluctant to do. In my class, I ask students to tell us something else they might *grab*. The sequence ends with another round of saying the word out loud (Beck et al., 2002).

Creating word families is another strategy I have started to use. Expanding on the word *grab*, I have added *grip, grasp,* and *grope*. These words all have the same initial sounds, and they all have to do with the hand. They are also words my students do not know. Another word family I use includes *snoot, snout, snort, snooze,* and *snore*. These words, too, share initial sounds and relate in one way or another to the same part of the body, in this case noses. I believe that offering phonological connections as well as lexical relationships will help students construct their vocabulary learning through Carey's (1978) extended mapping rather than the fast mapping that the learner does not retain. Graves (2006) also offers numerous strategies, from linguistics-grounded explorations to the use of Venn diagrams and many other suggestions for helping students learn how to learn vocabulary on their own.

These are the kind of vocabulary lessons I have started to use with my students. The lesson for me and perhaps for other teachers is not to assume that we know what our students know or do not know. We should remember that assuming is not good logic. We should remember that collecting and analyzing data about our own students, and applying those analyses to our work in the classroom may be the best way to serve the students we teach.

Elizabeth Park teaches middle school students in New Jersey, in the United States.

Appendix A: Worksheet for Words and Definitions

Name: _____

Word	Root	Affix	Other Language	English Definition

Write a sentence using the word:

_____

_____

Word	Root	Affix	Other Language	English Definition

Write a sentence using the word:

_____

_____

Word	Root	Affix	Other Language	English Definition

Write a sentence using the word:

_____

_____

Appendix B: Worksheet for Reading Record

READING RECORD

Name: _____

Date: _____

Title: _____

Author: _____

Publisher: _____

City of publication: _____

Year of publication: _____

Number of pages: _____

What I liked most about the book:

_____

_____

I liked least about the book:

_____

_____

Words from the book I didn't know:

_____

_____

_____

_____

_____

_____

_____

_____

CHAPTER 12

Are Nonnative Speakers Really Able to Converse? (*United States*)

Eliana Santana-Williamson

Issue

While working in the Brazilian Amazon for 11 years and in the United States for 6, I have observed that English as a foreign language (EFL) and English as a subsequent language (ESL) learners express similar feelings about engaging in conversations, including fear of speaking and making mistakes, lack of confidence when conversing, and inability to deal with the time constraints of unplanned talk. In an ESL context, where immigrant students' survival depends on their competence to participate in unplanned talk, such feelings of inadequacy likely lead to serious difficulties. I realized that my teaching of subsequent language (L2) speaking was not preparing students to deal with those difficulties, partially because most textbooks did not expose students to what speaking really was; neither did they prepare students to process, construct, and negotiate the language. Even though L2 learners are often taught through a functional approach, with opportunities to engage in oral interaction rather than mechanical drills, many elements that form the structure of the spoken language are still missing in ESL classes and textbooks (Hughes & McCarthy, 1998).

An out-of-classroom experience reinforced my feelings about the inadequacy of the material and my approach to teaching. When watching TV with my husband, an L2 learner of Portuguese, I was perplexed when he said within seconds into an interview that the Russian interviewee had obviously lived in America.

He explained that inserts (words or expressions inserted in a sentence but not interfering with syntax) such as *you know* and *I mean* were not present in textbooks or taught in classrooms, and therefore learners who were able to use them had had exposure to real-life language. In subsequent discussions, some of my experienced colleagues affirmed that L2 learners should be able to pick those elements up naturally. However, many of my L2 learners expressed great anxiety when having to engage in unplanned spoken interactions in English and complete perplexity when learning about dysfluencies of the spoken language, such as pauses, fillers, and repairs that aid in speaking and can be used as tools when conversing.

These events provided the fuel I needed to seek information on which discourse-level elements were commonly used by native speakers (NSs) of English but not present in the curriculum of L2 speaking classes. I soon realized that whereas studies on NS discourse were abundant, studies on nonnative speaker (NNS) discourse were almost nonexistent. I decided to pursue my own study that would inform my teaching and affect material design and student assessment. Inspired by my husband's comments and by the chapter on conversation in Biber, Johansson, Leech, Conrad, and Finegan's (1999) book, I decided to investigate whether certain inserts that occurred frequently in NS discourse were used frequently and for the same purposes by NNSs. My major goal was to see if NNSs were indeed able to resort to the same speaking strategies that NSs do. I started my investigation by researching the historical evolution of the teaching of L2 speaking.

Background Literature

Initially, the teaching of ESL and EFL students was influenced by mainly descriptive linguistics and psychology, which together generated methods and approaches to L2 teaching such as the audiolingual method and the cognitive approach. Descriptive linguistics focused on analyses of language at the sentence level by linearly dissecting and describing it. Analyses beyond the sentence level, called discourse-level analyses, became prominent in the 1970s. Linguists were then inspired by the social sciences and the view of language as a social product embedded in a situational context (McCarthy, 2001). This view led linguists to analyze language at the discourse level and originated the communicative language teaching era, which has led to improvements in the teaching of L2 speaking. Proponents of this view analyzed language within its social and linguistic context, recognizing that language does not occur in isolation.

Discourse-level analysis of language requires that authentic language be collected. When a certain body of authentically collected language is put together, it is called a *corpus*. A corpus can consist of newspaper articles, conversations, college classes, or some other body of text the researcher wants to analyze. However, whereas it was relatively easy to analyze authentic written texts, the analysis of authentic spoken texts required recorders and computer technology that were not previously available. Advances in recording and computer technology in the 1990s facilitated the collection of spoken texts, resulting in spoken corpora becoming available for analysis. Discourse-level, corpora-based analyses of language first affected the teaching of reading and writing in English for special purposes classes (Lezberg & Hilferty, 1978), then the teaching of listening (Brown, 1978), and more recently the teaching of grammar (Conrad, 2000). The spoken language was the last skill to be influenced by corpus work (see McEnery & Wilson, 2001, for a more detailed history).

Corpora-based studies of spoken texts unveiled two major problems in the L2 teaching field. First, spoken and written English are dissimilar. Although they can differ quite significantly, most teaching of speaking is still based on the structure of the written language. Second, L2 teaching of speaking has been mostly based on assumptions about how people speak rather than on how they actually speak. As a result, some researchers questioned the content validity of L2 speaking classes (Carter & McCarthy, 1995; McCarthy & Carter, 2001; Richards, 1980). They suggested that L2 learners are exposed to dialogues that do not represent how people actually speak. They also claimed that these learners are mostly provided with rules of thumb that fail to account for why choices are made when people are engaged in unplanned spoken interactions in authentic situations (Hughes & McCarthy, 1998). Moreover, many elements that are a crucial part of conversation—hesitation, retrace and repair, and other elements that belong solely to the spoken language—are lacking in ESL/EFL curricula. Therefore, I focused my study on these criticisms and the actions that can be taken to respond to these concerns.

Procedures

After the review of the literature, I realized that the most suitable method of investigation for the purposes I had in mind was based on principles of corpus linguistics, in other words, analyzing a body of text. Corpus linguistics involves conducting frequency counts and a posterior analysis of the use of elements in authentically collected texts. After getting acquainted with how to use corpus linguistics, I realized that I needed to follow some preliminary procedures.

PRELIMINARY PROCEDURES

First, I decided on what inserts I would count. *The Longman Grammar of Spoken and Written English* (Biber et al., 1999), the largest study on American spoken English I found, had a chapter on conversation that contained a description of frequent elements. I chose to investigate the three most frequent discourse markers (inserts that do not interfere with the syntax of a sentence), namely, *well, you know,* and *I mean,* and the three most frequent conversational hedges (words or expressions used to avoid being exact), namely, *like, kind of,* and *sort of.*

As a classroom teacher, I lacked the resources to collect, transcribe, and store a spoken corpus of my own. I had to find a corpus of spoken English that contained unplanned interactions and included NS as well as NNS participants. *The Michigan Corpus of Academic Spoken English* (MICASE), compiled by the University of Michigan from 1997 to 2001 (Simpson, Briggs, Ovens, & Swales, 2002) and available online, met my needs. MICASE contains 196 hours of naturally occurring spoken American English totaling 1.7 million words. It contains native and nonnative discourse; has interactive discourse modes; contains information about speaker attributes, such as age, gender, academic role, and participants' L1; and is annotated with traditional orthography, thus making the corpus easy to read.

I then chose the interactions from the MICASE I would use. To ensure that the small corpus to be selected was sufficient to produce valuable and reliable results, I followed Biber's (Meyer, 2002) advice that for frequent linguistic items, a corpus of 2,000 words should be sufficient. I found three interactions in the MICASE corpus, an interview, a meeting, and an office meeting, which amounted to 31,835 words, totaled 219 minutes, and contained a population of 9 native and 9 nonnative speakers. Sixteen of the speakers were graduate students, and 2 were faculty members at the University of Michigan, suggesting a comparable cognitive level. Because the students were accepted as graduate students at the same university, they likely also had comparable levels of linguistic competence. Among the NNSs, 2 were NSs of Spanish, 1 of Japanese, 4 of Mandarin Chinese, and 2 of Korean. The length of their stay in the United States could not be controlled.

After choosing the corpus and the inserts I was going to count and analyze, I was ready to formulate the following research questions:

1. What is the difference in frequency of use of the discourse markers *well, you know,* and *I mean* between advanced L2 speakers and NSs of American English in three subcorpora of the MICASE?

2. What is the difference in frequency of use of the conversational hedges *like, kind of (kinda),* and *sort of (sorta)* between advanced L2 speakers and NSs of American English in three subcorpora of the MICASE?

3. If differences are found, are they significant?

4. Are the words chosen for this investigation used differently by NSs and NNSs?

To be able to count discourse markers and conversational hedges, I had to define the two terms clearly. The definition of discourse markers came from Biber et al. (1999), who defined them as inserts that may occur in initial, medial, or final positions in a turn or utterance, usually separate contiguous constituents, and may be used "(a) to signal a transition in the evolving progress of the conversation, and (b) to signal an interactive relationship between speaker, hearer, and message" (p. 1,086). Relevant examples from the corpus used are the following: "instead of, *you know,* to assist them"; "*Well,* I think one way to m- maybe make it easier is . . ."; "Yeah. *I mean,* that's just my take on it." Conversational hedges were defined as adverbs that show imprecision and can occur before nouns, verbs, adjectives, adverbs, or numbers. The following are examples from the corpus: "I want to have, *like,* three hours is good, for me to work on this"; "okay, yeah, his are um, *kinda* this handwriting"; "we did last week and just *sort of* put everything together."

After determining what discourse markers and conversational hedges were and which ones I would explore, I had to decide which instances of the specified inserts I would not count. Concerning the discourse markers *well, you know,* and *I mean,* I determined that I would count only the ones that were not part of the syntax of the sentence. Therefore, instances of the adverb *well* and of *I mean* and *you know* as part of the syntax of a clause followed by a complement clause (e.g., *Do* you know *the man that lives next to you? What* I mean *by that is that I want to see you*) were not part of the frequency count. Concerning the conversational hedges *like, kind of,* and *sort of,* I would count only those instances used before a verb, noun, adjective, adverb, or numbers to show inexactness. Therefore, the study would exclude *like* when used as a verb; with the meaning *for example* or *such as*; as a quotative to report what someone said (e.g., *and I went* like *what did you do, and she went* like *I didn't really want to do it*); to mark focus (e.g., *when I went to the store yesterday, I saw* like *this beautiful bracelet*); with the meaning *similar* (e.g., *so, it's gonna be hard when you get into those words* like *that, it's sorta hard, to make sure that you know that . . .*); as a hesitation device, when it has no specific meaning (e.g., *he* like *told me he wanted to go*); and within the phrases *something like that* or *anything like that*; as well as *kind of* or *sort of* as meaning *type*.

With a clear picture of what was going to be included and analyzed, I selected the software program I was going to use for the frequency count. Several software programs have been developed specifically for such studies. MonoConc Pro, which allows for words to be counted in an entire text, was used for the frequency count. Microsoft Word served in the analysis of use because it will identify the exact location of the word and highlight each instance of the word to reflect the context in which it was uttered.

One more step remained before the data analysis could start. Because the objective of the study was to compare NS discourse to NNS discourse, two separate corpora had to be built, one of NS utterances and one of NNS utterances. This was achieved by having each speaker's utterances isolated and placed into a separate file, thus producing 18 files. All utterances by unidentified or several speakers were eliminated so that each file contained only what the individual speaker had uttered. Thus I ended up with 9 files that made up the NS corpus and 9 files that made up the NNS corpus. I then calculated the number of words per corpus.

DATA ANALYSIS

First, the frequency count was done in each file in four steps. The inserts *well, you know, I mean, like, kind of,* and *sort of* were each given a specific color and highlighted accordingly before they were counted. The total number of tokens per insert identified in each file was entered into a table on its last page. Two packs containing the 18 files were prepared: one for an independent rater and one for me. Each rater crossed out with a black marker those tokens to be eliminated, counted the number of tokens left, and then entered them in the same table as tokens to be studied. Then we compared our tables and discussed the instances we disagreed on to arrive at a consensus. When both of us had identified the same tokens to be studied, their number was calculated and transformed into a percentage by dividing the number of tokens to be studied by the total number of words in that subcorpus. This procedure provided the frequency count of each discourse marker and conversational hedge in raw numbers and as a percentage for each participant. It also provided insight into how many of the items were used by all the NSs and all the NNSs included in the two corpora.

Second, in order to determine if the differences found between the two groups were significant, a majority-minority chi-square, which is used to decide if a given population has the majority of the categories (Thorndike & Dinnel, 2001) was figured, using the formula

$$\chi^2 = \frac{(\text{Maj} - \text{Min} - 1)^2}{\text{Maj} + \text{Min}}$$

with $df = 1$ and $p < .01$. For this type of chi-square, results are significant at $p = .05$ when $\chi^2 > 3.34$ and at $p = .01$ when $\chi^2 > 6.64$. The chi-squares were calculated considering each discourse marker and conversational hedge individually and considering them as a group.

Last, after the three quantitative questions were answered, I used Microsoft Word to address the qualitative question, namely: Are the words chosen for this investigation used differently by NSs and NNSs? I used the entire text of all three interactions and left highlighted only those tokens that were included in the count, and then I looked at each highlighted token. Every time I identified a use, I assigned it a number and entered its description in a table (see

Appendix A). After the analysis of use, I determined the frequency of each use per token, per file, and then per group, and calculated a majority-minority chi-square.

Results

QUANTITATIVE FINDINGS

The word count per group indicated that the NNSs spoke considerably less (22.84%) than the NSs (77.16%). The frequency count per insert per group, summarized in Figure 1, answers research questions 1 and 2, about the differences in frequency of use of discourse markers and conversational hedges between NNSs and NSs of English in the three subcorpora (an interview, a meeting, and an office meeting).

NSs used the discourse markers *well* and *you know* more frequently than NNSs, and *I mean* was used more frequently by NNSs. However, *I mean* was uttered by only two NNSs (both speakers of Mandarin), each using it 16 times, which may have skewed the data. The majority of the NNSs did not use *well* or *you know* at all, suggesting that these speakers' repertoire of choices was very limited, with *I mean* being used very frequently by two speakers. The test of significance revealed that the differences in frequency of use of the three discourse markers were all significant at the .01 level, with *I mean* being used more by NNSs and *well* and *you know* by NSs.

Even though the conversational hedge *like* was used by both groups with no significant difference, *kind of* and *sort of* were close to nonexistent in NNS discourse. Only one NS of Spanish used *sort of* once. Although conversational hedges in general were more frequent than discourse markers in NS discourse,

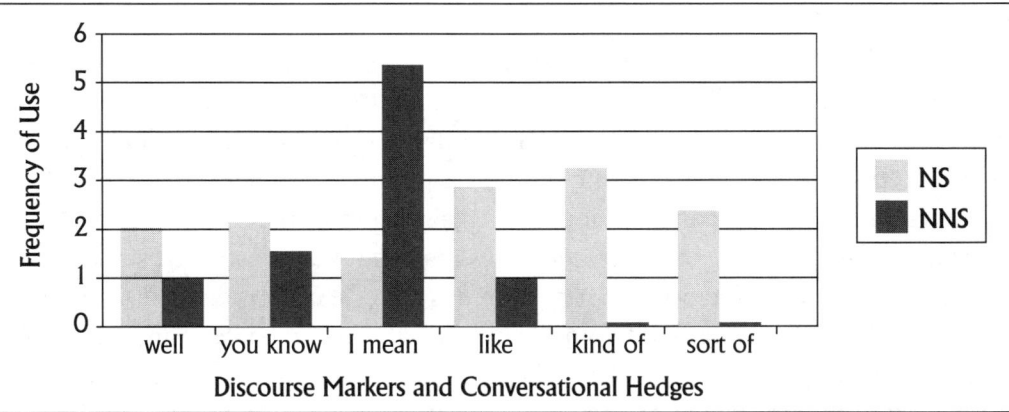

Figure 1. Frequency of use of discourse markers and conversational hedges for native speakers and nonnative speakers.

they were almost completely absent from NNS discourse (see Appendix B). The differences in frequency of use of *kind of* and *sort of* were significant at the .01 level. Thus, I found a clear answer to the following research question: If differences are found, are they significant? In this corpus, NSs used discourse markers and conversational hedges significantly more frequently than NNSs did.

QUALITATIVE FINDINGS

This section addresses the following research question: Are the words chosen for this investigation used differently by NSs and NNSs? Regarding the frequency of use of the discourse markers studied, out of the eight different uses of *well* in this corpus, five were found to have been used significantly more by NSs. Three of the latter were not present in the NNS corpus at all (see Appendix A, Table A1). Two uses of *you know* were significantly more frequent in NS discourse. The use of *you know* that was most frequently found in NS discourse, to gain processing time (see Appendix A, Table A2, No. 1), was rarely employed by NNSs, resulting in a significant difference at the .01 level. On the other hand, *you know* seemed to have been mostly used by NNSs in a more literal sense, that is, to check whether the hearer knew the information given, which did not produce significant results. Both groups used *I mean* with similar frequency for three purposes (see Appendix A, Table A3, Nos. 1, 2, and 3). However, one use of *I mean* (see Table A3, No. 4) was almost nonexistent in the NNS corpus, and the last use (see Table A3, No. 5) was used by NNSs comparatively less than by NSs. The differences found for uses 4 and 5 were significant at the .05 level.

Concerning the conversational hedges researched, *like* was the only insert that was used similarly by both groups, with no significant differences (see Appendix A, Table A4). Two out of the three uses of the conversational hedge *kind of (kinda)* were significant at the .01 level (see Appendix A, Table A5). The test of significance of the uses of the conversational hedge *sort of (sorta)* revealed a significant difference at the .01 level for all three uses of that insert (see Appendix A, Table A6).

The qualitative analysis of use (see Appendix C) shows that all the discourse markers and conversational hedges studied, except for *like*, were used variedly by NSs but in limited ways by NNSs. This analysis shows that although NSs and NNSs used some of the inserts in question in a similar manner, many uses of the discourse markers and conversational hedges studied were not part of the NNSs' language. The discourse markers and conversational hedges studied served a variety of important sociopragmatic functions (see Celce-Murcia & Olshtain, 2000, for details on pragmatic competence) as well as text-processing functions in NS discourse. For example, they enabled NSs to adjust their speaking according to whom they addressed and what they wanted to convey. They also helped NSs gain processing time while constructing their text in real time. The functions in question may affect the speakers' social relationships, the way they see language, and the way they see themselves. Consequently, the results of this study are likely to affect ESL and EFL teaching and learning in several ways, as indicated in the next section.

Reflection

My teaching has changed as a result of this study not only because of obvious factors—the fact that the final product provided me with enough empirical evidence to affect how and what I was teaching—but also because the books and articles I read throughout my review of the literature opened my eyes to issues I was not aware of before my review.

I realized that what I had been teaching and the order in which I presented material were based on the grammar of written English. I started to introduce modals, which are very frequent in English conversation, at the beginning of the program. When students learn the question *What's this?* They learn how to answer it by saying *It's* . . . or *It may/might/could/can be* . . . Also, I started teaching the differences between informal speaking and formal writing by, for example, teaching reduced forms, such as *gonna, wanna, gotta,* and *hafta.* I now familiarize students with the fragment as the unit of spoken discourse rather than the sentence. For instance, I have students respond to questions such as *What's your favorite color?* with the fragment *Yellow, and yours?* They are also taught basic fragments, such as *Sounds like a good idea* and *Love you.*

I noticed that much of the vocabulary students were encountering in my speaking classes was not frequent in unplanned, spoken conversations. I decided to teach frequent words and expressions, for instance, *though,* which is much more frequent than *but* in American conversation (Biber et al., 1999). These studies also revealed the importance of chunks, so I now expose students to unanalyzed chunks of language, that is, units that are stored whole and believed to assist fluency (see Lewis, 1993, 1997). Some examples are *What do you think? I'm not sure, I gotta go,* and *What's your favorite* . . . *?*

In addition, I realized that I needed to include more discourse-level activities in my teaching (for ideas on how to incorporate discourse-level language into L2 teaching, see Burns, Joyce, & Gollin, 1996; Riggenbach, 1999). Corpus work (see Biber et al., 1999) shows, for example, that *so* and *then* are the most frequent adverbial connectors in conversation, that *though* is more frequent than *but,* and that the fourth most common adverbial connector is *anyway.* Thus, I have started to teach students how to use these connectors in speaking in contrast to how they are used in writing.

I have become sensitive to the fact that dialogues in ESL textbooks are not typically based on authentic language and thus are not useful models for spoken language. Consequently, I have recorded many of my own dialogues to illustrate aspects of oral interaction. For instance, when teaching students how to leave messages on an instructor's answering device, the recording I used for teaching purposes was a message left on my answering machine by one of my colleagues.

As mentioned before, not only has the literature review phase affected my teaching, but so have the results of my study. The quantitative part revealed that even though all the NNSs were advanced-level speakers, their ability to use the discourse markers and conversational hedges researched was much below that of the NSs. Through the qualitative analysis, I realized how important processing strategies really are, because they assist the speaker in constructing, producing, and negotiating the language, as illustrated in the following exchange in my corpus (S = student):

S7: yeah
S2: okay
S7: yeah yeah. this wa- that was a big one.
S2: *well* n- so so like for the—you got my email about the noisy-or?
S7: yeah yeah
S2: okay

The insert *well* is being used to help the speaker gain processing time while speaking. Because speaking requires constructing language at the same time as speaking, a repertoire of time gaining (stalling) strategies facilitates construction. *Well* is one of the inserts that can be used for this purpose, and so can a number of others, as this study shows (see Appendix A, Table A1, A2, A3, and A6). Without stalling strategies, students likely will be unable to proceed with the processing of language in a timely manner. The processing strategies I have incorporated into my teaching are hesitating through the use of filled and unfilled pauses, such as *um, uh, well, you know*; backchanneling (used to confirm understanding and keep the speaker going while others are talking), such as *uh-huh, yeah, I see*; hedging (used to show inexactness), such as *things like that, sort of, kind of, -ish, around, about*; and retracing and repairing (used to repair slips of the tongue), such as *I mean*; among others.

This study showed me that many of the inserts were used for pragmatic purposes, and it therefore helped me discover the importance of sociopragmatic skills (Celce-Murcia & Olshtain, 2000), which relate to one's ability to be appropriate (see Bardovi-Harlig & Dörnyei, 1998, for a comparative study on pragmatic versus grammatical competence). A speaker is more likely to continue interacting with another when the cultural conversational rules are not broken (for an example, see Grice's maxims in Celce-Murcia & Olshtain, 2000) and even if the speaker exercises courtesy and politeness (Celce-Murcia & Olshtain, 2000). This has more to do with how something is said than with what is said. Discourse analysis in general and corpus linguistics studies in particular are very informative on which sociopragmatic tools are used by NSs to build interactions and negotiate meaning. For example,

A: . . . and how about removing this word?
B: I think this word is *kind of* important.
A: Oh, I see.

Speaker B used *kind of* to soften a disagreement with Speaker A. In my study (see Figure 1), softeners or conversational hedges were frequent among NSs. However, I have since noticed that few ESL textbooks model hedging techniques. Therefore, some of the sociopragmatic negotiating strategies I have included in my teaching are hedging (*like, sort of, kind of, -ish, things like that, stuff like that*); asking for clarification; asking for repetition; saying *no* politely; identifying when and why to use different levels of formality; identifying different registers; and starting, negotiating, and ending interactions appropriately.

As a result, I have redesigned my quizzes and tests to include prompts that elicit unplanned spoken language. This encourages students to employ tools that NSs use to aid them in processing, constructing, producing, and negotiating language. Furthermore, because students are overtly taught such devices as dysfluencies of the language, they are expected to produce those dysfluencies when being tested (see Brown, 1978). These changes have enriched my L2 learners by raising their awareness of differences between spoken and written modes of communication; enabling them to notice how the spoken language is actually produced; and helping them use strategies for coping with the difficulties of processing, constructing, producing, and negotiating unplanned spoken texts.

In conclusion, this experience has introduced me to the potential value of corpus material in my EFL and ESL classroom and has given me expertise at the research level. Carrying out this study has sharpened my ability to diagnose students' speaking needs. I can now observe students when interacting, identify discrepancies between their speaking skills and that of NSs, provide them with a treatment, and reflect on the results. Therefore, I am better equipped with information to help them identify problems related to their speaking skills and to design action plans. Moreover, I became aware that I can systematically investigate problems that I observe when teaching and then base decisions on data rather than on intuition alone. Also, in spite of all the difficulties that classroom teachers have due to their limited resources and other constraints, I have learned that teacher research is not only feasible but extremely informative because it feeds back into teachers' own teaching, making for better practitioners.

Eliana Santana-Williamson teaches at Southwestern Community College and part-time at Alliant International University, San Diego, California, in the United States.

Acknowledgment

I would like to thank Deana Alonso, Esther Alonso, Holly Wilson, Hedy McGarrell, and an anonymous reviewer for invaluable feedback.

Appendix A: Differences in Native and Nonnative Speakers' Use of Inserts

Tables A1, A2, A3, A4, A5, and A6 show all the uses of each insert found, the relevant raw number (f), the percentage per use and per group, and whether the difference in frequency of use between the two groups (χ^2) was significant or not. Because a minimum number of five instances in one group is required for this type of chi-square, some of the values could not be calculated (NP).

Table A1. Use of *Well* per Group, With Level of Significance of the Differences in Uses by Native and Nonnative Speakers

Use of *Well*	Native Speakers		Nonnative Speakers		χ^2
	f	%	f	%	
1. To offer/provide information	38	29.2	2	20.0	30.60*
2. To introduce a question	7	5.4	4	40.0	0.36
3. To self-repair previous utterances	3	2.3	1	10.0	0.25
4. To agree or disagree with a previous statement	38	29.2	1	10.0	33.20*
5. To reassure the hearer	5	3.8	0	0.0	5.00**
6. To emphasize the negativeness of an utterance	1	0.8	2	20.0	NP
7. To gain processing time	29	22.3	0	0.0	29.00*
8. As a quotative	10	7.7	0	0.0	10.00*

Note: *$p < .01.$ **$p < .05.$

Table A2. Use of *You Know* per Group, With Level of Significance of the Differences in Uses by Native and Nonnative Speakers

Use of *You Know*	Native Speakers		Nonnative Speakers		
	f	%	f	%	χ^2
1. To gain processing time	25	39.0	2	11.1	17.92*
2. To check whether the hearer shares background knowledge with the speaker	17	26.5	11	61.1	0.89
3. To explain a subject in more detail	8	12.5	2	11.1	2.50
4. To offer other options	8	12.5	1	5.5	4.00**
5. For self-repair	3	4.6	0	0.0	NP
6. To further criticisms	3	4.6	2	11.1	NP

*$p < .01$. **$p < .05$.

Table A3. Uses of *I Mean* per Group, With Level of Significance of the Differences in Uses by Native and Nonnative Speakers

Use of *I Mean*	Native Speakers		Nonnative Speakers		
	f	%	f	%	χ^2
1. To paraphrase what was just said	31	39.2	19	50.0	2.42
2. To reinforce the importance of an utterance	8	10.1	4	10.5	0.75
3. For self-repair	5	6.3	3	7.9	0.13
4. To explain and soften a negative statement or disagreement	9	11.4	1	2.6	4.9**
5. To gain processing time	26	32.9	11	28.9	5.29**

**$p < .05$.

Table A4. Use of *Like* per Group, With Level of Significance of the Differences in Uses by Native and Nonnative Speakers

Use of *Like*	Native Speakers		Nonnative Speakers		χ^2
	f	%	f	%	
1. To express inexact quantity, amount, or length	5	50.0	13	86.6	2.7
2. To express uncertainty about the information	3	30.0	1	6.6	NP
3. To hedge a word	2	20.0	1	6.6	NP

Table A5. Use of *Kind of (Kinda)* per Group, With Level of Significance of the Differences in Uses by Native and Nonnative Speakers

Use of *Kind of (Kinda)*	Native Speakers		Nonnative Speakers		χ^2
	f	%	f	%	
1. To emphasize an idea	18	60.0	0	0.0	16.0*
2. To soften a word, comment, or criticism because of its negative connotation	10	33.3	0	0.0	8.1*
3. To offer a suggestion without imposing	2	6.6	0	0.0	NP

*$p < .01$.

Table A6. Use of *Sort of (Sorta)* per Group, With Level of Significance of the Differences in Uses by Native and Nonnative Speakers

Use of *Sort of (Sorta)*	Native Speakers		Nonnative Speakers		χ^2
	f	%	f	%	
1. To soften a word, comment, or criticism because of its negative connotation	13	18.3	1	100.0	8.64*
2. To offer a suggestion without imposing	34	47.9	0	0.0	32.00*
3. To gain processing time	24	33.8	0	0.0	22.00*

*$p < .01$.

Appendix B: Total Use of Discourse Markers and Conversational Hedges

Total Raw Counts for Use of Discourse Markers and Conversational Hedges by Native and Nonnative Speakers and Their Significance

Marker or Hedge	Native Speakers		Nonnative Speakers		χ^2
	f	%	f	%	
Well	128	2.19	10	1.04	116*
You know	64	2.28	18	1.58	24.69*
I mean	79	1.56	38	5.5	13.67*
Like	10	2.95	15	1.1	0.64
Kind of (kinda)	29	3.39	0	0	27.03*
Sort of (sorta)	71	2.48	1	0.05	66.13*

*p < .01

Appendix C: Level of Significance of the Uses of *Well, You Know, I Mean, Like, Kind of,* and *Sort of*

Marker or Hedge	Significant	Not Significant	NP
Well	1*, 4*, 5**, 7*, 8*	2, 3	6
You know	1*, 4**	2, 3	5, 6
I mean	4**, 5**	1, 2, 3	0
Like	0	1	2, 3
Kind of	1*, 2*	0	3
Sort of	1*, 2*, 3*	0	0

*p < .01. **p < .05.

CHAPTER 13

Learning How to Learn: Metacognitive Strategy Training With Beginning EFL Students (*Costa Rica*)

Sharon L. Springer

Issue

When I took tests in high school, I would make inconspicuous little marks by the answers I was unsure of, so that when I got my test back I could check how I had done on those answers. Now that I am a teacher, I love to see my students do that, because it tells me that they know how sure they are of their answers and that they at least have the intention of following up on the ones they were not so sure of. It gives me a little window into their mental processes and lets me see where they are in terms of security as well as in terms of knowing how to learn.

One of my favorite student answers on an exam occurred within a complete-the-sentence exercise on infinitives of purpose to see if my Spanish-speaking students would use *to* instead of *for* (a direct translation of Spanish). A creative student completed the sentence "You use an umbrella . . ." with "to hit a ~~theef thefe thei~~ dog." I very much appreciated that the student did not white out the whole process, because it told me about her ability to plan an amusing answer (she was certainly not the type of person who goes around hitting dogs with umbrellas), decide if her plan was working, and in the end make the necessary changes. That is the essence of metacognition: planning what to do, monitoring one's progress while doing it, modifying one's plan if necessary, and, finally, evaluating how it went.

Metacognition, defined most accessibly by Anderson (2002) as "thinking about thinking" (p. 1), has been emphasized as an important factor in the success of learning endeavors in general, and especially in language learning. Metacognitive learning strategies help students manage their learning processes, a key element in maximizing results and minimizing frustration along the way. Chamot, Barnhardt, El-Dinary, and Robbins (1999) go as far as to assert that "metacognition, or reflecting on one's own thinking and learning, is the hallmark of the successful learner" (p. 2). Thus, it stands to reason that metacognitive strategies would be crucial to the success of today's university students, who, perhaps more than any other generation, will need skills oriented toward helping them on their journey of lifelong learning.

EARTH University, located in the humid tropics of Costa Rica, is a small, residential agricultural college with an emphasis on sustainable development and a student body of approximately 400 students, mainly from the tropical zone of Latin America (from southern Mexico to Paraguay). Given that EARTH's goal is to identify young people, particularly from rural areas, with leadership potential and provide them with an education that will enable them to return to their communities as agents for change, the student population is, in many respects, quite different from that of a more traditional university. In the comprehensive admissions process, grades are taken into account but are not the determining factor, and some of the students who enter have standardized test scores that would be considered quite low for admission to many other programs. The process is designed to look for leadership skills, social consciousness, and academic potential, with the understanding that many of the students in the target population have not had access to a high-quality education and therefore may not have high test scores.

Students at EARTH take nine required trimesters of English, starting in their second trimester of university studies. A placement exam is administered during their first trimester, and traditionally about 50% of the students are placed as beginners, having had generally only rudimentary high school English. English level tends to be a fairly accurate indicator of socioeconomic status and educational background, meaning that the 50% who place in the beginning-level group tend to be the poorer students from rural areas. They also tend to have the weakest educational backgrounds, often coming from educational systems based on rote memorization to pass exams. Although they are generally animated and quite willing to participate, they typically see English as an exercise to be completed in their first language in order to get the right answer but not actually to attempt to communicate in the process. In many cases, they do not venture far beyond the complete-the-exercise stage, and they tend to see their learning as something that happens in class, directed by the teacher.

These beginning English students (with all the characteristics just described) are typically at the highest risk for failure in a university system that encourages learning by doing and the application of learning to real-life situations. Although EARTH's admissions process offers a rare opportunity to students who in many cases would not otherwise be able to pursue a college education, it is important to bear in mind that if these students are not encouraged to learn how to learn, then they are likely to be at a considerable disadvantage in the university system. As a result of the type of education they have received, these students are often lacking in the learning strategies that are so crucial for their college success. They may have some strategies that they learned to use in high school, but they often do not know how or when to use them in order to get the maximum benefit. Furthermore, they may be reluctant to try out new strategies, preferring instead to stick with a familiar one, without considering whether it is working well. It stands to reason that such students could benefit from training in the use of metacognitive learning strategies, to improve not just their learning of English, but their learning in general.

It is for this reason that I decided to explore the incorporation of learning strategy training with a strong metacognitive component into my beginning-level English class. Considering the language level of the students and the complexity of the concepts, such training would necessarily have to be carried out in Spanish. However, my previous experiences had shown that the inclusion of some informal discussions about learning strategies held in Spanish tended to decrease students' willingness to use English for routine classroom interactions (e.g., asking what words mean, asking for repetition, asking to borrow things from classmates), despite explanations as to why Spanish was being used for the discussions. In the end, the students seemed to see it as evidence that it was acceptable to speak Spanish in class. Thus, the question arose as to whether the incorporation of strategy training would outweigh the decrease in exposure to English (less time dedicated to English practice at the expense of strategy training in Spanish and less perceived pressure to speak only English) and lead to improved student performance. Along these lines, Cohen (1998) explained that although initial strategy training is time-consuming, "ideally the learners will move through the curriculum more expediently, so this should make up for the outlay of time in training them" (p. 103).

As noted, the topic of learning strategies had been incorporated into beginning-level English classes in the past, and it always seemed to generate a fair amount of interest on the part of the students. However, I had always been curious about the extent to which such discussions had a real impact on the students, and I had nagging doubts about the potential confusion that my speaking Spanish with them seemed to cause. Although I firmly believed in the importance of learning strategies—particularly metacognitive strategies—in the language learning process, I wanted to explore their place in my teaching more systematically. Thus, I hoped that researching the incorporation of learning strategy training in my classroom would allow me to answer several key questions relating to what I believed about language teaching and learning and how that affected my classroom practice. I wondered how my students would react to strategy training. Would my focus on metacognition increase their strategy use? Would it result in improved performance in English? Along the same lines, I wanted to determine if speaking Spanish during the strategy-training sessions would hinder the progress of my beginning-level students or if it would be a worthwhile investment in their learning process.

Background Literature

Several key issues should be taken into account in learning strategy training endeavors. One is the need to link training not only to improved strategy use but also to improved performance. Another is the degree to which strategy training is integrated into the language class. Finally, the question of who carries out the training is crucial. These issues are briefly addressed in this section.

Although a good body of descriptive and correlational research has been carried out with the aim of understanding strategy use by language learners according to variables such as proficiency level, age, culture, and gender, more recently the focus has shifted towards strategy instruction and its implications (Chamot et al., 1999). Still, many studies have focused on the strategy gains that resulted from training, but without tying such gains to performance improvements. To this end, Gu (as cited in Cohen, 1998) pointed out the lack of definitive results regarding the effects of strategy use on language performance. In Bedell and Oxford's (1996) review of 36 learning strategy studies from around the world, very few of them considered the effect that increased strategy use had on performance. Finally, although Flaitz and Feyten (1996) cited various studies that looked at the effects of strategy training on performance, they also reminded us that "while there are indications that strategy instruction in the language learning classroom can lead to greater achievement, the research community has not as yet proven that there is a consistently positive effect *every* time" (p. 212).

Education researchers have various opinions about whether strategy training should be done separately or integrated into the regular language course, and if it is incorporated into the course, whether it should be explicit (Chamot et al., 1999; Cohen, 1998; Dadour & Robbins, 1996; Flaitz & Feyten, 1996; O'Malley & Chamot, 1990; Oxford & Leaver, 1996). Although some researchers argue that strategy training conducted separately may facilitate students' subsequent application of strategies to different contexts, most authors seem to favor integrated strategy training. As far as the second issue goes, there is general support in the literature for the idea of explicit versus implicit, or blind, strategy training, in which students are prompted to use certain strategies without necessarily being aware of what they are doing or why they are doing it. Researchers have questioned the transferability of such induced strategies and generally favor an approach explicitly teaching students how the strategy works, why it is useful, and in what other situations it can be used. Here, the importance of metacognition in helping students choose, orchestrate, and evaluate strategies comes into play in effective strategy instruction.

Anderson (2002) stated that "the use of metacognitive strategies ignites one's thinking and can lead to more profound learning and improved performance, especially among learners who are struggling" (p. 1). Anderson and Vandergrift (1996) found metacognitive strategies to be the main difference between successful and unsuccessful learners, and they went on to assert that "given that the use of metacognitive strategies, particularly comprehension monitoring, appears to be crucial for successful learners, teaching strategies should foster the growth of metacognition among students" (p. 17). It would seem that the metacognitive component of strategy training is vital for the other components to be used to their maximum advantage.

Various authors mention the importance of having regular classroom teachers carry out strategy training if it is to be effective and sustained (Cohen, 1998; Flaitz & Feyten, 1996; O'Malley, Chamot, Stewner-Manzanares, Russo, & Küpper, 1985; Yang, 1996). In my study, I was the regular classroom teacher, strategy trainer, and researcher. This combined role provided for a high degree of consistency but also necessitated additional controls to ensure the study's validity.

Procedures

The participants were 49 first-year students of beginning-level English, divided into two sections. I taught one section using the communicative approach and the other section using a methodology combining the communicative approach with integrated learning strategy training. Although I took on the role of trainer and researcher, I was the regular classroom teacher in both cases. The study was quasi-experimental because students could not be randomly assigned to the two sections as a result of scheduling constraints. However, in each section, students were drawn from two different blocks, with each block being the result of a carefully balanced assignment process carried out by the university, taking into account variables such as country of origin, socioeconomic status, age, gender, and rural or urban upbringing. Analysis of the two sections of beginning English did not show important differences with regard to age, previous exposure to English, rural or urban upbringing, type of high school (public or private, technical or academic), or country of origin.

I collected baseline data during Level 1 (the students' first trimester of English), including students' final exam scores (both oral and written) and a profile of their initial strategy use, as determined by Oxford's Strategic Inventory for Language Learning, or SILL (Version 7.0, 1989, reproduced in Oxford, 1990). The SILL is a Likert-type questionnaire that has been widely used in language learning strategy research and provides information on six categories of strategy use (memory, cognitive, compensation, metacognitive, affective, and social). It was important for students to have had some time in the language classroom before being asked about their use of learning strategies, so that their responses would actually be grounded in their language learning behavior in university English classes, rather than being hypothetical beliefs about what they *would* do. For that reason, students took the SILL toward the end of Level 1. Along with final exam data, it provided an initial portrait of each group. Groups were checked for equivalency in both areas (strategy use and grades) at the end of Level 1.

I carried out the learning strategy training in Level 2 (the students' second 15-week trimester of English). Students received 3 hours of English per week, and for the treatment group I incorporated strategy training into regular classroom activities and integrated it with course content. Although training was mainly metacognitive, the executive nature of metacognition in controlling and monitoring the use of other types of strategies meant that other strategies were also addressed in the process. The training consisted of various formats, including

- Class discussions as to where, when, and how the content being studied might be useful (e.g., that they could use questions about talents and abilities, together with vocabulary for sports and hobbies, to strike up conversations with English-speaking interns at the student center).

- Discussions about which new vocabulary items were most relevant for them and thus deserved greater attention in the learning process (e.g., the vocabulary for sports played in their countries or in which they had a particular interest, such as soccer or basketball, was more useful to them than the vocabulary for rugby, which they did not play and would probably never discuss with anyone).

- Presentations of different steps in the learning process (e.g., setting learning goals, selecting appropriate learning strategies, monitoring strategy use, evaluating strategy use, and learning).

- Analogies related to the learning process (e.g., taking a trip and knowing where one is going, how far it is, what kind of transportation will be needed, and what kind of clothing one should take).

- Modeling of strategy use during different types of classroom activities.

- Sharing of strategies that students used to accomplish different learning goals (e.g., to learn vocabulary items or to improve pronunciation).

- Brainstorming sessions as to what kind of strategies could be applied prior to starting challenging tasks.

- Mini-self-evaluations after certain activities (including individual exercises, pair work, whole class activities, and formal evaluations).

- Discussions as to why certain activities were carried out the way they were and what the benefits were (e.g., talking about why they were asked to brainstorm a list of potentially useful vocabulary and grammar structures before starting a conversational activity, and how that aided them during the activity).

Although the trimester is 15 weeks long, strategy training actually consisted of only 11 weeks, after adjusting for final exams, field trips, and other institutional activities that affected the school calendar. During the experimental period, members of the control group received their regular English instruction without the learning strategy training.

At the end of Level 2, I collected final data on strategy use as well as oral and written performance. I had students take the SILL again to determine final strategy use and respective gains in strategy use for both groups. I obtained information on written performance by means of the students' regular final exam, which, for purposes of the study, was graded by two independent specialists. Interrater reliability was high (0.97), and I used an average of the two grades as the students' final written scores. I measured oral performance by having students carry out an interactive task in pairs during the last week of class. The task consisted of an information-gap activity in which students had to describe one out of four similar drawings to their partners, and their partners had to mark which drawing was being described. The partners took turns, with each describing three drawings and marking three drawings. The exercise represented a considerable challenge for the students, and they undertook it with enthusiasm, despite the fact that they were told the activity would not be counted toward their class grade. The exercises were videotaped and later graded by the same specialists who had graded the written exams. Interrater reliability was 0.70, and again an average of the two scores became the students' final oral scores.

Once I had collected all the data, I determined posttreatment differences in strategy use (in each of the SILL's six categories) between the treatment and control groups using analysis of covariance (ANCOVA) to adjust for initial differences detected in the baseline data from Level 1. I then performed t tests (pre- and posttreatment) to determine in which categories of strategy use students had made significant improvements. Stepwise regression was performed to identify significant predictors of oral and written performance. A limiting factor in this study, because as little as possible was done to disturb the normal class routine, was that the written performance measures were the students' regular final exams for Level 1 and Level 2. Each exam, therefore, reflected the particular content of the course in question. It would have been interesting to be able to perform an ANCOVA on students' written grades to adjust for initial differences between the groups as well as to be able to correlate strategy gains with performance gains. However, a standard measure would have had to be introduced as pre- and posttests in addition to the students' regular course exams.

Results

The first research question addressed whether the focus on metacognition in the classroom would increase strategy use. The treatment group showed significant gains in cognitive and compensation strategies ($p < .05$ and $p < .01$, respectively), with gains approaching significance for memory strategies ($p = .075$) as well. Surprisingly, the control group showed significant gains in all strategy categories. Results of the ANCOVA performed to adjust for initial differences in strategy use showed that the only difference nearing significance between the treatment and control groups after treatment was in memory strategies ($p = .055$), in favor of the treatment group. Nevertheless, overall differences in strategy gains between the treatment and control groups proved not to be significant. In other words, although each group experienced certain gains, neither group made more significant gains than the other in any strategy-use category.

Even though strategy training seemed to have influenced certain categories of strategy use for the treatment group, the control group's unexpected increase in all categories of strategy use after instruction is quite perplexing. Interestingly enough, Cohen, Weaver, and Li (1998) also reported unexplained improvements in a control group, with one possible explanation being the power of suggestion represented by the strategies questionnaire students filled out (in other words, they may have been inspired to act by reading some of the items), but as they point out, it seems unlikely that such limited contact would have any substantial results. Another potential factor is that because EARTH is a residential campus with a small student body, students are in constant contact with each other. It is possible that there was some transfer from the treatment students when they studied with control students outside class.

The second research question addressed whether or not the focus on metacognition in the classroom would result in improved student performance, with performance being examined on oral and written measures. No differences were found between the treatment and control groups regarding their oral evaluation scores, either at the outset or after the treatment period. On the other hand, the control group started out significantly higher ($p \leq .01$) and ended up significantly higher ($p \leq .001$) in terms of written exam grades. Although initial differences on the written exam could not be controlled for, because of the limitations previously mentioned, the gap between the averages of the two groups on the written measure was similar (11 points of difference in Level 1 and 12 points in Level 2, out of 100 points). Thus, there did not appear to be any significant changes in the position of one group with respect to the other. This would seem to suggest that there was no difference in the results in performance achieved by either of the two teaching methods.

Although the strategy training method did not result in greater student achievement than the traditional communicative method, the control group's unexplained gains in strategy use should be taken into account. This factor could certainly influence interpretations regarding the results of strategy training. In terms of informing future practice regarding the incorporation of strategy training, the following question remains: Is increased strategy use (whether or not it was the result of strategy training) related to student performance? Should greater use turn out to be related to higher student performance, this would indicate that attempting to increase students' strategy use through systematic training is a worthwhile endeavor in terms of improving classroom practice and increasing learning opportunities.

To that end, stepwise regression was performed in order to identify significant predictors of performance for each group. In the case of the control group, no significant predictors of written performance were found based on strategy use. For oral performance, metacognitive strategy use turned out to be the only significant predictor ($p < .05$). The control group showed significant gains in metacognitive strategy use after treatment, and this category also ranked highest for strategy use by the control group in both pre- and postinstruction measures.

With the treatment group, metacognitive strategy use was found to be the only significant predictor of written performance ($p < .05$). In the case of the treatment group, although metacognitive strategy use did not show significant gains during the strategy training period, it did start out and end up as one of the highest categories of strategy use for the treatment group. On the other hand, memory and cognitive strategy use turned out to be significant predictors of oral performance ($p < .05$ and $p < .01$, respectively). Cognitive strategies showed significant increases during the strategy training period, and memory strategies approached significance.

I found it interesting that metacognitive strategy use was the only significant predictor across groups (of oral performance for the control group, and of written performance for the treatment group). Furthermore, metacognitive strategies turned out to be the only significant predictor of performance for the control group. In the case of the treatment group, there was a differentiation in the category of strategies that served as predictors, depending on the type of task. Metacognitive strategies predicted written performance in the treatment group, and memory and cognitive strategies were significant for this group's oral performance.

It is encouraging to see that the metacognitive strategies that I believed to be crucial for student success, whether or not they were influenced by the strategy training, were in fact shown to be positively linked to student performance. As noted, strategies showing interesting pre- to postinstruction gains for the treatment group turned out to be significant predictors of oral performance, and this relationship supports the role of strategy training in fostering opportunities for student learning. It will be important for future research to continue examining the implementation of strategy training, as well as the role of metacognitive strategies in particular, in the interest of determining the impact each one has on student learning.

Finally, I looked at the third research question, which addressed the use of Spanish during strategy sessions. Although strategy training did not result in higher performance, neither did reduced exposure to English (as a consequence of strategy training) seem to have a negative effect on the treatment group. That, in combination with the fact that certain strategies were found to be good predictors of performance, would seem to confirm that the investment in carrying out strategy training with beginners is worthwhile, even when it must be carried out in the students' native language.

Although the use of Spanish did not seem to hinder students' progress, I believe that certain improvements could be made to the process. For example, students did not seem to clearly understand the rationale behind Spanish use, even though I explained at the beginning of the treatment period that strategy work would be carried out in Spanish, and I always prefaced strategy sessions with an explanation of why the learning process was being discussed. When I asked students towards the end of the treatment period if they could identify specifically when and why Spanish was being used, very few were able to do so. Therefore, for future strategy training endeavors, I would consider measures to reduce potential confusion, clarify expectations, and maximize students' willingness to speak English for regular classroom interactions outside of strategy sessions.

One unexpected result relating to how students reacted to strategy training came from the standard university course evaluations at the end of the experimental period. Although course evaluations were quite positive for both groups, students in the treatment group rated the course higher overall than did the control group. As can be expected, responses were consistent across the two groups in terms of aspects such as teacher punctuality and preparedness. However, the treatment group felt that the course was a more worthwhile investment of their time, that their interest was stimulated to a greater degree, that they were capable of showing that they had met the course objectives (despite the fact that their written grades were lower), and that the course had enabled them to solve real-world problems. Real-world application is traditionally a notoriously low scorer for beginning-level English, especially in the context of the students' agronomy major, which has a heavily practical, hands-on focus. Other interesting differences included the degree to which students felt that they were encouraged to make suggestions about the development of the course and that their suggestions were taken into consideration. Suggestions were neither particularly encouraged nor discouraged, and, interestingly enough, students in neither group actually made any suggestions. Apparently, however, through class conversations the treatment group felt that they were being heard and validated. Finally, although the same kinds of oral and written evaluations were applied to both groups, the treatment group rated them as being a better reflection of course objectives and as stimulating their ability to think and reason. To that end, the consciousness-raising aspect of the strategy training seemed to have had an impact on students' awareness of why the course was carried out the way it was.

Reflection

Even though the results were not definitive, I feel confident that the incorporation of strategy training in my classroom was a positive process. In addition to learning more about students' reactions to learning strategy training, I was able to address some of the reservations I had about the place of Spanish in my classroom. As a result of this exploration, I will be able to make improvements in the process the next time around, in terms of strategy instruction and the research process. For example, I could clarify the role of Spanish in the classroom to maximize learning opportunities and ensure that the investment in training time is a profitable one. In addition, considering the positive reaction of the students to the strategy training component, I plan to involve them in providing ideas for subsequent training endeavors. In terms of the research design, applying a pre- and postinstruction measure of performance (other than the regular final exam for the course) should shed more light on the performance gains experienced by the students as well as their relationship to strategy gains.

It is important to recognize that this process may be a longer-term investment; therefore, these groups of students will be followed during their studies at EARTH to see what the long-term effects on performance or strategy use may be. The participants were quite interested in the process, and some of them periodically ask me when the final results of the study will be ready. I have promised them that I will save the videotape of their interactive task, and we can watch it together before their graduation (in 3 years) to see how far they have come.

My impression is that the students enjoyed learning about their learning process and sensed that I was interested in their learning. I know that injecting the strategy training component into my course reenergized my teaching and made the whole process more exciting because it felt as though we were constructing something together. The experience made me realize that those nagging doubts I sometimes have about my classroom practices are really action research questions ready to be answered. Rather than producing insecurity or frustration, those doubts can be a source of curiosity and inspiration. Having started down this road, I cannot imagine just going back to teaching without simultaneously exploring the fascinating world that is my classroom.

Sharon Springer teaches at EARTH University in Guácimo de Limón, Costa Rica.

References

Abedi, J. (2002). Assessment and accommodations of English language learners: Issues, concerns, and recommendations. *Journal of School Improvement, 3*(1), 83–89.

Abello-Contesse, C. (2005). *The "critical period" and early start in FL/L2 teaching*. Paper presented at World Congress of International Association of Applied Linguistics, AILA 2005, Madison, WI.

Alderson, J. C., & Hamp-Lyons, L. (1996). TOEFL preparation courses: A study of washback. *Language Testing, 13,* 280–297.

Alderson, J. C., & Wall, D. (1993). Does washback exist? *Applied Linguistics, 14,* 115–129.

Allan, M. (1985). *Teaching English with video*. London: Longman.

American heritage dictionary of the English language (4th ed.). (2000). Boston: Houghton Mifflin. Retrieved December 7, 2006, from http://www.bartleby.com/61/

Anderson, N. J. (2002). *The role of metacognition in second language teaching and learning*. Washington, DC: ERIC Clearinghouse on Languages and Linguistics.

Anderson, N. J., & Vandergrift, L. (1996). Increasing metacognitive awareness in the L2 classroom by using think-aloud protocols and other verbal report formats. In R. L. Oxford (Ed.), *Language learning strategies around the world: Cross-cultural perspectives* (Technical Report No. 13, pp. 3–18). Honolulu: University of Hawai'i, Second Language Teaching & Curriculum Center.

Anton, M. (1996). Using ethnographic techniques in classroom observation: A study of success in a foreign language class. *Foreign Language Annals, 29,* 551–561.

Appel, R., & Vermeer, A. (1998). Speeding up second language vocabulary acquisition of minority children. *Language and Education, 12,* 159–173.

Asher, J., & Price, B. (1967). The learning strategy of total physical response: Some age differences. *Child Development, 38,* 1219–1227.

Auerbach, E. (1993). Reexamining English-only in the ESL classroom. *TESOL Quarterly, 27,* 9–32.

Bailey, K. M. (1996). Working for washback: A review of the washback concept in language testing. *Language Testing, 13,* 257–279.

Baker, P. S. (2003). *The electronic introduction to Old English.* Retrieved December 7, 2006, from http://www.wmich.edu/medieval/resources/IOE/index.html

Bardovi-Harlig, K., & Dörnyei, Z. (1998). Do language learners recognize pragmatic violations? Pragmatic versus grammatical awareness in instructed L2 learning. *TESOL Quarterly, 32,* 233–262.

Barletta, N., Bovea, V., Delgado, P., Del Villar, L., Lozano, A., May, O., et al. (2002). *Comprensión y competencias lectoras en estudiantes universitarios* [Reading comprehension and competences in university students]. Barranquilla, Colombia: Ediciones UniNorte.

Basturkmen, H. (2002). Learner observation of, and reflection on, spoken discourse: An approach for teaching academic speaking. *TESOL Journal, 11*(2), 26–30.

Beck, I., & McKeown, M. (2001). Text talk: Capturing the benefits of read-aloud experiences for young children. *Reading Teacher, 55,* 10–20.

Beck, I., McKeown, M., & Kucan, L. (2002). *Bringing words to life: Robust vocabulary instruction.* New York: Guilford Press.

Bedell, D. A., & Oxford, R. L. (1996). Cross-cultural comparisons of language learning strategies in the People's Republic of China and other countries. In R. L. Oxford (Ed.), *Language learning strategies around the world: Cross-cultural perspectives* (Technical Report No. 13, pp. 47–60). Honolulu: University of Hawai'i, Second Language Teaching & Curriculum Center.

Benesch, S. (2001). *Critical English for academic purposes: Theory, politics and practice.* Mahwah, NJ: Lawrence Erlbaum.

Biber, D., Johansson, S., Leech, G., Conrad, S., & Finegan, E. (1999). *Longman grammar of spoken and written English.* London: Pearson Education.

Bowler, E., McCollum, D., Fried, P., Ackley, K., Hausmann, E., & Weidenman, L. (1994). *Literature: Bronze.* Englewood Cliffs, NJ: Prentice Hall.

Boyle, O. W., & Peregoy, S. F. (1990). Literacy scaffolds: Strategies for first and second language readers and writers. *Reading Teacher, 44,* 194–200.

Brett, A., Rothlein, L., & Hurley, M. (1996). Vocabulary acquisition from listening to stories and explanations of target words. *Elementary School Journal, 96,* 415–422.

Britton, J. (1970). *Language and learning.* London: Penguin Books.

Britton, J. N., Burgess, T., Martin, N., McLeod, A., & Rosen, H. (1975). *The development of writing abilities.* London: Macmillan.

Brown, G. (1978). Understanding spoken language. *TESOL Quarterly, 12,* 271–283.

Brown, H. D. (1994). *Teaching by principles: An interactive approach to language pedagogy.* Upper Saddle River, NJ: Prentice Hall Regents.

Burns, A. (1999). *Collaborative action research for English language teachers.* Cambridge, England: Cambridge University Press.

Burns, A., Joyce, H., & Gollin, S. (1996). *"I see what you mean": Using spoken discourse in the classroom: A book for teachers.* Sydney, Australia: The National Centre for Language Teaching and Research.

Burton, J. (2000). Learning from discourse analysis in the ESOL classroom. *TESOL Journal, 9,* 24–27.

Carey, S. (1978). The child as word learner. In M. Halle, J. Bresnan, & G. Miller (Eds.), *Linguistic theory and psychological reality* (pp. 264–293). Cambridge, MA: MIT Press.

Carlson, N. (1984). *Harriet's Halloween candy.* London, England: Puffin.

Carter, R., & McCarthy, M. (1995). Grammar and the spoken language. *Applied Linguistics, 16,* 141–158.

Celce-Murcia, M., & Olshtain, E. (2000). *Discourse and context in language teaching: A guide for language teachers.* Cambridge, England: Cambridge University Press.

Chamot, A. U., Barnhardt, S., El-Dinary, P. B., & Robbins, J. (1999). *The learning strategies handbook.* White Plains, NY: Addison Wesley Longman.

Chapple, L., & Curtis, A. (2000). Content-based instruction in Hong Kong: Student responses to film. *System, 28,* 419–433.

Cheng, L. (1998). Impact of a public English examination change on students' perceptions and attitudes toward their English learning. *Studies in Educational Evaluation, 24,* 279–301.

Christie, P. (2003). *Language in Jamaica.* Kingston, Jamaica: Arawak.

Clennell, C. (1999). Promoting pragmatic awareness and spoken discourse skills with EAP classes. *ELT Journal, 53*(2), 83–91.

Cliff, M. (1988). A journey into speech. In R. Simonson & S. Walker (Eds.), *Multicultural literacy* (pp. 57–62). St. Paul, MN: Graywolf Press.

Cochran-Smith, M., & Lytle, S. (1992). *Inside/outside: Teacher research and knowledge.* New York: Teachers College Press.

Cohen, A. D. (Ed.). (1998). *Strategies in learning and using a second language.* New York: Longman.

Cohen, A. D., Weaver, S. J., & Li, T.-Y. (1998). The impact of strategies-based instruction on speaking a foreign language. In A. D. Cohen, *Strategies in learning and using a second language* (pp. 107–156). New York: Longman.

Conrad, S. (2000). Will corpus linguistics revolutionize grammar teaching in the 21st century? *TESOL Quarterly, 34,* 548–560.

Corson, D. (1997). The learning and use of academic English words. *Language Learning, 47,* 671–718.

Creswell, J. (1994). *Research design: Qualitative and quantitative.* London: Sage.

Crookes, G. (1993). Action research for second language teachers: Going beyond teacher research. *Applied Linguistics, 14,* 130–144.

Crookes, G. (1998). The relationship between second and foreign language teachers and research. *TESOL Journal, 7*(3), 6–11.

Crusan, D. (2005, March). Missing elements in MA TESOL curriculum? *HEIS TESOL Community Newsletter,* 2–4.

Curtis, A. (2003). Making the most of movies in the ESL classroom. *Contact: Newsletter of TESL Ontario, 29*(3), 29–32.

Dadour, E. S., & Robbins, J. (1996). University-level studies using strategy instruction to improve speaking ability in Egypt and Japan. In R. L. Oxford (Ed.), *Language learning strategies around the world: Cross-cultural perspectives* (Technical Report No. 13, pp. 157–166). Honolulu: University of Hawai'i, Second Language Teaching & Curriculum Center.

Dantas-Whitney, M. (2003). *ESL students as ethnographers: Co-researching communicative practices in an academic discourse community.* Unpublished doctoral dissertation, Oregon State University, Corvallis.

Dasgupta, G., & Redfern, J. (1997). *Reading writing: Skills for ESL.* Toronto: ITP Nelson.

Devine, J. (1993). The role of metacognition in second language reading and writing. In J. G. Carson & I. Leki (Eds.), *Reading in the composition classroom: Second language perspectives* (pp. 105–127). Boston: Heinle & Heinle.

Dewey, J. (1910/1997). *How we think.* Boston: D. C. Heath.

Donley, K. M. (2000). Film for fluency. *Forum, 38*(3), 24–29 [Online article]. Retrieved October 8, 2006, from http://exchanges.state.gov/forum/vols/vol38/no2/p24.htm

Dutra, D., & Mello, H. (2001). Refletindo sobre o processo de formação de professores de inglês: Uma interpretação de abordagens, métodos e técnicas [Reflecting about ESL teacher education: An interpretation of approaches, methods, and techniques]. In E. A. M. Mendes, P. M. Oliveira, & V. Benn-Ibler (Ed.), *O novo milênio: Interfaces lingüísticas e literárias* (pp. 47–56). Belo Horizonte, Minas Gerais, Brazil: Faculty of Letters/Federal University of Minas Gerais.

Edge, J. (2005). Build it and they will come: Realising values in ESOL teacher education. In D. J. Tedick (Ed.), *Second language teacher education* (pp. 181–197). Mahwah, NJ: Lawrence Erlbaum.

Elbow, P. (1991). Reflections on academic discourse: How it relates to freshmen and colleagues. *College English, 53,* 135–155.

Elley, W. B. (1989). Vocabulary acquisition from listening to stories. *Reading Research Quarterly, 24,* 174–187.

Elley, W. B., & Mangubhai, F. (1983). The impact of reading on second language learning. *Reading Research Quarterly, 19,* 53–67.

Elliott, J. (1991). *Action research for educational change.* Philadelphia: Open University.

Ferguson, G., & Donno, S. (2003). One-month teacher training courses: Time for a change? *English Language Teaching Journal, 57*(1), 26–33.

Ferris, D. R. (1997). The influence of teacher commentary on student revision. *TESOL Quarterly, 31,* 315–339.

Ferris, D. R. (2003). *Response to student writing: Implications for second language students.* Mahwah, NJ: Lawrence Erlbaum.

Flaitz, J., & Feyten, C. (1996). A two-phase study involving consciousness raising and strategy use for foreign language learners. In R. L. Oxford (Ed.), *Language learning strategies around the world: Cross-cultural perspectives* (Technical Report No. 13, pp. 211–225). Honolulu: University of Hawai'i, Second Language Teaching & Curriculum Center.

Fox, J. (2000). *Carleton Academic English Language (CAEL) Assessment test manual.* Ottawa, Ontario, Canada: Carleton University Press.

Fox, J. (2003). From products to process: An ecological approach to bias detection. *International Journal of Language Testing, 3,* 21–48.

Freedman, S. W. (1987). How characteristics of student essays influence teachers' evaluations. *Journal of Educational Psychology, 71,* 328–338.

Freeman, D. (1998). *Doing teacher research: From inquiry to understanding.* Toronto: Heinle & Heinle.

Freeman, D., & Johnson, K. (1998). Reconceptualizing the knowledge base of language teacher education. *TESOL Quarterly, 32,* 397–417.

Freire, P. (1970). *Pedagogy of the oppressed.* New York: Continuum.

Freire, P. (1996). *Pedagogia da autonomia: Saberes necessários à prática educativa* [Autonomy pedagogy: Necessary knowledge to the educative practice]. São Paulo: Paz e Terra.

Garshick, E. (Ed.). (2002). *Directory of teacher education programs in TESOL in the United States and Canada.* Arlington, VA: Teachers of English to Speakers of Other Languages.

Gebhard, J., & Oprandy, R. (1999). *Language teaching awareness: A guide to exploring beliefs and practices.* Cambridge, England: Cambridge University Press.

Gebhardt, J. (2004). Using movie trailers in an ESL CALL class. *Internet TESL Journal, 10*(10), 1–3 [Online article]. Retrieved October 8, 2006, from http://iteslj.org/Techniques/Gebhardt-MovieTrailers.html

Genesee, F. (1987). *Learning through two languages: Studies of immersion and bilingual education.* Cambridge, MA: Newbury House.

Gilbert, M. (1993). Using movies for teaching low-level students of English. *Forum, 31*(3), 29–31 [Online article]. Retrieved October 8, 2006, from http://exchanges.state.gov/forum/vols/vol31/no3/p29.htm

Giltrow, J. (2002). *Academic writing.* Mississauga, Ontario, Canada: Broadview.

Giroux, H. (1994). *Disturbing pleasures: Learning popular culture.* New York: Routledge.

Graves, M. (2006). *The vocabulary book: Learning & instruction.* New York: Teachers College Press.

Hall, J. K. (1993). The role of oral practices in the accomplishment of our everyday lives: The sociocultural dimension of interaction with implications for the learning of another language. *Applied Linguistics, 14,* 145–166.

Hall, J. K. (1999). A prosaics of interaction: The development of interactional competence in another language. In E. Hinkel (Ed.), *Culture in second language teaching and learning* (pp. 137–151). Cambridge, England: Cambridge University Press.

Harper, D. (2001). *Online etymology dictionary*. Retrieved December 7, 2006, from http://www.etymonline.com/

Hatch, E., & Lazaraton, A. (1991). *The research manual: Design and statistics for applied linguistics*. Boston, MA: Heinle & Heinle.

Heffernan, N. (2005). Watching movie trailers in the ESL class. *Internet TESL Journal, 11*(3), 1–4 [Online article]. Retrieved October 8, 2006, from http://iteslj.org/Lessons/Heffernan-MovieTrailers.html

Henkes, K. (2004). *Kitten's first full moon*. New York: Greenwillow.

Hoffman, E. (1989). *Lost in translation: A life in a new language*. New York: Penguin Books.

Hughes, R., & McCarthy, M. (1998). From sentence to discourse: Discourse grammar and English language teaching. *TESOL Quarterly, 32*, 263–287.

Hulstijn, J. H., & Laufer, B. (2001). Some empirical evidence for the involvement load hypothesis in vocabulary acquisition. *Language Learning, 51*, 539–558.

Hutchinson, T., & Waters, A. (1987). *English for specific purposes: A learning-centered approach*. Cambridge, England: Cambridge University Press.

Hymes, D. (1972). Models of the interaction of language and social life. In J. Gumperz & D. Hymes (Eds.), *Directions in sociolinguistics. The ethnography of communication* (pp. 35–71). Cambridge, England: Cambridge University Press.

Jenkins, J. R., & Dixon, R. (1983). Vocabulary learning. *Contemporary Educational Psychology, 8*, 237–260.

Jenkins, J. R., Matlock B., & Slocum, T. A. (1989). Two approaches to vocabulary instruction: The teaching of individual word meanings and practice in deriving word meaning from context. *Reading Research Quarterly, 24*, 215–235.

Jenkins, J. R., Stein, M. L., & Wysocki, K. (1984). Learning vocabulary through reading. *American Educational Research Journal, 21*, 767–787.

Johnson, K. E. (1995). *Understanding communication in second language classrooms*. Cambridge, England: Cambridge University Press.

Kagan, S. (1986). Cooperative learning and sociocultural factors in schooling. In California Department of Education (Ed.), *Beyond language: Social and cultural factors in schooling language minority students* (pp. 231–298). Los Angeles: Evaluation, Dissemination and Assessment Center, California State University, Los Angeles.

Kolb, D. (1984). *Experiential learning*. Englewood Cliffs, NJ: Prentice Hall.

Krashen, S. (1989*)*. We acquire vocabulary and spelling by reading: Additional evidence for the input hypothesis. *Modern Language Journal, 73*, 440–455.

Krashen, S. (2003). *Explorations in language acquisition and use*. Portsmouth, NH: Heinemann.

Krashen, S., Long, M., & Scarcella, R. (1979). Age, rate, and eventual attainment in second language acquisition. *TESOL Quarterly, 13*, 573–582.

Kuck, M. (2004). *"Fi Mi" English language book*. Kingston, Jamaica: HEART TRUST/NTA Vocational Training Development Institute.

Kuck, M., & Blagrove-Williams, M. (2002). Creole + status ≠ English – status: A study of attitudes towards English of Jamaican future vocational/technical teachers. *Proceedings (Actas) II Conferencia Internacional de Lengua y Cultura del Caribe.* Santiago de Cuba: Universidad de Oriente.

Lanehart, S. (1998). African American vernacular English and education: The dynamics of pedagogy, ideology, and identity. *Journal of English Linguistics, 26,* 122–136.

Lantolf, J. P., & Appel, G. (1994). Theoretical framework: An introduction to Vygotskian approaches to second language research. In J. P. Lantolf & G. Appel (Eds.), *Vygotskian approaches to second language research* (pp. 1–31). Norwood, NJ: Ablex.

Laufer, B. (1989). What percentage of text lexis is essential for comprehension? In C. Lauren & M. Nordman (Eds.), *Special language: From human thinking to thinking machines* (pp. 316–323). Clevedon, England: Multilingual Matters.

Leki, I. (1990). Coaching from the margins: Issues in written response. In B. Kroll (Ed.), *Second language writing: Research insights for the classroom* (pp. 57–68). Cambridge, England: Cambridge University Press.

Leki, I. (1992). *Understanding ESL writers: A guide for teachers.* Portsmouth, NH: Boynton/Cook.

Lerner, D. (1997). *Lectura y escritura: Perspectiva curricular, apartes de investigación y quehacer en el aula* [Reading and writing: A curricular perspective apart from investigation and classroom practices]. Bogotá, Colombia: Facultad de Ciencias de la Educación.

Lewis, M. (1993). *The lexical approach.* Hove, England: Language Teaching Publications.

Lewis, M. (1997). *Implementing the lexical approach: Putting theory into practice.* Hove, England: Language Teaching Publications.

Lezberg, A., & Hilferty, A. (1978). Discourse analysis in the reading class. *TESOL Quarterly, 12*(1), 47–55.

Lightfoot, S., & Davis, J. (1997). *The art and science of portraiture.* San Francisco: Jossey-Bass.

Lincoln, Y., & Guba, E. (1985). *Naturalistic inquiry.* New York: Sage.

Lindlof, T. (1995). *Qualitative communication research methods* (Vol. 3). Thousand Oaks, CA: Sage.

Linn, R., Baker, E., & Dunbar, S. (1991). Complex, performance-based assessment: Expectations and validation criteria. *Educational Researcher, 20*(8), 15–21.

Liversidge, G. (2000). What do EFL students see in introductory sequences of movies? *Internet TESL Journal, 6*(3), 1–7 [Online article]. Retrieved October 8, 2006, from http://iteslj.org/Articles/Liversidge-Video.html

Lonergan, J. (1984). *Video in language teaching.* Cambridge, England: Cambridge University Press.

Malane, D. (2001). *Billie the hippo.* Wellington, New Zealand: Learning Media.

Maley, A. (1992). Global issues in ELT. *Practical English Teaching, 13*(2), 73.

Massi, M. P., & Merino, A. G. (1996). What's playing in the language classroom?

Forum, 34(1), 20–27 [Online article]. Retrieved October 8, 2006, from http://exchanges.state.gov/forum/vols/vol34/no1/p20.htm

Matsuda, P. K. (2003). Second language writing in the twentieth century: A situated historical perspective. In B. Kroll (Ed.), *Exploring the dynamics of second language writing* (pp. 15–34). New York: Cambridge University Press.

McCarthy, M. (1991). *Discourse analysis for language teachers.* Cambridge: Cambridge University Press.

McCarthy, M. (2001). *Discourse analysis for language teachers* (12th ed.). Cambridge, England: Cambridge University Press.

McCarthy, M., & Carter, R. (2001). Size isn't everything: Spoken English, corpus, and the classroom. *TESOL Quarterly, 35,* 337–340.

McCotter, S. (2001). Collaborative groups as professional development. *Teaching and Teacher Education, 17,* 685–704.

McDonald, B., & Boud, D. (2003). The impact of self-assessment on achievement: The effects of self-assessment training on performance in external examinations. *Assessment in Education, 10,* 169–207.

McEnery, T., & Wilson, A. (2001). *Corpus linguistics* (2nd ed.). Edinburgh, Scotland: Edinburgh University Press.

Meyer, C. F. (2002). *English corpus linguistics: An introduction.* Cambridge, England: Cambridge University Press.

Moffett, J. (1968). *Teaching the universe of discourse.* Boston: Houghton Mifflin.

Nagy, W., & Anderson, R. (1984). The number of words in printed school English. *Reading Research Quarterly, 19,* 304–330.

Nagy, W. E., & Herman, P. A. (1987). Breadth and depth of vocabulary knowledge: Implications for acquisition and instruction. In M. C. McKeown & M. E. Curtis (Eds.), *The nature of vocabulary acquisition* (pp.19–36). Mahwah, NJ: Erlbaum.

Nagy, W. E., Herman, P., & Anderson, R. (1985). Learning words from context. *Reading Research Quarterly, 20,* 233–253.

Nagy, W. E., Herman, P. A., & Anderson R. C. (1987). Learning word meanings from context during normal reading. *American Educational Research Journal, 24*(2), 237–270.

Nero, S. (1997). English is my native language . . . or so I believe. *TESOL Quarterly, 31,* 585–593.

New Jersey Department of Education. (2006a). *State profile of limited English proficient (LEP) students 2005–2006.* Retrieved December 7, 2006, from Bureau of Bilingual/ESL Education Web site at http://www.state.nj.us/njded /bilingual/statistics/

New Jersey Department of Education. (2006b). *2005–2006 languages with highest LEP enrollment statewide.* Retrieved December 7, 2006, from Bureau of Bilingual/ESL Education Web site at http://www.state.nj.us/njded/bilingual /statistics/

Nicenet. (1998). *Nicenet's Internet Classroom Assistant.* Retrieved November 15, 2002, from http://nicenet.org

Nichols, M. (Director). (1967). *The graduate* [Motion picture]. United States: MGM.

Norton, B. (1997). Language, identity, and the ownership of English. *TESOL Quarterly, 31*, 409–427.

Norton, B. (2000). *Identity and language learning: Gender, ethnicity, and educational change.* Harlow, England: Pearson Education.

Norton Peirce, B. (1995). Social identity, investment, and language learning. *TESOL Quarterly, 29*, 9–31.

Nunan, D. (1989). *Understanding language classrooms.* Hemel Hempstead, England: Prentice Hall.

Nuttall, C. (1982). *Teaching reading skills in a foreign language.* London: Heinemann.

Nyikos, M., & Hashimoto, R. (1997). Constructivist theory applied to collaborative learning in teacher education: In search of ZPD. *The Modern Language Journal, 81*, 506–517.

O'Malley, J. M., & Chamot, A. U. (1990). *Learning strategies in second language acquisition.* Cambridge, England: Cambridge University Press.

O'Malley, J. M., Chamot, A. U., Stewner-Manzanares, G., Russo, R. P., & Küpper, L. (1985). Learning strategy application with students of English as a second language. *TESOL Quarterly, 19*, 557–584.

Oxford, R. L. (1990). *Language learning strategies: What every teacher should know.* Boston: Heinle & Heinle.

Oxford, R. L., & Leaver, B. L. (1996). A synthesis of strategy instruction for language learners. In R. L. Oxford (Ed.), *Language learning strategies around the world: Cross-cultural perspectives* (Technical Report No. 13, pp. 227–246). Honolulu: University of Hawai'i, Second Language Teaching & Curriculum Center.

Pao, D. L., Wong, S. D., & Teuben-Rowe, S. (1997). Identity formation for mixed-heritage adults and implications for educators. *TESOL Quarterly, 31*(3), 622–631.

Paribakht, T., & Wesche, M. (1993). The relationship between reading comprehension and second language development in a comprehension-based ESL program. *TESL Canada Journal, 11*(1), 9–29.

Parks, S., & Maguire, M. (1999). Coping with on-the-job writing in ESL: A constructivist-semiotic perspective. *Language Learning, 49*, 143–175.

Partridge, E. (1959). *Origins: A short etymological dictionary of modern English.* New York: Macmillan.

Pennycook, A. (1999). Introduction: Critical approaches to TESOL. *TESOL Quarterly, 33*, 329–348.

Phillipson, R. (1988). Linguicism: Structures and ideologies in linguistic imperialism. In T. Skutnabb-Kangas & J. Cummins (Eds.), *Minority education: From shame to struggle* (pp. 339–358). Clevedon, England: Multilingual Matters.

Pribilsky, J. (2001). Nervios and "modern childhood": Migration and changing contexts of child life in the Ecuadorian Andes. *Childhood: A Global Journal of Child Research, 8*(2), 251–273.

Ramanathan, V. (2005). Seepages, contact zones, and amalgam: Internationalizing TESOL. *TESOL Quarterly, 39*, 119–124.

Reading Rockets/Colorín Colorado Project. (2006). *Using cognates to develop comprehension in English*. Retrieved February 27, 2006, from http://www.colorincolorado.org/introduction/cognates.php

Reid, J. (1993). *Teaching ESL writing*. Englewood Cliffs, NJ: Regents Prentice Hall.

Reid, J. (1995). The author responds. *TESOL Quarterly, 29*, 163–166.

Richards, J. (1980). Conversation. *TESOL Quarterly, 14*, 413–432.

Richards, J. (1998). *Beyond training*. Cambridge, England: Cambridge University Press.

Richards, J., & Farrell, T. (2005). *Professional development for language teachers*. New York: Cambridge University Press.

Richards, J., & Lockhart, C. (1994). *Reflective teaching in second language classrooms*. Cambridge, England: Cambridge University Press.

Riggenbach, H. (1999). *Discourse analysis in the language classroom: Vol. 1. The spoken language*. Ann Arbor: University of Michigan Press.

Robbins, C., & Ehri, L. (1994). Reading storybooks to kindergartners helps them learn new vocabulary words. *Journal of Educational Psychology, 86*, 54–64.

Roberts, C., Bryam, M., Barro, A., Jordan, S., & Street, B. (2001). *Language learners as ethnographers*. Clevedon, England: Multilingual Matters.

Ryan, S. (1998). Using films to develop learner motivation. *Internet TESL Journal, 4*(11), 1–4 [Online article]. Retrieved October 8, 2006, from http://iteslj.org/Articles/Ryan-Films.html

Sandburg, C. (1919). Fog. In L. Untermeyer (Ed.), *Modern American poetry: An introduction*. New York: Harcourt, Brace, and Howe. Retrieved February 26, 2006, from http://www.bartleby.com/104/76.html

Schleppegrell, M. (2004). *The language of schooling: A functional linguistics perspective*. Mahwah, NJ: Lawrence Erlbaum.

Seda-Santana, I. (2000). Literacy research in Latin America: Context, characteristics, and applications. Retrieved August 20, 2005, from www.readingonline.org/articles/handbook/seda/

Shum, M. (Writer/Director), Jennings, C. (Producer), Garvie, S. (Producer), Massey, R. (Producer), & Foon, D. (Cowriter). (2002). *Long life, happiness, and prosperity* [Motion picture]. Canada: Film Movement.

Simpson, R. C., Briggs, S. L., Ovens, J., & Swales, J. M. (2002). *The Michigan corpus of academic spoken English*. Ann Arbor: Regents of the University of Michigan.

Smith, L. (2005). The impact of action research on teacher collaboration and professional growth. In D. J. Tedick (Ed.), *Second language teacher education* (pp. 199–213). Mahwah, NJ: Lawrence Erlbaum.

Smith, P., Jimenez, R., & Martinez-Leon, N. (2003). Other countries' literacies: What U.S. educators can learn from Mexican schools. *Reading Teacher, 56*, 772–781.

Sommers, N. (1982). Responding to student writing. *College Composition and Communication, 33*, 148–156.

Spielberg, S. (Director). (1981). *Indiana Jones and the raiders of the lost ark* [Motion picture]. United States: Paramount.

Spradley, J. (1980). *Participant observation*. New York: Holt, Rinehart, & Winston.

Stefanakis, E. (2004, May/June). Assessing young immigrant students: Are we finding their strengths? *Harvard Education Letter*, 4–7.

Stempleski, S., & Tomalin, B. (2001). *Film*. Oxford, England: Oxford University Press.

Stern, H. H., Burstall, C., & Harley, B. (1975). *French from age eight or eleven?* Toronto, Canada: Ontario Institute for Studies in Education.

Sternberg, R. J. (1987). Most vocabulary is learned from context. In M. C. McKeown & M. E. Curtis (Eds.), *The nature of vocabulary acquisition* (pp. 89–106). Mahwah, NJ: Lawrence Erlbaum.

Strauss, A., & Corbin, J. (1990). *Basics of qualitative research: Grounded theory procedures and techniques*. Newbury Park, CA: Sage.

Swain, M., & Lapkin, S. (1998). Interaction and second language learning: Two adolescent French immersion students working together. *Modern Language Journal, 82*, 320–337.

Tatsuki, D. H. (1998a). Comprehension hot spots in movies: Scenes and dialogs that are difficult for ESL/EFL students to understand. *Internet TESL Journal, 4*(11), 1–5 [Online article]. Retrieved October 8, 2006, from http://iteslj.org/Articles/Tatsuki-HotSpots.html

Tatsuki, D. H. (1998b). ESL/EFL lessons using movies. *Internet TESL Journal, 4*(3), 1 [Online article]. Retrieved October 8, 2006, from http://iteslj.org/Lessons/Tatsuki-Movie/index.html

Tatsuki, D. H. (2000). Developing film study guides. *Internet TESL Journal, 6*(3), 1–7 [Online article]. Retrieved October 8, 2006, from http://iteslj.org/Techniques/Tatsuki-StudyGuides.html

Thiong'O, N. (2004). Decolonizing the mind. In S. Hirschberg & T. Hirschberg (Eds.), *One world, many cultures* (pp. 402–411). New York: Pearson/Longman.

Thorndike, R. M., & Dinnel, D. N. (2001). *Basic statistics for the behavioral sciences*. Upper Saddle River, NJ: Merrill-Prentice Hall.

Thralls, C. (1992). Bakhtin, collaborative partners, and published discourse: A collaborative view of composing. In J. Forman (Ed.), *New visions of collaborative writing* (pp. 63–81). Portsmith, NH: Heinemann.

Ulanoff, S. H., & Pucci, S. L. (1999). Learning words from books: The effects of read-aloud on second language vocabulary acquisition. *Bilingual Research Journal, 23*, 409–421.

Underhill, A. (1992). The role of groups in developing teacher self-awareness. *ELT Journal, 46*, 71–80.

Vygotsky, L. S. (1962). *Thought and language*. Cambridge, MA: MIT Press.

Vygotsky, L. S. (1978). *Mind in society: The development of higher psychological processes*. Cambridge, MA: Harvard University Press.

Wall, D., & Alderson, J. C. (1993). Examining washback: The Sri Lankan impact study. *Language Testing, 10*, 41–69.

Wallace, M. (1998). *Action research for language teachers*. Cambridge, England: Cambridge University Press.

Wells, G. (2000). Dialogic inquiry in education: Building on the legacy of Vygotsky.

In C. D. Lee & P. Smagorinsky (Eds.), *Vygotskian perspectives on literacy research* (pp. 51–85). Cambridge, England: Cambridge University Press.

Wells, G. (2001). The case for dialogic inquiry. In G. Wells (Ed.), *Action, talk, and text* (pp. 171–194). New York: Teachers College Press.

West, C. (1992, summer). A matter of life and death. *October, 61,* 20–23.

Whitten, N. (Ed.). (2003). Epilogue. In *Millennial Ecuador: Critical essays on cultural transformations and social dynamics* (pp. 355–373). Iowa City: University of Iowa Press.

Wink, J., & Putney, L. G. (2002). *A vision of Vygotsky.* Boston: Allyn & Bacon.

Yang, N.-D. (1996). Effective awareness-raising in language learning strategy instruction. In R. L. Oxford (Ed.), *Language learning strategies around the world: Cross-cultural perspectives* (Technical Report No. 13, pp. 205–210). Honolulu: University of Hawai'i, Second Language Teaching & Curriculum Center.

Zahar, R., Cobb, T., & Spada, N. (2001). Acquiring vocabulary through reading: Effects of frequency and contextual richness. *Canadian Modern Language Review, 57,* 541–572.

Zamel, V. (1982). Writing: The process of discovering meaning. *TESOL Quarterly, 16,* 195–209.

Zamel, V. (1985). Responding to student writing. *TESOL Quarterly, 19,* 79–97.

Zamel, V. (1997). Toward a model of transculturation. *TESOL Quarterly, 31,* 341–352.

Ziv, N. (1984). The effects of teacher comments on the writing of four college freshmen. In R. N. Beach & L. S. Bridwell (Eds.), *New directions in composition research* (pp. 362–380). New York: Guilford Press.

Zucker, D., & Zucker, J. (Directors). (1980). *Airplane!* [Motion picture]. United States: Paramount.

Zwick, E. (Director). (2003). *The last samurai* [Motion picture]. United States: Warner Brothers.

Zwick, J. (Director), & Vardalos, N. (Writer). (2002). *My big fat Greek wedding* [Motion picture]. United States: Home Box Office.

Index

Page numbers followed by an *f, t,* or *n* indicate figures, tables, or footnotes.

Auditory breakdowns, 44

B

Backchanneling, 164
Bible reading, language preference and,
117–118, 117*t*
Billie the Hippo (Malane), 89
Brainstorming, metacognitive strategy
training and, 177
Brazil, 95. *See also* Collaboration

C

CAEL. *See* Canadian Academic English
Language (CAEL) Assessment
Canada. *See* Film use in classrooms; Peer
review; Testing
Canadian Academic English Language
(CAEL) Assessment, 70–71. *See also*
Testing
Carribean. *See* Identity
"The Case for Short Words" (Lederer),
148
Children
age of compulsory foreign language
teaching and, 95
vocabulary development and. *See*
Vocabulary skills
Chinese families, film depiction of, 43.
See also Film use in classrooms
Class size, as a barrier, 2, 106
Classroom reading, vocabulary
development and, 144
Classroom teaching, relationship with
research and, 1–2
Classroom tests, 71–72. *See also* Testing
Cognitive approach to English
instruction, 156
Collaboration
background literature and, 96–98
introduction to, 4
overview of, 95–96
procedures and, 98–101
reflection and, 104–106
results and, 102–103
Samples of Student Artwork, 107*f*,
108*f*

Samples of Student Diaries, 111*f*, 112*f*
Samples of Student Letters, 109*f*, 110*f*
writing and, 73
Colombia, 95. *See also* Teaching context
Comment Classification Systems and
Examples, 33*t*
Comments
Appropriate comments by student
teachers, 35*f*
Comment Classification Systems and
Examples, 33*t*
Comments from ESL students, 37*f*
Inappropriate comments by student
teachers, 35*f*
Miscorrections of mechanics by
student teachers, 36*f*
Number of Student Teacher
Comments by Type and Location,
34*t*
peer review and, 32–38
Student Teacher Comments, 38*t*
Student Teacher Likert Responses, 37*t*
Tabulation of Length and Specificity of
Comments, 34*t*
Common literacy practices, in Latin
American schools, 8
Communication techniques, 4–5. *See also*
Academic interactions
Confidence, academic interactions and,
64–65
Connector use, writing practices and, 17*t*
Constructivism, 56
Consumerism, 131, 132, 133
Context, teaching and. *See* Teaching
context
Continuum, identity, 121*f*
Conversational English
background literature and, 156–157
Differences in Native and Nonnative
Speakers' Use of Inserts, 166*t*
Frequency of use of discourse markers
and conversational hedges for
native speakers and nonnative
speakers, 161*f*
introduction to, 5
Level of Significance of the Uses of

Induction, analytic, 76

Information gathering, *vs.* reflective activities, 77–78

Inserts, conversational English and, 156, 158–159, 160, 161*f*, 166*t*, 167*t*, 168*t*, 169*t*

Institutional Testing Program (ITP), 7–8, 9, 18, 20

Instituto de Idiomas, 7. *See also* Teaching context

Instruments, testing and, 75–76

Intelligence, identity and, 119*t*

Interaction, observation and, 10, 15*t*, 16*t*

Interactions, academic. *See* Academic interactions

Internal tests, 71–72, 77–79. *See also* Testing

Internet use, 45

Intervention, writing instruction and, 29

Interview Results, 18*t*

Interviews, academic interactions and, 61

ITP. *See* Institutional Testing Program (ITP)

J

Jamaica. *See* Identity

Japan, film use in classrooms and, 43–44

Journaling
collaboration and, 98, 104–105, 111*f*, 112*f*
teachers and, 129

K

Kitten's First Full Moon (Henkes), 94

L

Language, Film, and Culture course. *See* Film use in classrooms

Language awareness, academic interactions and, 63–64

Language choice
identity and, 117*t*, 118*t*, 119*t*
observation and, 10, 15*t*, 16*t*

Language Research Project. *See* Academic interactions

The Last Samurai (Zwick), 43, 48*t*, 49*t*. *See also* Film use in classrooms

LEP. *See* Limited English proficient (LEP) enrollment

Letter exchange, collaboration and, 98, 99–100, 109*f*, 110*f*

Lexical competence, 88

Library visits, vocabulary development and, 144, 145

Likert responses, 36–37, 37*t*

Limited English proficient (LEP) enrollment, 139, 140*t*. *See also* Vocabulary skills

Linguicism, defined, 126

Listening skills, 4, 84, 86

Literacy research, Latin American studies and, 8

Literacy scaffolds, vocabulary development and, 87, 93–94

Logistical considerations, peer review and, 39

Long Life, Happiness, and Prosperity (Shum, Jennings, Garvie, Massey, & Foon), 43, 48*t*, 49*t*. *See also* Film use in classrooms

The Longman Grammar of Spoken and Written English (Biber, Johansson, Leech, Conrad, & Finegan), 157

M

Means, testing and, 77

Means of Supertargeted and Targeted Words Acquired by Group, 92*t*

Metacognition, defined, 172

Metacognitive strategy training
background literature and, 174–175
introduction to, 5–6
overview of, 171–175
procedures and, 175–178
reflection and, 181–182
results and, 178–181

Mexico, teaching context and, 8

MICASE. *See The Michigan Corpus of Academic Spoken English*

The Michigan Corpus of Academic Spoken English (MICASE), 158

Migration, Ecuadorian, 126–127, 130–131

Miscorrections of mechanics by student teachers, 36f

Modeling, metacognitive strategy training and, 176

Movies. *See* Film use in classrooms

Multilevel classes, as a barrier, 2

My Big Fat Greek Wedding (Zwick & Vardalos), 43, 48t, 49t. *See also* Film use in classrooms

N

Needs assessment
   background literature and, 140–142
   Bilingual/ESL Education: New Jersey State Profile of LEP Students, 2005-2006, 141t
   Etymology of Reading Record Words, 146–147t
   Etymology of Words in the Poem "Fog," 149t
   Languages With Highest LEP Enrollment Statewide in New Jersey, 2005–2006, 140t
   overview of, 139–140
   procedures and, 142, 144–145
   reflection and, 147–151
   results and, 142–143, 145–147
   Worksheet for Reading Record, 153
   Worksheet for Words and Definitions, 152

New Jersey Assessment of Skills and Knowledge (NJ ASK), 84

Number of Student Teacher Comments by Type and Location, 34t

O

Objectives
   Reflection on Teaching Practices, 22–23
   teaching context and, 9–10

Observation
   academic interactions and, 59t, 63. *See also* Academic interactions
   collaboration and, 98, 101

teaching context and, 10–11

Opinion expression
   evaluation and, 10, 15t, 18t
   writing practices and, 17t

Overall Usage of Writing Practices in Student Reports, 17t

Oxford's Strategic Inventory for Language Learning (SILL), 176

P

Panic, language preference and, 117–118, 117t

Paragraphing, writing practices and, 17t

Paraguay, age of compulsory foreign language teaching in, 95

Patois. *See* Identity

Peer review
   Appropriate comments by student teachers, 35f
   background literature and, 27–29
   collaboration and, 98, 99–100
   Comment Classification Systems and Examples, 33t
   Comments from ESL students, 37f
   ESL in-class writing assignments, 31f
   ESL writing checklist, 30f
   evaluation and, 18t
   Inappropriate comments by student teachers, 35f
   introduction to, 3–4
   Miscorrections of mechanics by student teachers, 36f
   Number of Student Teacher Comments by Type and Location, 34t
   overview of, 25–26
   procedures and, 29–32
   reflection and, 39
   results and, 32–38
   Student Teacher Comments, 38t
   Student Teacher Likert Responses, 37t
   Tabulation of Length and Specificity of Comments, 34t

Pen pals, collaboration and, 98

Performance, metacognitive strategy training and, 178–180

teaching context and. *See* Teaching
context

Test Performance Compared With
Answers on Posttest Question 2,
80*t*

vocabulary development and, 84

Text Talk, 90

Textbook use

conversational English and, 163–164

teaching context and, 19

Time considerations, peer review and, 39

TOEFL. *See* Test of English as a Foreign
Language (TOEFL)

Translation, evaluation and, 11, 15*t*

U

*Understanding ESL Writers: A Guide for
Teachers* (Leki), 29

UniNorte, 8

United States. *See* Academic interactions;
Conversational English; Vocabulary
skills

Universidad del Norte, 7. *See also*
Teaching context

V

Vacation diaries, collaboration and, 98

Vocabulary skills

background literature and, 84–88,
140–142

Bilingual/ESL Education: New Jersey
State Profile of LEP Students,
2005–2006, 141*t*

Etymology of Reading Record Words,
146–147*t*

Etymology of Words in the Poem
"Fog," 149*t*

introduction to, 5

Languages With Highest LEP
Enrollment Statewide in New
Jersey, 2005–2006, 140*t*

Means of Supertargeted and Targeted
Words Acquired by Group, 92*t*

metacognitive strategy training and,
176

overview of, 83–84, 139–140

procedures and, 88–90, 142, 144–145

reflection and, 93–94, 147–151

results and, 90–93, 142–143, 145–147

Words Acquired per Subject Group,
92*t*

Worksheet for Reading Record, 153

Worksheet for Words and Definitions,
152

W

Warmth, identity and, 119*t*

Wealth, identity and, 119*t*

Web discussion, 59*t*

Word families, 151

Word Work game, vocabulary
development and, 145

Words Acquired per Subject Group, 92*t*

Writing practices

collaboration and, 98, 99–100

ESL in-class writing assignments, 31*f*

ESL writing checklist, 30*f*

metacognitive strategy training and,
178–179

Overall Usage of Writing Practices in
Student Reports, 17*t*

peer review and. *See* Peer review

Reading and Writing Questionnaire,
20–22

reflection and, 72–74, 78–79

Reflection on Teaching Practices,
22–23

Reflective and nonreflective
distribution of writing band
scores, 79*f*

Sample Student Writings, 23–24

teacher training and, 27–28

teaching context and, 12–13, 13–14*t*,
16*t*

TEFL certificate and, 129

testing and. *See* Testing

Also Available From TESOL

Perspectives on Community College ESL Series
Craig Machado, Series Editor
Volume 1: Pedagogy, Programs, Curricula, and Assessment
Marilynn Spaventa, Editor
Volume 2: Students, Mission, and Advocacy
Amy Blumenthal, Editor

PreK–12 English Language Proficiency Standards
Teachers of English to Speakers of Other Languages, Inc.

*Planning and Teaching Creatively within a
Required Curriculum for School-Age Learners*
Penny McKay, Editor

Professional Development of International Teaching Assistants
Dorit Kaufman and Barbara Brownworth, Editors

Teaching English as a Foreign Language in Primary School
Mary Lou McCloskey, Janet Orr, and Marlene Dolitsky, Editors

Teaching English From a Global Perspective
Anne Burns, Editor

Technology-Enhanced Learning Environments
Elizabeth Hanson-Smith, Editor

For more information, contact
Teachers of English to Speakers of Other Languages, Inc.
700 South Washington Street, Suite 200
Alexandria, Virginia 22314 USA
Toll Free: 888-547-3369   Fax on Demand: 800-329-4469
Publications Order Line: 888-891-0041
or 301-638-4427 or 4428
9 am to 5 pm, EST

ORDER ONLINE at www.tesol.org/

TESOL